SOCIAL WORK WITH THE BLACK AFRICAN DIASPORA

Washington Marovatsanga and Paul Michael Garrett

P

First published in Great Britain in 2024 by

Policy Press, an imprint of
Bristol University Press
University of Bristol
1-9 Old Park Hill
Bristol
BS2 8BB
UK
t: +44 (0)117 374 6645
e: bup-info@bristol.ac.uk

Details of international sales and distribution partners are available at
policy.bristoluniversitypress.co.uk

British Library Cataloguing in Publication Data
A catalogue record for this book is available from the British Library

ISBN 978-1-4473-6310-1 hardcover
ISBN 978-1-4473-6311-8 paperback
ISBN 978-1-4473-6312-5 ePub
ISBN 978-1-4473-6313-2 ePdf

Cover design: Qube Design Associates, Bristol
Front cover image: Shutterstock/Lora Sutyagina

Washington dedicates this book to his late parents, three daughters – Vanessa, Denise and Lillian – and to his wider, extended family. Paul dedicates this book to Arienze, Eniola, Florence, Kenny, Mark, Noma, Rowland, Salewa, Toyin, Victor, Victoria and Nisarg. Both are grateful to Charlotte Williams and Kathy Powell for their helpful suggestions and to Isobel Bainton and all of her colleagues at Policy Press. We are, of course, entirely responsible for any errors.

February 2022

Contents

List of tables

List of abbreviations

ASWI   African Social Workers Ireland
BLM   Black Lives Matter
CRT   critical race theory
CWT   critical whiteness theory
DP   direct provision
EU   European Union
HRC   Habitual Residence Condition
HSE   Health Service Executive
IASW   Irish Association of Social Workers
IFSW   International Federation of Social Workers
NGO   non-governmental organisation
SWAN   Social Work Action Network
UK   United Kingdom
UNDHR   United Nations Declaration on Human Rights
US   United States

1

Introduction

Introduction

In a keynote paper at the European Social Work Research conference in Leuven in 2019, Charlotte Williams (2020, p 1057) argued that the urgent need for 'sustained scholarly analysis and knowledge building on issues of race/ethnicity in social work research is as compelling as ever given the intensification of global racial inequalities, issues associated with the "migrant crisis", the spread of populist racialised political discourse and the ongoing downward pressure of neo-liberal imperatives'.

Responding to this challenge, we aim to furnish insights into how social work in Ireland engages with the Black African diaspora. The book is also rooted in five years (2015–20) of doctoral research exploring the interactional experiences of Black African and White social workers with Black African families (Marovatsanga, 2020).

Social Work with the Black African Diaspora examines social work education and its frequently culturally insular curriculum. Previous Irish research highlights inadequacies in working with specific categories of immigrants, such as asylum seekers, and in particular areas of practice, such as child protection (Dalikeni, 2013; see also Harrington, 2017; Okpokiri, 2020). Our book will go further in order to examine factors that could underpin inadequate social work across a range of practice domains. Furthermore, our focus on service providers is vital in that it gives voice to practitioners whose experience and daily interactions with Black African service users put them at the 'front line' of service delivery. If their assessment of the current situation is not considered, the 'gaps' they encounter in policies and practices are likely to continue to exist and this will seriously undermine the organisations within which they work.

In short, we hope to expand the 'intellectual space' within social work to make it more inclusive and vibrant. In this sense, our book is likely to be of interest to educators and students also located in the fields of sociology and social policy, and particularly segments of the these fields interested in far from unproblematic ideas circulating around 'diversity', 'anti-oppressive' and 'anti-racist' practices. *Social Work with the Black African Diaspora* also contains material that shares the concerns of a range of non-governmental organisations (NGOs) and members of the public. In our national context, we also hope that this book might also inform the evolution of the Irish

Association of Social Workers' 'Anti-Racism Strategic Plan', launched in February 2021.

Although focused on one European state, the book conveys vitally significant messages for global social work. This is because the themes we explore relate not only to Ireland, but also to the United Kingdom (UK) and elsewhere in Europe, North America and Australasia and, of course, Africa. (Our focus is on the Republic of Ireland and not Northern Ireland. For ease of reference, we will use 'Ireland' when we are discussing the jurisdiction in the south of the island). In what follows, we:

- critically explore an intellectually challenging range of thinkers and conceptual paradigms mostly absent within the academic literature of social work;
- contribute to the shaping of a more progressive social work that reaffirms the importance of anti-racism (Kleibl et al, 2019; Morley et al, 2020);
- give a voice to practitioners (including rarely heard Black African social workers) and educators who are grappling with significant issues pertaining to theory and practice when working with the Black African diaspora (see also Gatwiri, 2020; Obasi, 2021; Reid and Maclean, 2021).

In critically interrogating these core themes, we pose three key questions:

- As currently constituted, how does social work education and practice help or hinder the shaping of responses to Black African individuals, families and communities in Ireland? Relatedly, how do social work initiatives and interventions 'play out' in racialised encounters informed by neoliberal and dominant Eurocentric paradigms?
- In these neoliberal times, why is the social work response to the Black African diaspora problematic?
- More broadly, how can social work (as a body of knowledge and series of strategies of intervention) contribute to the creation of a more socially just world within, and beyond, the professional field?

Entirely at odds with the 'accepted narrative of Ireland as a former "emigrant nursery" and of in-migration as a "new" phenomenon, Ireland has long been a country of both emigration and immigration' (Lentin, 2007, p 612). As Ronit Lentin points out, alongside 'Scots and English migrants' there has always been an identifiable presence of 'Huguenots, Italian, Chinese, German, Jews and others' (Lentin, 2007, p 612). Despite common perceptions, Black people did not suddenly appear in Ireland during the final quarter of the 20th century. Hart's (2002) archival work suggests that in the 18th century Dublin had – after London – perhaps a larger number of Black residents than any other European city.

The country has a population of approximately five million. According to the 2016 census, more than one in three of those of African ethnicity (38.6%) were born in the Republic (22,331 persons), as were 31.3% (2,126) of those with other Black backgrounds. Africans were born primarily in Nigeria (27.2%). Those situating themselves in an 'any other Black background' category were born in a range of countries including Brazil (17.4%), England and Wales (7.1%) and Mauritius (3.2%). There were 10,100 dual Irish nationals who identified themselves as 'Black or Black Irish – African', the largest group of which was Irish-Nigerian nationals (6,683 people) (Central Statistics Office, 2020).

Paul Gilroy (2019) avows that in most of the Global North, 'Muslim has become fixed as a racial trope rather like Jew in the interwar years of the twentieth century'. This is probably the case, but religious identity and affiliation can be rendered optically undetectable. Islamophobia is not 'necessarily triggered by skin colour, and is often sparked off by one or more (perceived) symbols of the Muslim faith' (Cole, 2009, p 251). Australian-based research suggests that the more visibly different a social group is (phenotypically, and so on) from the dominant cultural group, the more likely it is likely to be discriminated against (Colic-Peisker and Tilbury, 2007). It may be that Black Africans – many of whom may also, of course, be followers in Islam (Crabtree et al, 2008) – are one of the groups most likely to be racially discriminated against in Ireland (Michael, 2016; see also Fanning, 2012; Child Care Law Reporting Project, 2015). For example, the Black African community in Ireland is '3–8 times more likely to be unemployed than their White counterparts' (Joseph, 2021, p 24). Previous research undertaken within the field of social work in Ireland has been inclined to subsume Black Africans' experiences under the reductive umbrella term 'ethnic minorities' (see also Christie, 2010).

The book's agenda

We aspire to contribute to the field of research and practice by expanding the social work knowledge base to include hitherto marginalised perspectives. Thus, we aim to address a profound 'silence' in seemingly benign, liberal paradigms. Relatedly, *Social Work with the Black African Diaspora* is committed to projects intent on decolonising the university (Bhambra et al, 2018; see also Gray et al, 2013). Underpinning our perspective is a belief that many Black Africans located on the margins of social work profession ('outsiders on the inside') must have the opportunity to begin actively to participate in the creation of social work knowledge (see also Fanning and Michael, 2019).

The empirical evidence analysed in our book highlights that social work involving the Black African diaspora (as both providers and users of services) appears to face a number of challenges. The perspectives of the practitioners and educators whose 'voices' we hear in Chapter 6 illuminate this dimension. Despite the existence of policies on equality and human rights protection in contemporary Ireland, social work interventions with Black African families continue to be a source of disquiet, and this matter should be accorded further consideration. The problems that we identify are partly attributable to significant cultural differences, language barriers and the potential for anti-Black discrimination because of implicit ethnocentric White assumptions of racial and cultural superiority.

Social Work with the Black African Diaspora is also situated alongside other contributions disrupting existing doxic academic knowledge in social work. It is widely accepted that Euro-American ethnocentric values are hegemonic within the profession's knowledge base. In the world at large, this dominance has led to the propagation of specific western norms as cultural universals (Mirsepassi, 2000). As the Indian historian Dipesh Chakrabarty (2000, p xiii) cautions, perceptions and paradigms drawn from particular cultural, intellectual and historical traditions are likely to lack 'universal validity', even if such validity is only implied. More emphatically, Iris Marion Young (1990, p 50) plainly describes the imposition of one's norms on other cultures as 'cultural oppression'. Globally, social work and social welfare systems have tended to impose White, western middle-class norms. Partly prompted by the population movements sparked by neoliberal globalism, the social and cultural 'diversity' constituting the worldwide social work practice context undermines the 'myth of sameness' underlying the social work tradition. This is a tradition rooted in the Universalist assumption that practice theories are broadly applicable to *all* persons because 'deep down we are all the same' (Pinderhughes, 1989, p 24).

As different countries have constructed and followed alternative routes to modernity, the academic literature on social work might – as some educators within the field acknowledge – try to become more alert to the diversity of the profession globally. It is vital that social work scholars, located in the West, refrain from cultural condescension and unthinkingly implying that theoretical models and ways of *doing* social work can be mechanistically transferred into emerging fields in countries such as those in the People's Republic of China (see, for example, Hutchings and Taylor, 2007).

Relatedly, Bar-on (1999) argues that the exportation to Africa of a form of social work underpinned by western values essentially alien to African culture was akin to the work of missionaries who sought to remake the Africans in their own image. In contemporary social work education, practice and research, the mainstream Eurocentric worldview continues to dominate by excluding non-western onto-epistemologies. Consequently, social workers are reproduced in the Eurocentric professional and cultural image. As many progressive scholars contend, important aspects of colonial-era ethnocentric assumptions underpinning traditional social work have proved to be remarkably resilient (see also Connell, 2007; Chibber, 2013; De Sousa Santos, 2014). Historically embedded Eurocentric assumptions and attendant messianic complexes endure to this day. These are often manifested through discursive practices and actions that suggest 'the West knows best for the rest'. Nevertheless, there are *different* ways of knowing and of being, and no single culture, purporting to be hegemonic and having all the 'answers' to 'social problems', can lay legitimate claim to enforce what is viewed as unequivocally 'appropriate' for the diversity of other cultures. What is more, those seeking to valorise indigenous knowledge systems are increasingly exposing the inadequacy of theories, intervention methods and research wholly founded on Eurocentric models.

Williams and Graham (2016) argue that contemporary global migration trends have magnified the inadequacy and inappropriateness of mainstream responses within western welfare regimes to meet the existential rights-based needs of new service user groups (see also Gray et al, 2013; Boccagni, 2015; Danso, 2016). Migration performs the dual role of 'problem solving' and 'problem generating' at the individual and societal levels. In Ireland, for example, migration 'solved' capital's labour shortage difficulties associated with the 'Celtic Tiger' economic boom. At individual immigrant levels, it afforded opportunities for some individuals to better their lives. As for those seeking asylum and refuge (based on a variety of persecutions), sanctuary – albeit often of a precarious kind – was also available for some individuals and their families. Migration can be a problem-generating phenomenon, at the levels mentioned earlier, in situations where the arrival of immigrants is not preceded by well thought-out planning and by the implementation of adequate policies, procedures and the nurturing of infrastructure at organisational and institutional levels. Lorenz (1994) argues that in such a situation, large-scale inward migration can lead to new forms of exclusion, managing and sifting of populations (see also Christie, 2003; Joseph, 2017). Evidence of such a situation exists in Ireland, given the hasty setting up of the 'direct provision' (DP) system for asylum seekers awaiting adjudication, which was made via ministerial order rather than through a legislative process. Here the emphasis was on quickly assembling a ramshackle deterrent system with the aim, as with the old workhouse system initially set up under British rule, to ward off people seeking help. Introduced as a mere 'pilot' scheme, it was rhetorically intended to house applicants for six months, but many have languished in DP for several years (Dalikeni, 2021). During summer 2020, over 32,000 people signed a petition calling for the government to end DP (McDermott, 2020a). If one is classified as an 'asylum seeker', the DP system imposes where one can live and not live. The type of accommodation available through DP results, therefore, in a form of enforced socio-spatial marginalisation (Ombudsman for Children's Office, 2021).

The challenges for social work are now being played out in interventions, training and research pivoting on migration. All of this has profound implications for the identity of the profession, its ethical claims-making, positioning and future strategies. In this context, it is of deep concern that social work practice presently risks becoming annexed to the immigration policing machinery put in place across various states in the Global North (Humphries, 2004; Farmer, 2020).

Black Lives Matter and the impact of the COVID-19 global pandemic

Reaching beyond Ireland, more contemporary events linked to the resurgence of the Black Lives Matter (BLM) movement and the disproportionate impact of COVID-19 on Black and ethnic minority people illuminate the importance of some of the 'messages' conveyed to social work in our book. Here, therefore, we will briefly refer to these two dimensions that are to the fore at the present conjuncture.

In *Black Skin, White Masks*, Fanon argues that, for many Black and colonised people, it was becoming 'impossible ... to breathe' (Fanon, 1986 [1952], p 226). In our contemporary world, the phrase took on a fatal resonance in 2014, when 'I can't breathe' was the final cry of Eric Garner who, on Staten Island in New York, died while being gripped in a 'chokehold' by a police officer. Fanon's line of political reasoning and analysis can be directly linked to this event and to the police execution of George Floyd in Minneapolis that prompted the re-energising of the BLM movement (BBC News, 2020; see also Teasley et al, 2018). Breonna Taylor, Tony McDade and Rayshard Brooks are among the many others killed at the hands of the United States (US) police (see also Nordberg and Meshesha, 2018). This is not simply a US phenomenon because, in Europe as well, a number of Black people have suffocated while being 'restrained' in the custody of the police or related personnel. These include Semira Adamu in Belgium in 1998, Mitch Henriquez in the Netherlands and Sheku Bayoh in Scotland in 2015, Adama Traoré in France in 2016, Rashan Charles in London in 2017 and William Tonou-Mbobda in Germany in 2019 (O'Leary, 2020). There are many more unexplained police custody-related deaths, such as that of Oury Jalloh in Germany in 2005 (Bruce-Jones, 2017). At the time of writing, concerns are being expressed in Ireland about the lethal police shooting of George Nkencho in Dublin in December 2020 (Otukoya, 2021; see also Gallagher and Pollack, 2021). Research also identifies how aggressive forms of intervention and structurally incompetent responses to racism are prompting a deterioration in the relationship between the An Garda

Síochána (the Irish police) and Black youth in Ireland. There is a 'long list of systematic failures which were causing trust in Gardaí to be damaged by the responses to reporting of racist incidents, including but not limited' to:

> refusal to advise or act in cases of racist crime; failure to attend ongoing violent crimes; refusal to speak to perpetrators or relevant witnesses; hostile treatment of witnesses; failure to collect relevant evidence of crime and of bias element; failure to provide crime numbers to victims; diversion of victims; failure to provide information on status of case to victims, and most importantly, investigations of immigration status before investigation of racist crimes, and hostile interactions with ethnic minority people in public, including racial profiling, harassment and unwarranted searches. (Michael, 2021a, p 58)

Historically, Black bodies have always been targeted for particular types of punitive oversight and scrutiny (Browne, 2015; Benjamin, 2019). Such deeply racialised watchfulness on the part of the state is illustrated by the surveillance operations of the Metropolitan Police in London, which has systematically targeted Black males as *potential* criminals from an early age (Amnesty International, 2018; Liberty, 2019). In the US, the organisation Data for Black Lives (D4BL, 2020) expresses concern about how data collected relating to COVID-19 might, given embedded structural racism, become 'weaponised' against Black and other minority ethnic communities. D4BL demands, therefore, that COVID-19 data should not be used to 'determine risk. It should not be used to surveil, criminalize, cage, and deny critical benefits'. Although relating to one country, these demands have global resonance for Black people (see also Pirtle, 2020).

Turning specifically to the ongoing COVID-19 pandemic, the Jubilee Debt Campaign (2020) reveals that 64 states spend more on external debt payments than they are able to devote to healthcare. Unsurprisingly, this drastically undermines the ability of countries (such as Gambia, Ghana, Zambia, Laos, Lebanon and Pakistan) to deal adequately with this public health emergency. This situation highlights how the colonial practices of the West continue to exploit parts of the Global South. In many parts of the Global North, the disproportionate numbers of fatalities in Black and minority ethnic communities are a significant issue (Gore, 2020; Munn, 2020). Public Health England (2020, p 4) found, in the early stages of the pandemic, that the 'highest age standardised diagnosis rates of COVID-19 per 100,000 population were in people of Black ethnic groups (486 in females and 649 in males) and the lowest were in people of White ethnic groups (220 in females and 224 in males)'. This is partly attributable to class and capitalist labour market positioning that leaves Black and ethnic minority people more vulnerable. Comparable data is not presently available in Ireland, but research highlights how COVID-19 has adversely affected asylum seekers corralled into 'hotel style' DP accommodation (Irish Refugee Council, 2020; see also Foreman, 2008; Arnold, 2012; Barry, 2014; Loyal and Quilley, 2018; O'Reilly, 2018; Ombudsman for Children's Office, 2021). Significantly, it has also been revealed that the state's vaccination portal does not allow those registering to enter either 'Black Irish' or 'Asian Irish' as a valid identity description (Cullen, 2021). This may be reflective of mere administrative incompetence, but it may also illuminate a facet of the hegemonic Whiteness, so pervasive in Irish life, that we will discuss later.

More expansively, the disproportionately high number of Black and minority ethnic fatalities during the global pandemic is suggestive of Ruth Wilson Gilmore's (2007, p 28) definition of racism as the 'state-sanctioned or extralegal production and exploitation of group-differentiated vulnerability to premature death'. Such an interpretation might also be associated with Mbembe's (2003) Foucauldian-inflected conceptualisation of 'necropolitics' (see also Robertson and Travaglia, 2020). Unsurprisingly, as soon as concerns about the disproportionately high deaths and infection rates within Black and ethnic minority groups surfaced, many right-wing commentators attempted to 'reframe' the debate in order to dwell on 'biological inheritance, lifestyle choices, and cultural differences that have no connection to discrimination' (Farah, 2020).

Positioning ourselves

Clearly, our interest in this topic is influenced by our positionality and ethical and political commitments. In this sense, it is important that we say a little about ourselves. We might also add that occasionally the authors fail to agree with each other on questions relating to class, 'race' and culture: Afrocentric theory, for example, furnishes a good example of this convivial lack of absolute alignment. Grounded in our joint commitment to combat racism, we view our differing opinions, if existing in creative and comradely tension, as beneficially adding to the vibrancy of our book. Our joint project has also been held together by our commitment to the aims and objectives of the Social Work Action Network (SWAN).

Washington was born and raised in what became, after a protracted war of national liberation, independent Zimbabwe on 18 April 1980. The Shona people had inhabited the land since approximately 1100 AD. From the early 1920s, until the 'unilateral declaration of independence' (UDI) by the White settler administration in 1965, the territory was the British colony of Southern Rhodesia (1923–65). Prior to UDI, colonial administrators 'relied on social workers who were seconded from Britain' to help run the colony (Kaseke, 2011, p 121; see also Chigudu, 2021). Now residing in Ireland, Washington has also worked in North America and Europe as a Black African 'ethnic minority' and social services practitioner, tutor and educator. In this sense, as a member of the Zimbabwean diaspora, he approaches the themes addressed in the book with his own experientially based conceptualisations (Zembe, 2019). This book is partly grounded in Washington's witnessing – as a student social worker – critical incidents between White Irish social workers and service users from culturally different backgrounds. In this context, he observed a lack of knowledge and a certain indifference toward the cultural orientation of Black African people and this, unsurprisingly functioned as an obstacle to fruitful engagements. Rarely were the normalisation and dominance of Whiteness, and the racialised power differentials associated with it, questioned or scrutinised (Michael and Schulz, 2019). When he completed his social work training in 2015, there were no Black social work educators in Ireland.

All of these factors propelled him to undertake more in-depth and robust investigation of the themes at the heart of *Social Work with the Black African Diaspora*. However, it is important to note Washington's ambiguous positioning. Something of an 'outsider' in terms of the state's categorisation and 'common sense' or popular perceptions, he is also an 'insider' because of his position within the 'field' as an accredited social worker (Fanning and Michael, 2019). More generally, his worldview is complex and bi-cultural in that he tries to interpret, express, understand and promote moral and social harmony (as in Ubuntuism, or what is sometime referred to as Hunhuism); yet, in many instances, he finds himself preoccupied with verification, rationalism, prediction and control as reified through what some might view as western scientific norms. Equally, he often tends to oscillate between collectivism and individualism simply in order to survive. That is to say, as most diasporic and continental Africans, he is attentive to the benefits of both collectivism and individualism while trying to shun their respective discontents and extremes. Despite all that, he still retains an enduring African cultural inheritance which is at the core of his habitus. Indeed, a strong African 'pulse' beats beneath his European attire: he feels that he cannot be other than a Black African man who spent his formative years in Rhodesia/Zimbabwe. Although he is now part of the African diaspora, many members of his extended family remain in 'Zim' and he occasionally returns there. He is also someone who has previously sat on 'both sides' of the social work office desk.

Paul, the second author, also identifies as male and is of the same generation as Washington. Like him, he is also an accredited social worker. He is 'White Irish', but has spent most of his life beyond Irish shores. One of his early books examined historical and contemporary patterns of discrimination directed at the Irish in Britain (Garrett, 2004). Paul has not been the victim of racism because of the colour of his skin, and he is deeply aware of his lack of knowledge of the lifeworld of Black African people. While an undergraduate student at the University of Sussex, he also recalls being captivated by listening to the accounts given by Zimbabwe African National Union/Zimbabwean African National Union members of the Patriotic Front delegation to the Lancaster House 'peace talks' then taking place in London. These exchanges, hosted by the British government, led to the Lancaster House Agreement being signed shortly before Christmas in 1979 and led to independence the following year.

Denzin and Lincoln (1998) argue that there exist both 'traditional' researchers and 'critical' researchers, and we identify with the latter category. These writers suggest that 'traditional' researchers are likely to adopt a positivistic stance and will cling to the guardrail of neutrality in order to be 'objective'. 'Critical' researchers – like ourselves – understand that there is no place or time outside of which we can objectively view and judge knowledge claims. Denzin and Lincoln maintain that all knowledge claims are imbued with the historical, theoretical and value predispositions of the researchers. More saliently, they further contend that 'critical' researchers tend to view research as potentially empowering individuals, or groups. That is to say, a research project can be a potentially transformative undertaking that should not be embarrassed by the 'political' label and should be unafraid to promote emancipatory consciousness. Such a stance assumes greater significance when there is a glaring injustice in a society, or in – what Bourdieu (2003 [1977]) would term – a particular 'field' of society.

We also align ourselves with the perceptions of Bourdieu's colleague Wacquant. According to the latter scholar, the 'intellectual' has as a 'duty', to re-inject the 'fruit' of 'reflections and observations into the civic and public sphere' (Wacqaunt, 2004, p 124). The 'primary historical mission of critical thought' is to constantly 'question the obviousness and the very frames of civic debate so as to give ourselves a chance to think the world, rather than being *thought by* it, to take apart and understand its mechanisms, and thus to reappropriate it intellectually and materially' (Wacquant, 2004, p 101, original emphasis). Questioning the seemingly 'natural' order of things can also be perceived as a gesture of solidarity with the marginalised, exploited or downtrodden because the 'dominated classes have an interest in pushing back the limits of *doxa*', while the 'dominant classes have an interest in defending' its integrity (Bourdieu, 2003, [1977], p 169).

An alternative perspective, which we disassociate ourselves from, is solely and reductively focused on 'methodological precision' with an 'ideal' of the 'professional' as the 'bearer of "technical competency"' and 'expert', 'neutral' knowledge. Such figures refrain from entering into public debate and merely move within the insular world of peers and colleagues (Wacquant, 2009, p 124). The role of 'academic' is, according to Wacquant, 'one-dimensional' and apt to orientate 'exclusively towards the microcosm of the university' (Wacquant, 2009, p 124). He asserts that when you 'remain cloistered in your university circles, you allow yourself to get caught up in the games and stakes of the microcosm, and in the end you lose your civic energy, your capacity for astonishment at the world, and the perspicacity needed for deciphering it' (Wacquant, 2009, p 125). Although it is readily apparent where his allegiances lie, Wacquant (2009, p 124) concedes that 'each of these traditions has its own virtues and vices'. For example, he recognises that a willingness to engage in the civic and public sphere need not result in an abandonment of a scholarly and ethnical commitment to methodological rigour. Once again, we find ourselves in alignment with this position (Garrett, 2021).

Chapter map

This is not a 'how to' guide and a book that is focused on improving 'techniques' in dealing with one particular diasporic community in Ireland. We are not entirely decrying such contributions to the academic literature of social work, but our aim is to produce a book that is far more expansive in its concerns. In Chapter 2, we will refer to some of the keywords, concepts and terminology that are found in the book. It is important to spend a little time articulating these aspects, because there are risks in failing to do so. Underpinning this chapter, therefore, is our critical engagement with the lexicon of 'race' and its associated conceptual vocabulary.

In Chapter 3, we turn our attention to the topical theme of decolonisation and the decolonisation of the various disciplines within universities. Our contention is that it is vital for social work, in Ireland and elsewhere, to be involved in the 'conversation' because these are not simply abstract debates. Some of the core issues also impact on, and shape, micro-level interactions when social work engages with users of services who form part of the Black African and other diasporas. As will soon become clear to readers, the perspective we aim to promote does not pivot on a foolish dismissal of European philosophy and social theory. Thus, the chapter refers to the insights of seminal figures such as Antonio Gramsci, Michel Foucault and Pierre Bourdieu. The US-based scholar Alexander G. Weheliye (2014, p 6) charges that the ideas of European intellectuals, such as Foucault, are 'are frequently invoked' with insufficient scrutiny of the

> historical, philosophical, or political foundations upon which they are constructed, which bespeaks a broad tendency in which theoretical formulations by white European thinkers are granted a conceptual carte blanche, while those uttered from the purview of minority discourse that speak to the same questions are almost exclusively relegated to the jurisdiction of ethnographic locality.

We remain sensitive to this critique, but we also recognise that Gramsci, Bourdieu and – albeit with much greater hesitancy, Foucault (Garrett,

2020) – will be used creatively and reflexively to help us to think more deeply about issues pertaining to 'race', racism and social work. We then begin to incorporate figures and concepts that are much more critical of the European intellectual tradition. In this context, we draw attention to the work of the Portuguese legal scholar, Boaventura de Sousa Santos. The chapter concludes by briefly discussing two paradigms that are significant for *Social Work with the Black African Diaspora*: critical race theory (CRT) and critical whiteness theory (CWT). Such forms of epistemological scholarship (and activism) help to unmask the hegemonic processes determined by, or crafted in the service of, loosely put, White norms and values.

Chapter 4 deepens this exploration of writers and theorists mostly absent within the social work literature in Europe in that our prime – and, indeed, critical – focus is on Afrocentricity. Here, many readers will be introduced for the first time to the African–American author Marimba Ani and her book *Yurugu*. Howe (1998, p 248), a notable critic of Afrocentricity observes that her book is significant because it has 'real strengths in comparison with all the other literature emerging from Afrocentrism'. It is, avows Howe (1998, p 283), 'perhaps the most intellectually impressive single work yet to appear from U.S. Afrocentric circles'. We next examine the contributions of Molefi Kete Asante, probably still the 'most influential, widely quoted Afrocentric writer' (Howe, 1998, p 231). Both writers have had a direct impact within the field of social work and have shaped the perceptions of Jerome Schiele (in the US), Mekada Graham (in the UK and the US) and Dumisani Thabede (in Africa). All of these writers have argued, even if not wholly convincingly, that Afrocentric thinking and the specific interventions it might generate are beneficial for continental and diasporic Black African communities. Nonetheless, we perceive deep and fundamental problems with the strident reasoning of Asante and other Afrocentric thinkers. For example, as Makungu M. Akinyela (1995, p 31) maintained more than a quarter of a century ago, there is an abiding

> refusal to deepen the critique of existing capitalist social structure and capitalism's relationship to oppression and exploitation, Afrocentricity implicitly accepts the legitimacy of the politics of domination outside of the racial paradigm and fails to examine the relationship to racism of other forms of oppression such as sexism, heterosexism, and ecological destruction.

The chapter concludes by illuminating the significant contributions of the Beninese philosopher, Paul J. Hountondji. Very much opposed to the reductive identity politics of the Afrocentrists, his complex contributions are mostly unknown within the social work literature. We aim to rectify this by dwelling on the utility of Hountondji when grappling with issues relating to 'race' and culture. (For an interesting critique of Hountondji's work see also Owomoyela, 1987).

In Chapter 5 we begin to situate the book's discussion more firmly in Ireland by focusing on a bundle of themes which provide a contextual layering for the empirical work highlighted in Chapter 6. Here, we discuss social work in Ireland and the dominance of the neoliberal capitalist regime of accumulation and the social order than it generates and perpetuates. Comprehending this dimension is, for us, fundamental because issues connected to 'race' and racism can never be detached from the political economy. In this chapter we also provide a brief overview of 'multicultural' Ireland, civil society and the Black African diaspora and the difficulties facing Black African social work students. We also briefly outline the relevant legal frameworks, guidance and protocols for social work practice and, in this context, focus particularly on children, child welfare and child protection. As readers will quickly detect, much of this chapter is very much 'Ireland specific' – and that is its purpose – but those located elsewhere can make the connections and make comparisons in terms of how some of the issues that we identify play out in their own national settings.

A number of contributions have begun to explore the perceptions of 'service users' in relation to 'race' and racism, but frequently those providing the actual services have been missing. In Chapter 6, therefore, we 'hear' what a number of them have to say. Hence, our focus is on the perceptions – always lucid and fascinating, but often surprising and controversial – of social work practitioners and educators in Ireland. Talking openly and with enormous candour, they outline their perceptions across four core themes relating to: social work education and theoretical perspectives; praxis; organisational structures within the capitalist racial state; and neoliberalism. In the final chapter we briefly look backwards at some of the main themes that emerged and we also refer to future possibilities.

We have chosen to include a series of 'Reflection and talk boxes' at the end of each chapter. The particular purpose of the boxes (which can be ignored if they are not to the liking of particular readers) is to assist students, and others, in critically reflecting (individually and in class/seminar and fieldwork/workplace discussions) on key themes and questions referred to in the chapter. These Reflection and talk boxes are not included, of course, to overly direct or limit discussion on any of the issues emerging in each chapter. Moreover, the topics raised in these boxes may need to be tailored in order to address concerns specific to your own country and field of activity.

Reflection and talk box 1

How do some of the issues raised in this initial chapter relate to where you are situated in terms of the job that you do and national setting in which you are located?

How should the BLM movement impact on social work theory and practices?

Across a number of states, what does the impact of the COVID-19 global pandemic reveal about the social and economic location of Black and minority ethnic peoples?

'Social work MUST be anti-racist': how does this statement relate to changes that need to be made in your national setting? How does racism intersect with questions of class exploitation and patriarchy?

2

Keywords, concepts and terminology

Introduction

A number of interrelated keywords and concepts will be of differing degrees of significance in the book, and so it is important to say a little about these (Williams, 1983). Relatedly, issues pertaining to language and terminology also warrant clarification. In this chapter, therefore, we focus in turn on the following keywords and concepts: Black, 'race', ethnicity, racism and anti-racism, capitalist racial state, acculturation, cultural competence, diversity and multiculturalism, diaspora. Clearly, entire books can be written on each of these and our modest aspiration is – drawing on the work of other writers and commentators – to merely furnish a succinct, and far from exhaustive and comprehensive, overview.

Black

Our use of the term 'Black African', as opposed to simply 'African', reflects an understanding that there may be people from the continent of Africa who see themselves as 'African', but who do not identify, or are not viewed by others, as 'Black'. Using the term 'Black' is also a political statement. Against the 'backdrop of the US Black Power Movement, the term "Black", hitherto acting as a signifier of "racial" inferiority, became transformed into a key category of an organised practice of struggle based on building black resistance and new kinds of black consciousness' (Singh, 2020, p 28). In this context, Joyce M. Bell (2014) has charted the impact of the movement on US social work.

Kwesi Tsri (2016, p 151) argues that the categorical use of the term 'Black should be abandoned'. This is because

> as long as the symbolic use of the term 'Black' remains, [it] will be derogatory. Its use contributes to the persistence of racial stereotypes that are informed by the idea of blackness. Furthermore, the use of the term 'Black' as a human categorising device is an imposition of a definition by another group, a dominant group, on another. The depiction of Africans as 'Black' in classical antiquity was not a case of

self-definition, but an example of the naming of Others by those who exercised dominion over them.

He further observes that in Africa today, many groups are identified by the 'names of the languages they speak, such as Ewe, Gã, Fante, Krobo, Wolof, Ibo, Yoruba and many others. Thus, in general, geographical location and language continue to be available as the core elements around which group identities can be constructed' (Tsri, 2016, p 152). In what follows, while recognising and respecting Tsri's point and acknowledging that the word is embedded in relations of power, we will retain the word 'Black'. We also find ourselves in agreement with Gurnam Singh's (2020, p 28) observation that not all Black people are 'disadvantaged in the same way', and so use of the word 'Black' can, in dealing with inequalities, be a 'very blunt instrument'. Oftentimes, issues pertaining to class and gender will, for example, be of enormous significance, and lending primacy to 'race', while neglecting other intersectional considerations, is misguided and reductive for both theory and practice (Anthias and Yuval-Davis, 1993).

'Race'

Within the social work literature, Singh and Masocha (2020, p 1) state that as a 'scientific and analytic concept, the notion of "race" has been heavily critiqued, yet it remains a significant factor in shaping the lived experiences of minority groups'. This is a perspective that we share in this book. Usefully, in charting the evolution of 'race', Singh (2020, p 16) maintains that as, a 'scientific tool for sifting, categorising, organising and brutalising human populations', the term emerged and began to gain prominence in the late 17th century (Singh, 2020, p 16). He continues:

> Historically, the idea of 'race' rested on monolithic and essentialist notions of lineage and ancestry. Much racist ideology is predicated on three main assertions: i) there exists a thing called 'race' which in some way can be linked to certain, real or imagined, distinguishing characteristics, such as 'the soul' (or lack of), skin colour, hair texture, bone structure; ii) that such differences [that] exist amongst different 'races' are immutable; and iii) that [it] is possible to use such differences to arrange human beings in an hierarchical order in which some 'races' are seen to be dominant or more advanced and others less advanced. (Singh, 2020, p 17)

Three 'distinct overlapping historical phases' in the evolution of the term can also be charted (Singh, 2020, p 17): a 'scriptural phase' (16th and 17th centuries); a 'scientific phase' (from the 18th century) and today's 'sociological phase' in which 'race' is understood as a 'social and ideological construct' (Singh, 2020, p 14). The 'older scriptural and scientific discourses of "race" are still evident in the way particular groups and communities are imagined and talked about … [and have] not gone away' (Singh, 2020, p 23).

Paul Gilroy (1998; 2000) has been a compellingly lucid voice challenging what he terms 'raciology'. According to his analysis, there is no scientific or biological basis to focus on 'race', and doing so might even serve to reinforce the anachronistic usage and the often troubling politics that it helps to generate. Freeing ourselves from this fixation with 'race' – and its associated idea of racial 'camps' – might help us to promote a more expansive and inclusive planetary humanism (Gilroy, 2000). This move requires us to step away from the 'pious ritual in which we always agree that "race" is invented but are then required to defer to its embeddedness in the world and to accept that the demand for justice nevertheless requires us to enter the political arenas that it helps to mark out' (Gilroy, 1998, p 842).

In an insightful discussion on the approach of Gilroy and like-minded others, Brett St Louis (2002, p 653) identifies their project as one which aims to 'de-reify or erase race'. In this sense, it can be interpreted as a bold attempt to imagine a 'post-racial polity' that crystallises 'around the understanding that the idea and reality of race cannot fully escape the (historical) taint of its absolutist and essentialised premises' (Brett St Louis, 2002, p 653). While seeking to drain intellectual, political and popular discourses of 'race' talk may be a laudable aspiration, it still remains a 'primary ascriptive marker of individual and group characteristics in the social world and also serves, at times, as a validation of discrimination and an incitement to violence' (Brett St Louis, 2002, p 253). Given the rise in neo-fascist movements over the past decades, alongside notable and distressing examples of police violence against racialised bodies, this point has become even more apparent. As Charles W. Mills (1998, p 41) observed, over two decades ago, the notion that 'race' should 'be irrelevant is certainly an attractive ideal, but when it has not been irrelevant, it is absurd to proceed as if it had been'. Indeed, a report from the Irish Network Against Racism, published in March 2021 and reviewing the past year, concludes:

> The group most commonly reporting experiences of both crime and illegal discrimination is the group of Black-African, Black-Irish and Black-Other. They experienced 33 percent of all crime cases and 33 percent of all discrimination cases. The next largest group of reports came from South Asian, Chinese and Other Asian people. South Asians and Chinese or Other Asian each reported 16% of crimes, and South Asians reported 13% of discrimination. Nearly a third (32%) of assaults and threats to kill or harm were against people identified as Black-African, Black-Irish or Black-Other. Eighteen percent were Muslim,

but half of these were also identified as Black. Eighteen percent of assaults and threats to kill or harm were against people identified as South Asian, and 18 percent were Chinese or Other Asian. (Michael, 2021b, p 16)

Conceptually, we also recognise the highly significant dimension of 'non-colour-coded racism' (Cole, 2009, p 250). As Robert Miles (1987, p 75) argues, racialisation is not limited to skin colour. The 'characteristics signified vary historically and, although they have usually been visible somatic features, other non-visible (alleged and real)' biological and cultural features have also been important in constructing threatening 'Others'. Although not a focal concern in this book, we acknowledge that racism directed at Irish Travellers is still perniciously significant in Ireland (Mac Laughlin, 1996; Pavee Point, 2013; Department of Health, 2020). Frequently, the antipathy toward the Roma community is also evidentially stark and troubling (NASC, 2013; Logan, 2014; Higgins, 2015; European Union Agency for Fundamental Rights, 2020). A rise in racist intimidation and violence against people of Chinese origin has also occurred since the outbreak of the COVID-19 pandemic (McDermott, 2020b).

Racism and anti-racism

In a significant development, in November 2020, the Irish government's 'independent' Anti-Racism Committee published an interim report as part of the development of a new National Action Plan Against Racism (Department of Children, Equality, Disability, Integration and Youth, 2020). Pinderhughes (1989) argues that power is a key element in racism because it affects social systems, social structures, interactions and individual self-concepts. Similarly, Kitano (1980) argues that racism serves to maintain power and status for the dominant groups in society as it is those with power who can effectively discriminate through deciding who is 'in'/'out' of the group. When racism results in some members of society not accessing adequate resources necessary to participate meaningfully in everyday life, their self-esteem and self-concept is further threatened, and a sense of powerlessness is likely to negatively impact on their ability to cope with the demands of everyday life. Racism – when enacted through policies and behaviours to exclude targeted groups from institutions, interactions and resources open to other groups – becomes oppression. When social workers fail to confront racist, discriminatory and oppressive practices/policies they may also be violating their basic professional code.

Lee and Lutz (2005) argue that liberal individualism, as a dominant theme of Enlightenment philosophy, presumes the equality of individuals and their ability to make rational choices as citizens. Liberalism, therefore, sees racism as an individual pathology and as a result of individual prejudices: it is *not* a societal or structural problem. When racism is framed this way, the authors argue that anti-racism takes the form of individualistic strategies often grounded in moral education: for example, promoting greater cultural knowledge of others, but maybe also having recourse to psychometric and actuarial risk evaluations to determine an individual's susceptibility to racial intolerance. The same authors also suggest that approaching racism from a liberal individualist perspective leads to a legalistic understanding of it as a violation of rights to which a person is entitled in a liberal democracy. Consequently, those subjected to racism can seek remedies in the form of punishment (of offenders), protection or compensation. Lutz and Lee (2005) imply, however, that this juridical approach has shortcomings because it fails to acknowledge the embedded internalised assumptions and biases within the field. Hence, they argue that the law fails to transcend its own complicity in the *production* and *reproduction* of racism at the structural level.

In much of Europe, for example, racism has mutated into 'cultural racism'. Reflecting this development, terms such as 'Islamophobia' and 'Afrophobia' now exist, circulate and contribute to our comprehension of what is occurring. Racism becomes subtly expressed through the idiom of cultural differences. In this context, Lentin and Titley (2011) warn against conceptualising racialised subjects as products of culture, as it allows the 'laundering' of racism as mere cultural differences. They argue this can lead immigrants to become viewed as indoctrinated by 'culture' and intransigently unwilling to change or adapt. How, therefore, can practitioners acknowledge enduring cultural differences while avoiding the racialisation of culturally distinct groups?

Ronit Lentin (2007, p 611), drawing on the work of Barnor Hesse among others, maintains that racism is a 'political system aiming to regulate bodies'. This understanding is significant because the emphasis is placed on the involvement of the state, rather than individuals laden with prejudices. The focus on the latter was very much at the core of misguided 'race awareness training' which took place in many social services departments in the UK in the 1980s and 1990s. In contemporary Ireland, despite the recognition that racial discrimination may occur at the level of institutional and state structures, the conceptualisation of racism as a phenomenon that is largely personal and attitudinal resiliently persists in public consciousness (Beirne and Jaichan, 2010). In sharp contrast, recognising the role of the state implies that racism is promoted, structurally embedded, organised and maintained. Weheliye (2014, p 3) is alert to this dimension when he observes that 'race', racialisation and racial identities are 'ongoing sets of political relations that require ... constant perpetuation via institutions, discourses, practices, desires, infrastructures, languages, technologies, sciences, economies, dreams, and cultural artifacts'. This mix functions to bar 'nonwhite subjects from the category of the human as it is performed in the modern west'.

Social Work with the Black African Diaspora is founded on anti-racism, which can be defined as 'forms of thought and/or practice that seek to confront, eradicate and/or ameliorate racism. Anti-racism implies the ability to identify a phenomenon – racism – and to do something about it' (Bonnett in Singh and Masocha, 2020, p 3). As a model it was developed by grassroots political movements, 'inspired both by Black Power movements in the USA and by anti-colonial movements in Britain's ex-empire', and it opposes both assimilationist and multiculturalist approaches (Anthias and Yuval-Davis, 1993, p 113). Significantly, anti-racist projects and struggles have been sparked *beyond* social work and, more emphatically, such struggles have often been informed by opposition to racist practices *within* state institutions, including social work. As Michael Lavalette and Laura Penketh (2013, p 9) observe about the British experience:

> Anti-racist approaches within social work had their roots in the social movements against racism in the 1970s and early 1980s ... These movements included a wide array of campaigns against racism and racist political violence (such as the campaign around the New Cross fire where 13 young party goers were killed in a fire started by racists), against the Far-right (for example, Rock Against Racism, Anti-Nazi League, Campaign Against Racism and Fascism), against police harassment and racist immigration controls. These movements were also shaped by the inner city uprisings that exploded in various parts of Britain in 1981, particularly in Bristol, Brixton (London), Chapeltown (Leeds), Handsworth (Birmingham) and Toxteth (Liverpool).

The 'riots' – for some, urban 'uprisings' – may also have prompted the social work profession to recruit more people from Black and ethnic minority backgrounds. These actions did not resolve the difficulties relating to how to operationalise 'anti-racist' ideology in social work theory and practice. Furthermore, 'anti-racism' was castigated by the insurgent political Right for being aridly 'politically correct', too ideologically driven and too formulaic. Perhaps in response, the formal commitment to 'anti-racism' was later dropped from UK social work programmes in the 1990s and replaced with a managerially inflected demand for 'cultural competence'.

Contributions in the Lavalette and Penketh (2013) volume note that, despite their increasing numbers within social work since the 1980s, Black and ethnic minority social workers remain underrepresented in strategically significant positions in the profession including academia. More emphatically, Black and ethnic minority practitioners' absence from such powerful opinion-forming positions could be considered another form of oppression within the profession itself. Perhaps there is an irony, even hypocrisy, in a profession advocating for equality and the eradication of discrimination in society insofar as social work's 'own house' is palpably not 'in order'. Relatedly, there is a relative absence of Black African social workers in academia and in professional decision-making positions in Ireland. At the time of writing at least one higher education social work programme in Ireland – and probably more – has no Black members within any tier of its governance structure (staff group, management board, practice assessment panel and so on).

Lavalette and Penketh (2013) call on social workers to become activists truly working to collectively champion anti-racism. One section of their edited volume documents a case in which a social worker questioned an unfair age assessment undertaken on a migrant. While this 'lone ranger' action is emancipatory, it has potential risks of victimisation: collective action, through organisations such as SWAN, could arguably be safer and, in the long term, create more substantial victories.

While we are both alert to the structural underpinnings of racism, we acknowledge that it frequently plays out in micro and personal interactions. In this sense, we also recognise some of the significant work undertaken which has articulated and interpreted racial micro-aggressions occurring in everyday life. This dimension has, of course, particular resonance for social work because it is a profession in which the quotidian is often rooted in small-scale interactions and interventions taking place in offices and within people's homes.

Albeit derived from the US and located within the discipline of psychology, Sue et al's (2007) focus on common, everyday racism may contain 'messages' for social workers in Ireland and elsewhere. The authors describe racial micro-aggressions as brief and commonplace daily verbal, behavioural or environmental indignities (whether intentional or unintentional) that communicate hostile, derogatory or negative racial slights and insults toward people of colour. Perpetrators of micro-aggressions are often unaware that they engage in such communications when they interact with racial/ethnic minorities. The rationale that Sue et al (2007) advance for why White perpetrators of racial micro-aggressions might be unaware of their conduct, or its impact, is that, as dominant members of society, they are not immune from inheriting the racial biases of their forebears. Often, according to this line of reasoning, they are victims of a cultural socialising process that predisposes them to biases and prejudices discriminating against people of colour. Framed a different way, their 'habitus' is one saturated in a proclivity that fails to detect that they are perpetrators of racialised micro-aggressions (see also Chapter 3). The authors also analyse how racism, again manifested as serialised racial micro-aggression, can be difficult for practitioners to identify. Consequently, they propose a taxonomy of racial micro-aggressions that may be likely to impinge upon practice, education, training and research. This, although embedded in the US cultural context, may have potent resonances for many Black Africans in Ireland.

Despite the fact that a Black African person may have been born in Ireland, a common micro-aggression that they often encounter is entangled in the ambiguous and routinised question 'where are you from?' The 'message' often implied is 'how can you be Irish when you are Black African?' A second common micro-aggression would normally be something like 'you are articulate' which might be 'translated' as 'your English is very good for a Black African'. A third might be 'I am not racist, I have Black friends', which, according to Sue et al (2007), suggests 'I am immune from racism because I have Black friends. Fourth, 'there is only one human race' can be perceived as denying the racial and cultural reality of the person at whom the comment is directed. Fifth, asking a Black person 'why do you have to be so loud/animated … Just calm down' might be interpreted as pathologising a particular disposition while implying that the communication styles of the dominant White culture are the normative ideal which all must strive to achieve and personify. All of these micro-aggressions (and how they might be deconstructed) relate to the experiences of Black Africans in Ireland and they may impact on social work interventions.

Capitalist racial state

Abdelmalek Sayad (2004, p 279) observes that the 'secret virtue of immigration' is that it 'provides an introduction, and perhaps the best introduction of all, to the sociology of the state'. It is 'as though it were the very nature of the state to discriminate … between the "nationals" it recognises … and "others" with whom it deals only in "material" and instrumental terms. It deals with them only because they are present within the field of its national sovereignty' (Sayad, 2004, p 279). Sayad reminds us, therefore, that our book has to interrogate the role that the state and the role that what he dubs 'state thought' plays. In this sense, the 'racial state' conceptualisation that is deployed by Lentin, and informed by the contributions of Omi and Winant (1986) and Goldberg (2002), is theoretically useful. The latter posits the 'law as central to modern state formation and a technology of racial rule, promoting racial categorisation and identification, and shaping national identities through legislating on immigration controls and citizenship rights' (Lentin, 2007, p 614). Hence, through

> constitutions, border controls, the law, policy making, bureaucracy and governmental technologies such as census categorizations, invented histories and traditions, ceremonies and cultural imaginings, modern states, each in its own way, are defined by their power to exclude (and

include) in racially ordered terms, to categorize hierarchically, and to set aside. (Lentin, 2007, p 612; see also Christie, 2006)

Such practices can be associated with what is often termed 'institutional racism' and the embedding of patterns of discrimination within all the distinctive 'fields' of the racial state (Lea, 2000). Hence, spheres such as welfare, education, the law and policing, arts and culture, housing and, of course, social work are shaped accordingly. Our main refinement of the racial state conceptualisation is to seek to ground it in the symbolic and material fabric of *capitalism*. Hence, our preference for the term *capitalist* racial state aims to highlight how states' imperatives are also capitalist imperatives that are triggered and sustained in order to increase the surplus value derived from – and stolen from – the working class. Whatever the colour of our skin, most of us are exploited by capital, even though the rate of exploitation may differ on account of our skin colour (and gender) and our roles and functions within a capitalist world system and the complex social orders that it gives rise to and maintains.

Today, the 'asylum seeker' category of migrant is mostly framed as a 'social problem'. The so-called European migration crisis of 2015 exposed the weaknesses of the Dublin Regulations, as countries, such as Greece, would have disproportionately carried the 'burden'. The coercive directive from the European Union (EU) for member states to share the 'burden' of receiving and settling refugees resulted in Ireland taking a relatively small number of Syrian refugees. More generally, those categorised as 'asylum seekers' by the naming practices of capitalist racial states are not only presented as a 'burden', they are also often portrayed as competing with the indigenous and 'disadvantaged' population for scarce resources. Hence, the need to control them is presented as essential to the 'common good' and to 'the integrity of the asylum process' (Schuster, 2003, p 253). Stressing the significance of neoliberal capital and globalisation, Eithne Luibhéid maintains that contemporary migration is a consequence of restructuring, capital accumulation and global wars that destabilise national boundaries and, along with these, notions of imagined homogeneity that have been culturally perceived as the 'life blood' of capitalist racial states (in Fanning, 2002).

Luibhéid's argument, therefore, is that capitalist racial states, such as Ireland, actually need asylum seekers in order to be able to consolidate or 'redraw' racial and national boundaries that have become destabilised by neoliberal globalism. Even within the 'asylum seeker' category there exists differential racialisation whereby light-skinned asylum seekers or refugees from the Middle East or Eastern Europe tend to be considered 'genuine', while Black Africans are perhaps more likely to be labelled as 'bogus' and/ or simply 'economic migrants'. For example, a prominent Irish politician, from Galway, confidently avowed that Syrian refugees were 'more genuine' that those from Black Africa, who were much more likely to be 'bogus' and/or 'economic migrants. Expressed using the colloquial Irish, this latter group were often simply a bunch of 'chancers'. The recent emergence of a right-wing Irish National Party, modelled along the same lines as other ultra-nationalist European political parties, such as British National Party, continues to illustrate the concerns of at least some Irish people about becoming minorities in their homelands on account of supposedly large-scale immigration. Exacerbated by the pandemic, such tensions might also prompt parasitic fascist groups to tactically amplify such 'concerns'.

Also examining the Irish situation, Beirne and Jaichand (2010) argue that it is the state that sets the tone and the tenor of 'race relations' in any society. It is for this reason that racism within the state and its institutions should be identified and confronted. Such racism can occur at various levels: in legislation, within the executive branch of government, within the judiciary, within immigration and asylum policy, at the level of individual government ministers and related political representatives. Beirne and Jaichand (2010) also stress the role that non-state actors, such as the media and NGOs, can also play in nurturing toxic institutional racism.

Cultural competence

The concept of 'cultural competence' was developed in the US as part of a strategy to try to improve access to healthcare for a population that was increasingly diverse: the aim also, as expressed in policy document discourse emerging in the southern hemisphere, was to address marked inequities in the delivery of social services for indigenous populations (Midgley, 1981, Weaver, 1999). A range of authors argue that countries, such as Australia and New Zealand, developed 'cultural competency' influenced by US models after recognising that interventions in healthcare and social services rooted in a mostly unexamined mono-cultural, western knowledge base resulted in poor health and well-being 'outcomes' for indigenous people and other minorities. This realisation, at times grudging and not infrequently merely tactical, appeared to mark a departure from the previously held doctrinal assumption that western cultural values could be universally applied.

The literature on the concept ranges from texts that offer summations of the knowledge that professionals 'require' in order to work with specific cultural groups to texts that offer a somewhat richer and more nuanced engagement. The meso- and micro-level articulations of the concept are widely debated, with contestation issues centred predominantly on conceptual ambiguity, limitations, Universalist claims and stereotyping effects. Major criticism of the concept relates to its focus on meso and micro interventions, which can preclude a focus on the structural level. Articulations of the concept in the US are frequently based on the model of Cross et al (1989), and the focus is mostly on individual and organisational 'cultural competence' and culturally adapted interventions. Studies on the concept from Australia, Canada and New Zealand largely focus on descriptions of culture-based intervention strategies for local indigenous populations. There appear to be few, if any, 'cultural competence' models truly originating in Europe.

Most social work courses in Ireland now try to encompass diversity and multicultural awareness in some shape or form, with certain programmes keen to devise their own 'cultural competence' training programmes. They have also, not always unproblematically, 'imported' some 'tried and tested' 'cultural competence' models from abroad. Embracing such approaches emanates from assumptions that these models can transform social workers into 'sensitive' and 'culturally competent' practitioners by equipping them with awareness, knowledge, skills and inductive learning. Such assumptions include the implied understanding that providing practice guidelines is a panacea for cultural incompetence. Such misguided assumptions are evident in Ireland (McGregor et al, 2020). In this context, 'how to' models aimed at everyday practices fail to go far enough to truly disturb the conventional received wisdom and unconscious bias of entrenched dispositions. Indeed, despite the proliferation of such models, Irish practitioners' interventions with members of the Black African diaspora continue to generate controversy (Onyejelem, 2017).

Regarding social work research, Davis et al (2010) alert us to the importance of 'culturally competent' projects contributing to critical and reflective thinking and practices. These authors maintain that, in social work research, the shape and scope of scholarly inquiry is often largely influenced by how the 'problem' is formulated. They warn that this can result in mooted 'solutions' being tarnished by the 'social and cultural fingerprints' of the researchers. The proposed 'solutions' might be entirely at odds with the interest and expectations of the intended beneficiaries of the research. Hence, they offer 'guiding principles' that seek to prioritise the 'integration of cultural relevance' in the entire research process from the outset. Grounded in the Afrocentric perspective, which we will examine in more detail in Chapter 4, these authors argue that in order to achieve 'culturally competent' research, it must be related to a people's understanding. Researchers must have an affinity, knowledge and respect for the history, culture and knowledge of Black African-descendant people. This does not, however, imply that non-Black-African group members cannot conduct 'culturally competent' research. What is important is that the actual research agenda must reflect and serve the interests of the people studied. Davis et al (2010) also maintain that we should keep in mind seven questions when defining research questions.

- How did/do 'studied persons' understand relevant historical and contemporary phenomena connected to the question?
- How have their attitudes and behaviours been shaped and misshaped by this phenomenon?

- What are the factors that they see as being important?
- How do we know?
- Where are their words?
- When are they speaking?
- Where is their 'voice?

The authors' guidelines for integrating cultural relevance are shaped by three major criteria: centredness, culture and self-determination. In addition, four questions serve as a guide:

- What are the historical issues from which the community needs to heal?
- In relationship to the research question, what are the myths or misperceptions about the behaviour of the community?
- In relationship to the phenomenon, what are the culturally relevant examples of how the community has been transformed?
- In relationship to the phenomenon, how has the community mobilised others to affect change?

Although grounded in the Afrocentric perspective, Davis et al (2010) conclude that these dimensions can be combined with other western methodologies to assist researchers in integrating cultural relevance into their research agendas.

Clearly, it is important to take into account cultural factors in both social work practice and research effort in order avoid flawed assessments/ intervention and possible disengagement of service users/research participants. Culture influences how we view our social circumstances, health and help-seeking behaviour. All cultures have beliefs and practices that are unique, and that are used to explain and manage ill health and mental or emotional distress (see also Chapter 4). These, in turn, impact on and shape how mental health difficulties are experienced (Fanon, 2018 [1953–1956]). Relatedly, O'Hagan (2001) emphasises the need for practitioners to try to familiarise themselves with regard to the patterns of obligations, hierarchies and responsibilities in service users' families, and their culturally influenced perceptions of problems.

Nevertheless, despite the voguish popularity of the 'cultural competence' concept, especially within the liberal managerial literature, some of its main articulations are tokenistic and inherently flawed. Indeed, the whole notion of 'cultural competence' can easily be easily assimilated and incorporated into 'state ideological apparatuses' (Althusser, 1971). In short, the exhortation to become 'culturally competent' need not result in any recalibration of how societies are shaped to become more economically and socially just and equitable. In this sense, discourses circulating around 'cultural competence' might be perceived as potent 'screen discourses' distracting attention from substantial issues concerning the distribution of income, wealth and resources (Bourdieu and Wacquant, 2001; see also Choonara, 2021). An emphasis on 'cultural competence' training has, in some cases, also fuelled fear and resistance. Problems have been compounded in training for social workers that excluded consideration of cross-cultural issues *beyond* a Black/White divide (Garrett, 1998). We are not, of course, pre-emptively dismissing the weighty and doxic corpus of 'cultural competence' literature, but we are alert to the fact that 'cultural competence' approaches remain largely locked within an insular discursive framework that is embedded in the population management strategies of what we described earlier as the neoliberal capitalist racial state.

Diversity and multiculturalism

In parts of Europe, our contemporary conjuncture has witnessed a renewed emphasis on 'blood and soil' nationalism. More generally, the situation is complex because many capitalist racial states are also keen to embrace rhetoric of 'diversity' and 'multiculturalism' (Nash, 2019). Such states can, therefore, be interpreted as partly replicating the 'multicultural' sensibility of the corporate sector (Sobande, 2019; 2020). Relatedly, David Theo Goldberg (2002) maintains that modern nation-states 'exclude in order to construct homogeneity which he sees as "heterogeneity in denial" while appropriating difference through celebrations of the multicultural' (Lentin, 2007, p 612). Lentin (2007, p 611) elaborates:

> racial terminology of categorisation and control on the one hand and discourses of 'cultural diversity' on the other underpin the Irish state's response to the arrival of growing numbers of immigrants since the 1990s, in the shape of 'intercultural' politics, which construct cultural difference and ethnic minority 'communities' as static and already there, ignoring intra-ethnic heterogeneities and contestations.

Since the mid-1990s, Ireland has been described in government documents as a 'multicultural society' (Christie, 2010). Christie (2010) suggests that this development is partly in response to the significant number of migrants who have recently come to live in a country that has traditionally viewed itself in monocultural terms and as a country of emigration. Loyal contends that the 'current hegemonic construction of Ireland as an "open, cosmopolitan, multicultural, tourist friendly society" obscures a "harsh reality of capitalist production, exclusionary nationalism and growing xenophobia in relation to both the state and the general populace"' (in Lentin, 2007, p 616). In Chapter 5, we will explore this dimension in more detail.

The level and extent to which a country embraces multiculturalism tends to be reflected in the policies and organisational behaviours of its institutions. It has been argued that there exist three types of multicultural policy models: the 'difference-blindness' approach, the 'recognition of differences' approach and the 'critical multiculturalism' approach. Within the 'difference-blindness' approach, policies ensure that individual rights and advantages are equally applied to all without reference to ethno-cultural, racial or religious location (Bissoondath, 1994). The argument is that this ensures the state's neutrality in resource allocation, as well as ensuring a stronger commitment to national unity on account of immigrants assimilating to the dominant culture. The 'recognition of differences' perspective suggests that, while democracy encompasses equality of all cultural identities, people need to be recognised as having a unique identity in order to evolve an authentic sense of 'self'. The aim is to reconcile the contradictions that arise in resisting homogenising individuals in the name of ensuring equality, while also acknowledging differences without creating hierarchies of identity (Kymlicka, 1995). This approach argues for representative rights for marginalised groups to remove barriers to 'parity of participation' in all spheres of life (Fraser, 2003). This policy is frequently 'blind' as to how the history of colonialism has 'distorted' the identities of some ethnic minorities who have internalised oppression. As for 'critical multiculturalism', McLaren (1994) argues that both 'difference-blindness' and 'recognition of differences' perspectives are wholly inadequate policies to address challenges inherent in a culturally plural society. McLaren maintains that critical multiculturalism begins by acknowledging the nature and construction of 'race', class, nation and so on within a socio-historical and capitalist context. The same writer further argues that it is only through vigorously interrogating conditions and notions of 'otherness' that people become aware of, and consequently address, the ways in which hegemonic cultural norms sustain their marginalisation and oppression. In childcare, for example, Christie (2010) asserts that the National Children's Strategy states that children from minority ethnic communities have 'special needs' that should be met. Such 'special needs', identified with those seen as culturally different, have largely remained unnamed and unrecognised in research, policies and social work practice. The foregoing argument by Christie (2010) suggests, therefore, that a liberal 'recognition of differences' approach obtains in Ireland.

Gisèle Legault (1997) analysed the problems encountered by 40 social workers in providing public social services to ethnic minorities in multicultural and multi-ethnic Montreal in the early 1990s. The findings highlight significant instances of 'culture shock' involving social workers from a western cultural location, and users of services from non-western societies. These include: different notions of the role of social services and definitions of 'basic' human needs; different notions of childhood upbringing; unequal relationships between men and women; different notions of the individual and family. A brief review of each of these themes is offered to establish and identify the impact on the practice and training of social workers to better understand and competently engage in intercultural encounters involving sensitive areas of service provision. More importantly, the study provides a useful comparative analysis of what has changed in the recent child protection literature.

Nylund (2006) examines social work's response to increasing cultural diversity as it is reflected in teaching 'cultural competence' in the US, and he provides, therefore, with a comparative perspective in respect of the Irish situation. Nylund contends that classes in multiculturalism are now commonplace in most graduate schools of social work. This, he suggests, is evidenced by the fact that, since the late 1970s, 'cultural competence' and 'ethnic sensitivity' have increasingly become part of the social work literature and curricula (Lum, 1999). The author argues that the central themes in a good deal of the associated literature have been concerned with developing a 'culturally competent' practice model by offering effective services to ethnically diverse service users.

Nylund maintains that this model is underpinned by an assumption that teaching social work students about various ethnic and racial groups transforms them into more 'sensitive' and 'empathetic' practitioners better able to meet the unique needs of ethnic minorities. The key message is unfortunately also prevalent in most western liberal democratic jurisdictions, including Ireland. Nylund (2006) particularly identifies an 'over-emphasis' on curricular change and an 'under-emphasis' on the impact of structural racism on Black service users and Black social work students (Adeleye et al, 2020). This failure to adequately acknowledge such lived experiences amounts to a major weakness of multicultural education theory and practice in social work education in the US. This is useful as a critique in respect of the current 'state of the art' in this area in a number of countries.

Nylund also cites McLaren's (1994)'s contribution criticising multicultural education for an overly simplistic and naive view of structurally entrenched wider social and cultural power relations. Additionally, the writer deploys McLaren's arguments to suggest that the dominant forms of White ethnicity are rendered 'invisible' in discussions of multiculturalism. Based on this perspective, Nylund further critiques the current emphasis on 'cultural competence' in social work education and practice. In this context, he refers to 'liberal' and/or 'conservative' multiculturalism.

As to a 'solution', Nylund proposes 'critical multiculturalism'. This is a theoretical perspective influenced by the work of figures such as Freire (1970), bell hooks (1984), Giroux (1997a; 1997b) and – again – McLaren (1994). This paradigm is committed to removing 'cultural competence' and replacing it with 'anti-racist practice'. Critical multiculturalism seeks to accomplish this pedagogical and political task insofar as it:

- recognises the socio-historical construct of 'race' and its intersections with class, gender, nation, sexuality and capitalism;
- creates pedagogical conditions in which students interrogate conditions of 'otherness';
- challenges the idea of social work (and other social sciences) as an apolitical, trans-historical practice removed from the power struggles of history;
- makes visible the historical and social construction of Whiteness. Hence, critical multiculturalism is more inclusive of White students/social workers and possibly may have the most profound impact on them.

Nylund argues that this approach provides a more radical, anti-racist conception of multiculturalism in that it is potentially drained of the reductionist orientations found in most 'cultural competence' models. He particularly focuses on 'critical whiteness studies' as a key aspect of critical multiculturalism. This approach interrogates the political, social and historical situatedness of White ethnicities and the hegemonic processes that spawn their universalisation and normalisation. To 'undo' the status quo, Nylund (2006) advises social work educators and practitioners to use the insights of 'critical multiculturalism' as a 'tool' to 'destabilise' racism.

Bourdieu and Wacquant (1999; 2001) are scathing about what they view as the importation into Europe and elsewhere of US ideas underpinned by 'multiculturalism'. Žižek (2002, p 172) observes that the global market 'thrives on the diversification of demand' and 'multiculturalism' 'perfectly fits the logic' of contemporary capitalism. In the US, during the Obama presidency, African-American political scientist Lester K. Spence (2012, p 144) similarly perceived 'multiculturalism' as a 'vehicle to promote neoliberal policies'. Relatedly, while making 'anti-racism' into a 'public principle', associated projects championed the notion that the 'most effective means of combating racism' was developing 'entrepreneurial capacities in populations, institutions, and spaces deemed as "non-white"' (Spence, 2012, p 145). As we have noted, debates on 'multiculturalism' are complex and cannot simply be viewed as reflective of US dominance on international intellectual fields. 'Multiculturalism' might best be interpreted as a 'travelling theory' which 'disguises very different and fluid struggles in different countries, and even in different cities and localities' (Werbner, 2000, p 154).

Diaspora

The term diaspora has been 'loose in the world' for decades (Clifford in Gray 2000, p 168). At its most basic, it references the dispersion or migration of communities (Vertovec, 2000, ch 7). For Spivak (2002, p 47), large 'movements of people – renamed "diaspora" – are what defines our time'. Certainly, the whole idea of an African diaspora informs our understanding of some of the main concerns of our book. Gilroy (2000, p 123) observes that the

> idea of diaspora offers a ready alternative to the stern discipline of primordial kinship and rooted belonging. It rejects the popular image of natural nations spontaneously endowed with self-consciousness … I[t] problematize[s] the cultural and historical mechanics of belonging. It disrupts the fundamental power of territory to determine identity by breaking the simple sequence of explanatory links between place, location, and consciousness.

Stuart Hall (1990, p 35), theorising from a not dissimilar perspective, concludes:

> Diaspora does not refer us to those scattered tribes whose identity can only be secured in relation to some sacred homeland … the diaspora experience as I intend it here is defined, not by the essence of purity, but by the recognition of a necessary heterogeneity and diversity; by a conception of 'identity' which lives by and through, not despite difference; by hybridity. Diaspora identities are those which are constantly producing and reproducing themselves anew, through transformation and difference.

Sharing Hall's approach, *Social Work with the Black African Diaspora* is underpinned by an understanding that Black African people in Ireland do not, of course, form a homogeneous and socially static bloc. In this sense, our intention is not to promote 'simple' ideas of ethnic identity or – even worse – to champion a crude essentialism or dangerous 'ethno-dogma' (Gilroy, 1994). Rather, our book is a sustained call for greater plurality within social work in respect of how the profession, in theory and practices, engages with a specific, internally diverse, community. Also from the 1990s, Avtar Brah's (1996, pp 208–209) articulation of the concept of 'diaspora space' also informs our engagement with a range of themes in this book. Brah explains her idea as follows:

> Diaspora space is the point at which boundaries of inclusion and exclusion, of belonging and otherness, of 'us' and 'them', are contested. [It refers to] a conceptual category … 'inhabited', not only by those who have migrated and their descendants, but equally by those who are constructed and represented as indigenous. In other words, the concept of *diaspora space* (as opposed to that of diaspora) includes the entanglement, the intertwining of the genealogies of dispersion with those of 'staying put'. The diaspora space is the site where *the native is as much a diasporian as the diasporian is the native*. (Original emphases)

Conclusion

Some of the main keywords and conceptualisations that will be mentioned in the book having been briefly discussed, the next two chapters will be more theory attuned. In the next chapter, the focus is on themes connected, in various ways, to decolonisation. In the subsequent chapter, attention will switch to critically concentrate on Afrocentricity and a number of its primary definers. Both chapters assemble, therefore, a rich mosaic of contrasting theoretical perspective which may be of use as we begin to dwell in more detail on social work with the African diaspora in Ireland.

Reflection and talk box 2

Why are questions circulating around keywords and associated concepts significant for social work?

Does the 'capitalist racial state' idea help us to understand how racism is promoted and sustained within 'official' and institutional structures?

What is your understanding of notions such as 'diversity' and 'multiculturalism'? Can they underpin anti-racist strategies; are they obstacles?

How can ideas related to the concept of 'diaspora' help social workers and similar groups to get a better sense of some of the complexities associated with issues connected to migration?

3

Decolonising theory

Introduction

This chapter begins by briefly dwelling on decolonisation. Here we aim to concisely discuss issues related to the struggle for national independence, involving emerging African states and more recent efforts intent on decolonising the knowledge base and teaching in western universities. Unsurprisingly, the latter project has begun, to different degrees, to impact on the field of social work education.

Underpinning this book is the rooted understanding that theoretical approaches, often originating in the West, should not simply be discarded because they are often crudely and lazily and erroneously assessed as wholly tainted by the 'Eurocentric' brush. Even while remaining reflexively committed to decolonising social work's insular knowledge base, we can still appreciate what is useful not only in the Marxist tradition – and specifically in the contributions of Gramsci and others – but also within the non-Marxist European tradition as reflected in the work of Bourdieu and Foucault. In the next part of the chapter, therefore, we briefly discuss how this trinity of European intellectuals are connected to some of the key theoretical preoccupations in *Social Work with the Black African Diaspora*. The final third of the chapter focuses on the contributions of Boaventura de Sousa Santos, and it concludes by summarising some of the thinking largely emerging from the US that is grounded in CRT and CWT.

Decolonising the material world, decolonising the university, decolonising disciplines

Western 'modernity' arrived in Africa and other places in the world 'out of the barrels of guns' (Therborn, 2011, p 59). From its inception, colonisation was frequently catastrophic, in human terms, because of its racialised and even genocidal character. Even during the period that witnessed the gradual ending of European colonisation, from the close of the Second World War, various colonial powers continued to try to violently extinguish nationalist rebellions. For example, the British government orchestrated the brutal suppression of the Mau-Mau rising for eight years stretching from 1952 to 1960 (Elkins, 2005; see also Ngũgĩ wa Thiong'o, 2014). In 1954, in the Sétif area of Algeria, the French colonial authorities, aided by *Pied-noir* fascist militias, are estimated to have massacred 45,000 civilians. Two years later, in Madagascar, the French tried to defeat a nationalist uprising and, by the mid-1950s, it has been estimated that 100,000 had been killed. The French government, while celebrating the defeat the Hitler regime and the end of the German occupation, spent the following years violently crushing nationalist insurgency (Mbembe, 2017).

Colonialism, and the domination or eradication of subjugated populations, can also been linked to later developments within the European heartland. The colonies were, for instance, locations where concentration camps emerged as a 'novel form of political administration, population management, warfare, and coerced' labour (Gilroy, 2000, p 60). Despite conservative historiography's attempts to restore a more benign, even triumphalist, depiction of the British Empire, corrosive colonial nostalgia is unable to mask the fact that two 'systems of morality' frequently appeared to coexist within modernity, 'one for "us" and the other for "them". All of the "liberal", "enlightened", and "progressive" triumphs in western modernity have had their independent counterpart in utterly illiberal, violently totalising, and destructive assaults on other peoples' (Mirsepassi, 2000, p 35).

Aimé Césaire (2000 [1955]) was among the first to interpret fascism as 'a form of colonialism brought home to Europe' (Young, 2001, p 2; see also Kelley, 2000). This dimension is occluded or significantly downplayed in accounts of Nazism and the Holocaust; for example, Bauman's (1989) influential work tends to perceive the Holocaust as a phenomenon that was largely generated by an insular bureaucratic rationality, within Europe, that the Nazis pushed to an extreme. In this context, Césaire (2000 [1955], p 36) maintains that the 'very Christian bourgeois of the twentieth century' cannot

> forgive Hitler for [it] is not the crime in itself, the crime against man, it is not the humiliation of man as such, it is the crime against the white man, the humiliation of the white man, and the fact that he applied to Europe colonialist procedures which until then had been reserved exclusively for the Arabs of Algeria, the 'coolies' of India, and the 'n.....s' of Africa.

It is has been argued that Césaire's (2000 [1955]) *Discourse on Colonialism* is not accorded 'much attention' within postcolonial criticism (Kelley, 2000, p 9). His account of the impact of colonisation is replete with insights that continue to have contemporary resonances that can inform our understanding. Between coloniser and colonised there is

> room only for forced labor, intimidation, pressure, the police, taxation, theft, rape, compulsory crops, contempt, mistrust, arrogance,

self-complacency, swinishness, brainless elites, degraded masses. No human contact, but relations of domination and submission which turn the colonising man into a classroom monitor, an army sergeant, a prison guard, a slave driver, and the indigenous man into an instrument of production. My turn to state an equation: colonisation = 'thingification'. (Césaire, 2000 [1955], p 42)

Not unlike Frantz Fanon subsequently, Césaire (2000 [1955, p 33) is also attuned to how colonisation projects contaminate and de-civilise the coloniser working to 'brutalise him in the true sense of the word, to degrade him, to awaken him to buried instincts, to covetousness, violence, race hatred, and moral relativism' (Césaire, 2000 [1955], p 35). Once the toxins have been 'distilled into the veins of Europe and, slowly but surely, the continent proceeds toward savagery. And then one fine day the bourgeoisie is awakened by a terrific boomerang effect: the gestapos are busy, the prisons fill up, the torturers standing around the racks invent, refine, discuss' (Césaire, 2000 [1955], p 36). What is more, despite all the European 'pseudo-humanism' the 'rights of man' is clearly a concept and discourse that 'has been – and still is – narrow and fragmentary, incomplete and biased and, all things considered, sordidly racist' (Césaire, 2000 [1955], p 37).

Perhaps not unlike Marx, Césaire (2000 [1955], p 43) is also alert to the destructive and exploitative nature of colonisation, given the disruption caused to 'harmonious and viable economies adapted to the indigenous population', with 'food crops destroyed, malnutrition permanently introduced' and agricultural development becoming 'oriented solely toward the benefit of the metropolitan countries; about the looting of products, the looting of raw materials'. Hence, colonised societies are 'drained of their essence', with their 'cultures trampled underfoot, institutions undermined, lands confiscated, religions smashed, magnificent artistic creations destroyed, extraordinary possibilities wiped out' (Césaire, 2000 [1955], p 43). Written in the 1950s, his 'discourse' ends by noting the coming of the 'American hour' and the dangers associated with 'looking upon the country as a possible liberator' (Césaire, 2000 [1955], pp 76–7).

Fanon, also from the Caribbean island of Martinique and a former pupil of Césaire, similarly drew attention to the material dimension, as well as the adverse psychological impact of colonisation, given that the manifest 'scandal' of 'European opulence' was 'built on the backs of slaves, it fed on the blood of slaves' and owed 'its very existence to the soil and subsoil of the underdeveloped world. Europe's well-being and progress is built with the sweat and corpses' of Blacks, Arabs, Indians and Asians (Fanon, 2004 [1961], p 53).

Chiming with the perceptions of our contemporary BLM movement and topplers of the statues of slave-traders, Fanon baldly asserted that the 'wealth of the imperialist nations' has to be seen as the wealth of those who have been colonised. Europe has 'been bloated out of all proportions by the gold and raw materials' from the colonialised world (Fanon, 2004 [1961], p 58). He charges that Europe can be perceived as the 'creation of the Third World', given that its 'riches' were 'plundered'. What is more, the 'ports of Holland, the docks in Bordeaux and Liverpool' owe their importance to the 'trade and deportation of millions of slaves' (Fanon, 2004 [1961], pp 58–59). Although not expanding on the point, and moving his discussion into the discourse circulating around reparations, Fanon maintains that the capitalist powers 'must pay up' (Fanon, 2004 [1961], p 59).

Echoing some of the thinking of Césaire, Paul Gilroy (2000) alerts us to the fact that seminal Enlightenment figures often held views of Black and colonised peoples that contaminated their thinking. Thus, Kant confidently declares that 'Negroes of Africa have no feeling that rises above the trifling' (in Gilroy, 2000, p 58). Furthermore, 'blacks are ... so talkative that they must be driven apart from each other with thrashings' (in Gilroy, 2000, p 60). Pronouncements such as these reveal that 'Kant's democratic hopes and dreams simply could not encompass the black community' (Gilroy, 2000, p 60). Such 'philosophical' pronouncements by iconic figures such as Kant illustrate modernity's 'color-coded promises' (Gilroy, 2000, p 87; see also Eze, 1997).

These critical interventions from scholars such as Gilroy furnish a welcome corrective to theorisation that has persistently failed to situate modernity within the project of western expansion and colonialism. Although distinctive, this critique is not the 'first to question the ethics of colonialism: indeed, anti-colonialism is as old as colonialism itself' (Young, 2001, p 6). This is reflected in Priyamvada Gopal's (2019) *Insurgent Empire: Anticolonial Resistance and British Dissent*, in which she illuminates the opposition of middle-class reformers and labour movement activists to British imperialism throughout the 19th and 20th centuries. Early Marxist theorisation, following Marx himself, assumed that capitalist incursion would lead to positive economic and social evolution. On account of this perception, there is a 'powerful tendency in postcolonial studies to dismiss Marx as a Eurocentric or even Orientalist thinker' (Lindner, 2010, p 27). Objecting to the hastiness of this critique, Linder's close reading reveals that gradually Marx came to 'reject Eurocentric assumptions' (Lindner, 2010, p 27). Subsequently, Rosa Luxemburg was one of the earliest European Marxist thinkers and activists to recognise the devastating impact of imperialism upon the Third World (Hudis and Anderson, 2004, p 20). For the first time, following the Bolshevik Revolution in 1917, a government of a powerful state was explicitly opposed to western imperialism in principle and practice. Three years later, Lenin's Comintern 'offered the first systematic programme for global decolonization in its "Theses on the National and Colonial Questions"' (Young, 2001, p 10).

Not only did Marxists play practical activist roles in anti-colonial resistance but, as Chibber (2013, p 291) maintains, at the level of theory, there is 'probably no project to which Marxist theorists have devoted more energy and time since the first Russian Revolution of 1905 than to understand the peculiar effects of capitalist development in the non-West'. Chibber (2013, p 292) maintains, for example, that 'Trotsky's theory of uneven and combined development was an explicit *rejection* of the argument that later developers would simply replicate the developmental path of the early ones'. Moreover, a range of Black thinkers – either explicit Marxists or moving in the same orbit of Marxist analysis – have made enormous contributions that have enhanced our theoretical and political understanding of the enmeshed dynamics of 'race', racism and imperialism. These include George Padmore, C.L.R. James, Cedric Robinson and Angela Davis.

Turning specifically to education, one critique of mainstream theorisation is that it fails to adequately recognise the impact of colonialism and the positionality of its primary definers and iconic figures. One of the chief criticisms directed at dominant social theories is that they have tended to be 'western' perspectives failing to incorporate a satisfactory understanding of the evolution of other societies located elsewhere. This insular view of the world percolates into social work theorisation and forms of intervention in Ireland and elsewhere. Mainstream western political, socio-cultural and economic hegemony, birthed in colonial times, continues to influence social work. Some social work educators, often prompted by the demands of minority ethnic and indigenous communities, have fruitfully begun to examine how hegemonic western conceptualisations are inextricably enmeshed with historical and contemporary approaches to practice (Gray et al, 2013; Baines et al, 2019; Kleibl et al, 2019).

Relatedly, many progressive students and educators have embarked on projects to 'decolonise the university' and to question the validity of forms of knowledge and discourse entirely derived from a western – and frequently male – perspective (Bhambra et al, 2018). 'Decolonising' encompasses a multiplicity of viewpoints. Bhambra et al (2018, p 2) usefully point out that it embraces a

> multitude of definitions, interpretations, aims and strategies. To broadly situate its political and methodological coordinates, 'decolonising' as two key referents. First, it is a way of thinking about the world which takes colonialism, empire and racism as its empirical and discursive objects of study; it re-situates these phenomena as key shaping forces of the contemporary world, in a context where their role has been systematically effaced from view. Second, it purports to offer alternative ways of thinking about the world and alternative forms of political praxis.

Essentially, this approach can be interpreted as aiming to understand a particular form of hegemony that has evolved. At the same time, those advocating for change are intent on slowly, but decisively, constructing new forms of more inclusive understanding.

Hegemonic power: Antonio Gramsci

Primarily associated with Antonio Gramsci, hegemony refers to 'something more substantial and more flexible than any abstract *imposed* ideology' (Williams, 1973, p 10, emphasis added). Those attentive to the construction of hegemonic projects interrogate how a dominant class has to *organise*, *persuade* and *maintain* the consent of the subjugated by ensuring that its own ideas constitute the core perceptions and 'common sense' within a particular society or social formation (Crehan, 2002; 2011; 2016). Gaining currency through language, many elements in 'common sense' contribute to 'people's subordination by making situations of inequality and oppression appear to them as natural and unchangeable' (Forgacs, 1988, p 421). Frequently 'common sense' is also imbued with deeply racialised perceptions of particular groups. In Irish society, therefore, it can be argued that Irish Travellers have been viewed – by those outside their community – has having mostly negative and anti-social characteristics.

Hegemony is 'not to be understood at the level of mere opinion or mere manipulation. It is a whole body of practices and expectations' (Williams, 1973, p 9). Part of the political skill integral to such an endeavour is the ability to rearticulate, co-opt or nullify 'alternative meanings and values' (Williams, 1973, p 10). Hegemonic projects do not simply seek to win over people to a particular worldview. Rather, they can be perceived as aspiring to neutralise and render passive competing perspectives, 'while recruiting small but strategically significant populations and class fractions into active support' (Gilbert, 2015, p 31). What counts is what *penetrates*, what *sticks* and what achieves some degree of explanatory power. Hegemony presupposes an 'active and practical involvement of the hegemonised groups, quite unlike the static, totalising and passive subordination implied in the dominant ideology concept' (Forgacs, 1988, p 424).

As Gramsci recognises, hegemonic powers aim to maintain the 'consent given by the great masses of the population to the general direction imposed' (Gramsci in Hoare and Nowell Smith, 2005, p 12). The 'apparatus of state coercive power' is empowered to 'legally' enforce 'discipline on those groups' failing to render active or passive consent (Gramsci in Hoare and Nowell Smith, 2005, p 12). Importantly, continues Gramsci, this apparatus is 'constituted for the whole of society in anticipation of moments of crisis of command and direction when spontaneous consent has failed' (Gramsci in Hoare and Nowell Smith, 2005, p 12). In this way, coercive power is held in reserve for those times and places when the means of generating sufficient consent *fails* (Smith, 2011). Ordinarily, the mass of people would not directly be targeted or experience such a deployment of coercive power.

Gramsci's work on hegemony illuminates, therefore, how dominant groups and individuals in society control – but also have to win and maintain a measure of consent – in order to try to ensure the reproduction of social and institutional practices. His work has been very influential in, for example, examining the unfolding of postcolonial India (Chaturvedi, 2012). A fascinating Gramscian 'take' on social work in India is also provided by Shahid and Jha (2014). The concept's utility for *Social Work with the African Diaspora* pivots on its helping us to understand how the maintenance of dominant cultural hegemonies in social work education translate into relations of power and control within cross-cultural micro-level encounters with services users and vice versa.

We can also use the concept in more encompassing political terms. In Africa, for example, Robert Mugabe, who served as president of Zimbabwe for nearly 40 years, was very adept at using the radio to win and maintain the support of those living in dispersed rural parts of the country (Fanon, 1989 [1959]). This form of communication served as a medium to skilfully generate consent among the population. Other coercive powers and subtle 'persuasive strategies' of the state were also deployed against those who were not won over to his regime's political project. In South Africa, Thabo Mbeki's (president 1999–2008) notion of an 'African Renaissance' functioned not only as a rhetorical hinge to dissent from prevailing representations of the continent; it also was also utilised as a conceptual framework to try to insert his country, as an equal player, into the circuits of global neoliberalism (Ahluwalia, 2002; Pitika Ntuli, 2002). Commenting on the management of hegemonic power in the US in the mid-1990s, the critical Afrocentrist, Makungu M. Akinyela (1995, p 35), observed:

Critical Africentricity understands hegemony as the psychological and social manipulation of one or several groups by another group for the purpose of establishing moral and intellectual leadership. Hegemony is the gained consent of a group to the domination by another group even when the consent may not be in the interest of the consenting group. Hegemony is enforced primarily through the institutions of civil society, which are the cultural institutions, such as churches, social clubs, sororities/fraternities, educational institutions, artistic institutions, print and electronic media, and private enterprise. All of these institutions of 'civil society' are to varying degrees independent from the state and its apparatus.

Importantly, how consensual support for institutionalised social practices is 'manufactured' need not appear to be coercive. For example, one strategy may be to simply, yet systematically, suppress knowledge produced by an oppressed group. Such an approach often enables dominant groups to rule without there appearing to be any dissent, with subordinated groups seeming to be entirely willing to collaborate in their own victimisation (Scott, 1985).

Baker (2012, p 1) cites Mignolo's (2007) argument that to build a universal and hegemonic conception of knowledge, western epistemology, from Christian theology to secular philosophy and science, has asserted that knowledge is independent of the geo-historical circumstances. Within this doxic framing, Christian Europe and the life experiences of particular White men became the locus of epistemic enunciation. Concurrently, the rest of the world became the object to be studied and described from a European perspective. After the demise of political colonialism, Eurocentrism maintained its intellectual hegemony through a range of subtle 'soft power' strategies within the matrix of neoliberal globalised educational structures (Bernstein and Solomon, 1999).

Askeland and Payne (2006) indicate how this relates to social work, and they suggest that neoliberal globalism presses social work education towards the postcolonial oppression of minority cultures by dominant cultures, deepening economic difference and dependency. They also concede that diverse cultures and languages may be lost in internationalised social work education. Hence, they call on social work educational structures to combat Eurocentric cultural hegemony. Clearly, social work is a western construct with a knowledge base that is informed by European historical and cultural development (Graham, 1999). Albeit this is frequently not acknowledged, some aspects of present-day western interventions borrow from indigenous knowledge systems. For example, family group conferencing, now widely used in western social work, originated from the Aotearoa New Zealand and Maori culture. Restorative justice, used in probation services, is based on African jurisprudence that does not prioritise coercive confinement: rather, it affords the offender and victim space to resolve problems, and this is mediated by their wider community.

Social work originated in countries such as England in the 19th century as a response to the social problems brought about by the Industrial Revolution. It was later exported to the colonies as part of hegemonic projects. Gordon Pon (2009) highlights the profession's complicity in the history of White supremacy, racism and imperial projects that proved central to the formation and ascendancy of countries such as US, Australia and Canada (Maylea, 2020). White South African social work 'largely accepted segregationist ideologies well before 1948, readily adopted the practices of racial separation' that culminated with the creation of Apartheid (Ioakimidis and Trimikliniotis (2020, p 6). In a powerful statement, the Canadian

Association of Social Workers (CASW) identifies how the profession 'reinforced the colonial project' and this has been apparent in its collusion with policies and practices directed at Indigenous peoples (First Nations, Métis and Inuit) (CASW, 2019, pp 3–4). Children from these communities were routinely subject to forced removal and placed in group homes in order to 'civilise' them (see also Viens Commission, 2019; Turpel-Lafond, 2020). This involved indoctrination in 'White thought' and the indigenous being prohibited from speaking their own languages and practising their own cultures. Pon (2009) further argues that social work not only actively participated in this form of cultural genocide, it also failed to protest against the social and physical violence that led to the annihilation of Aboriginal peoples. The infamous 'sixties scoop', in which high numbers of Aboriginal children were removed from their families by social workers, starkly highlights social work's collusion with colonialism and White supremacy projects. Furthermore, contemporary equivalent practices continue in some western countries (Graham, 1999; Earner, 2007). In referring to the removal of Aboriginal children during the colonial era, Weaver (1999) believes that it is vital for social workers today to understand the Indigenous 'holocaust' in these countries – this, in the context of social work's compliant role and the unresolved 'pain' associated with it (Weaver 1999, p 221). In trying to explain the social workers' actions/inactions in such matters, Weaver argues that the profession's historical roots in the British Empire perhaps bestow upon it a cultural legacy that may predispose social workers to operate from a professional belief system antithetical to the cultural values, norms and beliefs of many non-western recipients of services.

Eurocentric hegemony is deeply embedded at the core of knowledge production within universities and within the social work programmes (McKeown and Wainwright, 2019). Gurminder K. Bhambra (2007, p 5) succinctly defines Eurocentrism as the 'belief, implicit or otherwise, in the world historical significance of events believed to have developed endogenously within the cultural-geographical sphere of Europe'. The discourse of Eurocentric cultural hegemony in much of the literature mostly dwells on how Eurocentric values, dominating social work theorisation – and, more pervasively, the social sciences as a whole – led to the propagation of specific western norms as cultural universals. Erik Erikson's theorisation of the development of a sense of identity in adolescence is a good example of such Ethnocentrism (Ahmad, 1990). Relatedly, in theory-to-practice areas, social work might have much to gain from exposing the limitations of Carl Rogers' 'unconditional positive regard' when applied to 'clients' from a more collectivist-oriented culture shunning individualism (Rogers, 1980). Social work educators might also begin to take a more critical approach to other traditional theoretical pillars of practice such as Bowlby's (1990) attachment theorisation. Criticisms of such ideas have been available since

Margaret Mead's (1962) devastating paper in a World Health Organization publication six decades ago. Indeed, her comment that Bowlby had taken 'a set of ethnocentric observations on our own society' and turned them into a 'set of universals' remains very apt (Mead, 1962, p 58). More recently, critiques of attachment theory have appeared in the literature of anthropology and psychological and cultural studies (Quinn and Mageo, 2013a; Quinn and Mageo, 2013a; Vicedo, 2013; Otto and Keller, 2014). Naomi Quinn and Jeannette Marie Mageo (2013b) elaborate:

> Anthropologists and others whose research has immersed them in other cultures cannot help but see contemporary attachment theory as resembling a folk theory. A folk theory abstracts elements of experience in a culture to formulate a view of the human condition that is regarded as universal and is held, implicitly or explicitly, by most group members but is in fact reflective of experience within the group. In more complex economically tiered societies, folk theories tend to take the experience of a hegemonic class or classes as universally representative and normative. Attachment theory, like a folk theory, draws upon the way many middle-class Americans, and to a lesser extent members of this class in other Western and Western-influenced societies, think they should care for infants and small children, including ideas about how child–caregiver attachments are formed and fostered. Because this theory is so naturalized in American thinking, it can seem self-evident. Folk theoretical thinking often creeps into academic and other expert theories especially, as we have noted, when an academic psychology is based nearly exclusively on research in the United States and other Western countries and excludes the intercultural variation introduced by non-middle-class and minority populations in these countries.

Critical interventions such as these rarely seem to percolate into the teaching of social work, which remains in thrall to what we might term 'Bowlbyism'. More generally, hegemonic middle-class western ideas about appropriate childhoods and what constitutes 'appropriate' or 'good enough' parenting (Adcock and White, 1985) might also be more closely interrogated. Failure to do this sustains sterile inertia and solidifies intellectual laziness.

Atkinson et al (1995) credit cross-cultural psychology for contributing to research that has enhanced understanding of culture through an awareness of the influence of differing values and norms on human development, thoughts and behaviours. This approach has led to the exposure of the cultural bias of psychometric tests simply based on the perceptions and assumptions of dominant cultures. Cross-cultural psychology continues to counter traditional negative assumptions of different cultures in many areas including human growth and development, youth identity formation and so on (Ahmad, 1990; O'Hagan, 2001).

Young (1990, p 50) plainly describes the imposition of one's cultural norms on other cultures as 'cultural oppression' and social work rhetorically repudiates all forms of oppression. Located in the US, Elaine Pinderhughes (1989) believes such cultural oppression sets in motion an inevitable clash between dominant and non-dominant cultures. Pinderhughes (1989) relates that, in the past, social workers and social welfare systems have imposed western middle-class norms as rigid standards for all service users. The same author also suggests that manifest social and cultural diversity challenges the 'myth of sameness' underlying the historic social work tradition; a tradition rooted in the universalist assumption that practice theories are broadly applicable to all persons because 'deep down we are all the same' (Pinderhuhges, 1989, p 24).

Erika Haug (2005) highlights how the influence of US global hegemony (across political, economic, cultural and ideological plains) significantly impacts on discourses and practices and shapes social work internationally. The author evidences this by referring to how generic principles and 'values' formulated in the 1920s in the US (such as individualism, self-determination, non-judgmentalism and confidentiality) continue to influence social work practice globally. This, despite the criticism that such values are mostly rooted in an individualistic western liberal culture and are not universally shared or accepted throughout the world. Haug also criticises 'comparative studies' remaining dominated by one gender (male), one class (financially comfortable and highly educated) and one ethnicity (European). How, the question is posed, can the views derived from this structured positioning represent all populations, genders, classes and ethnicities? The contemporary dominant social work paradigm, according to Haug (2005), represents a globalised local tradition given the status of a unified knowledge system, universally applicable and superior to all other pre-existing traditions of social work/social care.

Certainly within Irish social work, White and 'mainstream' voices continue to dominate, effectively shutting out any new divergent voices that might 'rock the boat' sailing on the waters of the current status quo. In many quarters there is also a marked tendency to try to transplant ways of working derived from the US into Irish social work. In recent years, this has been especially apparent in the moves to encourage the use of 'made-in-the-US' models of 'short-term' and 'manualised' interventions in the lives of children and their families. Significant here has been the importation of the so-called 'Incredible Years Programme' and the 'Strengthening Families, Strengthening Communities' scheme (see, for example, Frost and Dolan, 2021). As Wacquant (2001, p 406) caustically observes, in many parts of Europe, as well as in the Global South, there are always likely to those willing to provide a 'thin scholarly whitewash' in order to invest various US-derived policies with a veneer of respectability.

Bidgood et al (2003) concur with Haug that western knowledge systems, ideologies and social work/social care systems and methods have, on numerous occasions, been repeatedly proven to be inappropriate and wholly inadequate when deployed in other parts of the world. Such approaches have manifestly failed to address the profound ecological, spiritual, economic and security crises confronting contemporary humanity. These authors, therefore, conclude that most western social work practice methods are perceived as 'alien', 'unacceptable' or 'ineffective' in many countries, especially those in the so-called 'Third World' (Silavwe, 1995). Such shortcomings are often seen in working with people such as diasporic Black Africans domiciled in western countries (Graham, 1999).

Relatedly, Stephen Webb (2003) argues that the profession of social work is complicit in the neoliberal globalisation/objectification agenda. He, therefore, accuses international social work of adhering to the neoliberal global agenda by holding on to *particular* views of social life as applicable to *all* social situations and contexts. This stance contradicts the profession's expressed maxim of 'starting where the client is located'. Arguably social work, through bodies such as International Federation of Social Workers (IFSW), seeks to enlarge its role and presence in many countries and maintain control by centralising authority and managerial governance: for example, by standardising theories/education, professionalising missions, international definitions and so on. The flourishing agenda of global social work – occasionally redolent of a corporate 'branding' exercise – furnishes a decidedly bourgeois model – one privileging, in fact, the dominance of the global systems over the local realities of people's daily lives. This mode of thinking also represents liberal utopian politics wholly out of sympathy with the actualities of social work practice 'on the ground' (Webb, 2003). For example, Silavwe (1995) argues that some traditional social work casework principles are entirely irrelevant for everyday practice in African settings. The focal core of his argument is that social casework, based on western concepts such as 'self-determination' and 'confidentiality', is predicated on the concept of liberal individuality. Such values, he maintains, are often alien to African cultures and are, therefore, wholly inappropriate and practically inapplicable.

We are not seeking to crudely eliminate conceptualisations derived from European contexts. As we have argued, Gramsci is of considerable theoretical utility in enabling us to understand how some worldviews become forms of hegemonic power. In our next two sections, therefore, we will turn to briefly refer to two other European thinkers, Foucault and Bourdieu. Both are iconic within their respective philosophical and sociological traditions and both can contribute to this book's theoretical architecture.

Relations of power and truth regimes: Michel Foucault

Foucault believed that power is not something that is 'possessed' or owned by a group of people in the 'society': rather, power 'circulates' and must be understood in relational terms. He argued that power is not simply a property of the state but is fluid and existing in all networks including social institutions such as universities, religions, medical and health agencies (see also Garrett, 2018, ch 9 for a much more detailed articulation). Jessop (2007) partly supports Foucault's definition of power by arguing that social institutions shape the way we live and 'do things' according to the dominant discourses and practices operating in a 'society' in a particular time and place. He maintains that our behaviours are, therefore, shaped by our being part of institutions and through the discourses present in the wider culture and systems of governance. Jessop, therefore, cites Foucault's argument that in order to understand power, we need to study it from *where* it is exercised. Ball (2013, p 50) contends that, for Foucault, power is not always repressive or harmful; instead, it may enable other kinds of relations which are less constraining and oppressive. For example, if the service user is from a culture/worldview that the social worker knows nothing about, then it is will be the former who is the 'expert' in their own culture because of the experiential knowledge they possess. Wider and encompassing forms of institutional power and dominant discourses may, though, facilitate the routinised denial of this fact because of the solidity of notions circulating around professional 'expertise' that shape the social worker's subjectivity.

Ball (2013) also argues that knowledge is produced within power relations in the sense that some groups or institutions have been able to speak knowledgeably about 'others': for example, the West about the Orient and the West about Africa in a way that has reaffirmed the discursive and material dominance of the West. Ball (2013), basing his insights on Foucault again, also maintains that we should not take for granted the relations entwining power and knowledge, but consider that such relations need to be explored in detail on a case-by-case basis. This is important, given that power relations, instantiated in fields of knowledge such as social work 'play out' in specific scenarios, encounters and micro engagements. The idea that 'experts' and their 'knowledge' play a key role in determining how we should act, who we are and – more fundamentally – what *counts* as 'knowledge' means that they also exercise immense power. For example, child protection social workers, on account of their institutionally accredited 'expert' knowledge, exercise considerable power when court judges rely on their testimony to determine if an individual is 'fit' to parent or if this is not the case because 'abuse' or 'neglect' has occurred within a family. Understanding knowledge/power relations is also helpful in exploring how, for instance, social work educators exercise power to shape the thinking and subsequent actions of students. What 'knowledge' is being instilled and what 'knowledge' is being marginalised, even extinguished? Social work educators can exercise their power either to help students evolve as critical, reflexive and culturally aware practitioners or they can exercise the same power to 'reproduce' future practitioners who will unthinkingly uphold the status quo. At our present conjuncture, there is considerable danger of the latter occurring if more dissenting perspectives are not nurtured (Garrett, 2021).

Illuminating how the relations of power are linked to (officially validated) knowledge is also critical in aiding our ability to ascertain how the 'disregarding' or 'suppressing' of (potentially competing subaltern) knowledge systems relates to the 'disempowering' of individuals or groups associated with the latter forms of knowledge. In this context, dominant discourses – and the words and concepts deployed – enable a society to evoke or to conceal, downplay or even discursively erase a phenomenon. Foucault (1972, p 54) defines discourses as 'practices that systematically form the objects of which they speak'. He argues that discourse is not *present* in the object, but it enables it to appear. Discourse refers, therefore, to a 'type of language associated with an institution and includes the ideas and statements which express an institution's values'. Hence, discourses play a significant role in creating and perpetuating 'truth games'.

Drawing on Foucault, Danaher et al (2000) contend that practices help to form discourses, in the sense that individuals and institutions create meanings out of experiences, and through them, knowledge is produced. For the French philosopher, discourses are social constructs allowing us to 'make sense' of how we 'see things'. He suggests, therefore, that to understand a discourse, we need to understand the *purpose* it serves. What discursive work does it try to achieve (Garrett, 2019)? In this sense, statements are functional units through which knowledge is produced. Foucault argues that discourse structures the way that we perceive reality. In Ireland, for example, discourses on child welfare protection have tended to exclude children living in DP, in that they have not tended to be classified as potentially children 'at risk', despite documented concerns (Health, Information and Quality Authority (HIQA), 2015; Ombudsman for Children's Office, 2021).

There are discourses that constrain the production of knowledge, dissent and difference, and those which might enable 'new' knowledge(s) and difference(s). Why, therefore, do certain discourses maintain authority? Relatedly, why do certain 'voices' get heard while others are silenced? In terms of how these processes work to dismiss non-western knowledge and practices, one frequent tactical move is to assert that such alternatives 'lack empirical rigour'. This can often be interpreted as merely a discursive ploy aspiring to discipline, even to nullify, dissenting knowledge by situating it within a western criterion of judgement.

Resistance cannot, though, be eradicated within the Foucauldian analysis of relations of power because of 'a certain degree of freedom on both sides' (Foucault, 1997, p 292). Power and resistance both constitute and are constituted by each other. Hence, individuals possess the capacity to resist structures of domination in modern societies. This is the powerful and more 'upbeat message' that we can derive from Foucault's contribution. More generally, the concept of resistance can inform how social work students can resist stultifying power, servicing the interests of the neoliberal globalised racial order, within their educational institutions. Occasionally, such institutions house social work educators 'delivering' outdated curricula and practices which objectively fail to prepare future social workers for the demands of contemporary multicultural practice. More provocatively, social work students in Ireland might commence to resist the sheer hypocrisy present in higher education institutions which purport to teach 'human rights' – and even have 'human rights centres' – yet which still fail to sufficiently challenge the continued 'human rights' violations encountered, often literally within walking distance, by 'asylum seekers' corralled into DP.

The idea that power produces resistance has been illustrated by student protests at the prestigious University of London School of African and Oriental Studies. As the conservative *Daily Mail* (8 September 2017) fumed: 'They Kant be serious! P[olitically]C[orrect] students demand white philosophers including Plato and Descartes be dropped from university syllabuses'. This was a trivialising response to the fact that the students are resisting the power of the university authorities to continue to systematically exclude Black African and Asian philosophers from the curriculum. These students' destabilisation of truth regimes and their demands for the inclusion of philosophers from the Global South furnishes evidence of campaigns that are beneficially committed to facilitating the expression of subjugated knowledge and to challenging embedded 'truth regimes' (Goldstein, 2012).

Truth regimes, for Foucault (1997, p 297), are sets of 'rules by which truth is produced'. Each society has its own 'truth regimes', usually informed by its culture, theories, policies and pedagogy. These 'rules' structure or influence how people see themselves and behave. Danaher et al (2000) define 'truth regimes' as the rules that govern how certain institutions produce truth and contribute to our understanding and sense-making. Indeed, 'truth' (not truth) is a major theme, of course, throughout the work of Foucault. For him, 'truth' is something that 'happens' and is produced by a multitude of 'techniques' rather than something that already exists and is simply waiting to be discovered. He believes, moreover, that 'truth regimes' emerge in society and are undergirded due to the social practices of the human sciences.

This notion of 'truth regimes' (along with other focal Foucauldian concepts) can also help us to grasp how the casting of people from the so-called Third World as 'inferior' became an internalised 'truth' in western countries. From a postcolonial perspective, as Watkins (2002) reminds us, to enable the colonial self to profit from the oppression of others, it created a view of the 'other' that justified exploitation and oppression. The colonised 'other' was portrayed as underdeveloped, superstitious and in need of monitoring and tutelage. At the same time, the colonial self – typically masculine – was elevated as superior, all knowing, disciplined and capable of logical thought and resourcefulness. According to this norm, the cultural other became reduced to a deficient version of the western 'self' (Watkins, 2002, p 3). Significantly, contemporary social work, and many kindred fields in western societies, contain powerful residues of this form of reasoning. That is to say, western society (including, perhaps, some White social workers lacking critical insight and an appropriate degree of reflexivity), may well have internalised such inherited 'truths' that continue to situate Black Africans as deficient and this is, of course, reinforced by the media and, often strikingly, international NGO fundraising 'initiatives'.

Focusing on the socially constructed nature of 'truth regimes' opens up an intellectual space for us to interrogate how relations of power, sedimented in 'truth regimes' in society and specific fields such as professional social work, provide the contours mapping normativity or deviance. This understanding – underpinning the critical ethos of *Social Work with the Black Africa Diaspora* – can shed light on how practitioners might think about 'empowering' those situated on the cultural margins by facilitating the expression of viewpoints associated with subjugated 'truth regimes'. Such action might also gel with Foucault's notion that power can also be used positively and productively. Most importantly, permitting expression of *other* 'truth regimes' allows alternative 'stories' to be told and alternative strategies to be formulated. Valuing different cultural 'truth regimes' also creates the *possibility* of reducing cultural domination. Both CRT and CWT, which we briefly discuss later in the chapter, are relevant in this context.

Prior to briefly referring to Bourdieu, it is also important to mention social constructionism. Although this body of theory is not specifically Foucauldian, there is an affinity with the French philosopher's work in that the emphasis, once again, is on the knowledge informing social and public policy and everyday human interactions.

Social constructionism

Social workers concern themselves, to varying degrees, with trying to understand the 'reality' of the social world of the user of services. This dimension is important, given this book's concerns relating to the impact of cultural differences in engagements involving dominant Euro–American cultures and Black African minority ethnic cultures. While being alert to the dangers of culturally reductive binaries, trying to grasp what constitutes 'reality' for a given service user, informed by their ethnicity and worldview, is a key theme for those aspiring to arrive at better forms of practice. In this sense, it is useful to explore two polarised responses to the question of what constitutes the 'nature of reality'.

The first response advocates that truth is simply 'out there' and independent of the individual. The second holds that 'truth' is far from 'independent' of the individual, but is immanent in their beliefs and thoughts. The first approach is commonly referred to as 'classical empiricism' (or 'positivism') and the second perspective is grounded in 'social constructionism'. *Social Work with the Black African Diaspora* is, therefore, informed by the social constructionist understanding that reality can be understood only in the context of the beliefs, thoughts and perceptions of an individual situated in a social specific milieu. The social work profession's emphasis on 'service user participation', 'human rights' and 'social justice' potentially makes the social constructionist approach an attractive tool in enabling service users to participate in the 'helping process' as equal partners empowered to define problems via the lens and language derived from their worldview. Burr (2015) argues that a social constructionist approach has several interlinked components and, in what follows, we will briefly refer to each of these.

A critical stance towards taken-for-granted knowledge

This implies that we must critically interrogate our understanding of the world, including – as best we are able to do so – our own perceptions. We must also be critical of the suggestion that our observation of the world 'unproblematically' yields its nature to us. This is a standpoint which seeks, of course, to undercut the more conventional understanding that knowledge can be grounded in an objective, unbiased observation of the social world (Burr, 2015).

Historical and cultural specificity of knowledge

The variety of ways in which we understand the world, through 'categories' or 'concepts' that we deploy, are historically and culturally relative. Burr (2015) uses the notion of 'childhood' to illustrate how the concept has changed over time, with notions of childhood being intertwined with social and economic developments prevailing within different cultures (James et al (1998). This implies that forms of knowledge, found in any culture, are products of that culture and hence no culture can lay legitimate claims to being 'standard knowledge'. Thabede (2008) argues that key and influential theorists, such as Erikson, aimed to normalise adult development resulting in appropriate career attainment, monogamous marriage, childbearing/rearing and managing a nuclear family/household. Thabede maintains that such theorists have excluded the developmental experiences of a wide spectrum of people and other theoretical alternatives and models. Relating to the purported universality of Erikson's theory, he also asserts that the German-American's perspective was developed solely through observing people and cultures among whom he lived. That is to say, his observed population was manifestly insular in that it contained nobody residing in Africa or Asia. Consequently, Erikson's conceptualisations are of limited use because they remain a series of hypotheses about the development toward adulthood merely prevalent in those cultures he studied. The 'universal applicability' of his theory becomes, therefore, rather questionable, since different cultures have different paths toward adulthood. For instance, people who may be regarded as 'adolescents' in European cultures may be considered 'fully grown adults' within Black African cultures. The importance of this understanding for social worker assessments is, therefore, fairly clear. Pursuing the same line of reasoning, Thabede also argues that Freud, for example, was largely indifferent to that which existed outside western and bourgeois intellectual and artistic traditions. Hence, his theoretical speculations are of diluted relevance for the cultures of Black Africa.

Knowledge is sustained by social processes

Social constructionism recognises that different cultures evolve alternative ways of constructing knowledge: they have different lenses through which to understand the same world. There may also be different 'truth claims' about how the world is or, indeed, should be. Traditionally, social work (within western contexts) has operated within a dominant 'positivistic' medical/deficit model. Within this perspective, the practitioner's image has tended to be that of the 'expert individual knower' who, on account of the possession of 'expert' knowledge, was viewed as capable of carefully observing and deliberating on the service user's perceived 'problem' or 'malfunctions'. They would then provide their 'assessment' on the 'inadequacies' or 'dysfunctions' of the service user as an independently situated 'other'. The service user would then be expected to confront life's challenges in order to attain an 'independent' and 'fulfilled life'; once again, this might be steered or piloted by kindred systems of 'expert' knowledge/intervention (McNamee and Gergen, 1992). Importantly, many social work practitioner forms of individual 'casework intervention' – perhaps especially in more clinically driven fields such as those in the US – still tend to align with this approach (albeit now, perhaps, being coloured with rhetorical flourishes incorporating the valorisation of 'participation' 'human rights', 'empowerment' and so on).

Theoretically, what is occurring in such instances accords with Burr's (2015) characterisation of dominant thinking – the *doxa* – within traditional psychology, which seeks out 'explanations' of social phenomena 'inside' the person through hypothesising on the existence of 'attitudes', 'motivations' and cognitions and so on. Sociology has, on occasions, countered this view by pointing to the significance of social structures and institutions (the economy and institutions such as 'marriage' and the 'family'). For social constructionists, knowledge is derived from communication processes that prompt co-constructed meaning. Relating this to social work, the tacit and lay knowledge of the service user is immensely significant within the 'helping process' (Burr, 2015).

Knowledge, social action and reflexivity

Becker (1982) observes that no single culture has all the 'right' answers to the problems that people experience on a daily basis. He suggests that various cultures must, therefore, adapt their understanding to new situations in order to fruitfully accommodate differences. For example, relating to our preoccupations in this book, social workers utilising a western knowledge base may have a different conceptualisation of 'childhood' and 'family' than service users (and, indeed, Black African co-workers) who have a Black African cultural heritage (see also Chapter 6). Becker argues, in this context, for a collaborative approach that aims to yield a 'negotiated understanding' reducing cultural distance. Such an orientation is consistent with social constructionism, and it also disputes the purported transcendental superiority often claimed by White, European practitioners operating from a more traditional 'expert' modality uncritically valorising the taken-for-granted assumptions (McNamee and Gergen, 1992).

Social constructionism also places emphasis on reflexivity as an intrinsically human endeavour: we are all, in short, capable of generating, nurturing and sustaining this kind of self-reflection which might 'open the door' to alternative forms of understanding. Acknowledging the cultural and historical specificity of knowledge might, in fact, prompt social work practitioners to adopt a position which provides the space for curiosity. What is more, such an approach can potentially address issues rooted in power differentials (McNamee and Gergen, 1992).

Social constructionism reminds us that, as individuals within a particular society or culture, we construct our own different versions of reality as far as 'knowledge' is concerned. This implies the historical and cultural relativity of *all* forms of knowledge. That is to say, knowledge tends to be derived from looking at the world from some perspective or other and functions to serve some interests more than others. The 'message', therefore, is that there is rarely such a thing as pure and pristine 'objective facts'. Notions of unblemished 'truth', for Burr (2015), are consequently frequently problematic. Understanding that *all* forms of knowledge are historically and culturally specific, social constructionism alerts us to the specificity of knowledge generated by social sciences located within dominant cultures. It also helps us to embark on exploring 'subjugated' knowledge within minority cultures.

All knowledge from psychology and the human sciences (whether theories or explanations of the lifeworld) are, therefore, time and culture bound. This means that such knowledge cannot be given the status of 'once-and-for-all authority' in purporting to describe humanity and human nature. Social workers intervening with cultural 'others' might, therefore, reflect on their own assumptions, positions and biases, in terms of their 'knowledge' of 'others' and their 'theories'. Perhaps there should be, therefore, a requirement to remain appropriately 'humble'? Reflection and humility are invaluable practitioner qualities in a world increasingly prone to lay heavy emphasis on 'expertise' and 'qualifications' (Dean and Fleck-Henderson, 1992, p 18). Indeed, the social constructionist approach gels with Ross's (2010) notion of 'cultural humility'.

Habitus, capital, field: Pierre Bourdieu

Bourdieu's theorisation revolves around a conceptual arsenal in which habitus, field, and capital are central. Importantly, these related conceptualisations can fruitfully contribute to some of the core themes at the heart of this book (see also Garrett, 2018, ch 7). More specifically, they potentially help us to better comprehend the complex interplay between agency and structure in reproducing racialised inequalities in neoliberal, capitalist societies. Using Bourdieu can help to expose power relations that are often rendered 'invisible' in social processes that (mis)recognise the cultural 'other'.

Habitus refers to the way that a society becomes embedded in individuals, their dispositions and the structured propensities that guide their thinking, feeling and acting (Navarro, 2006). The concept of habitus also relates to how a society reproduces itself over time, and it functions as a practical ideology. A person's habitus (saturating their thinking and behaviour) can also transfer to other contexts and can change. Thus, the habitus may alter during, for example, times of societal conflict, or it may mutate when one migrates to an entirely different culture. For example, there may be situations in which someone finds that an evolved habitus is entirely unsuited to a new environment, the ways people live and their reciprocal expectations.

At its core, habitus formulation tries to capture, therefore, how social action is 'simultaneously regulated and improvised, while neither wholly determined nor spontaneous' (Parker, 2000, p 83). David Parker maintains that habitus, as described by Bourdieu, fails to satisfactorily embrace the 'lived experiences of racialised hierarchy' because his 'topology of social space prioritises the mapping of class positions'. On account of Bourdieu's alleged failure to 'specify the non-class modes of exposure to the world defined by habitus', Parker helpfully coins the phrase 'diaspora habitus' (Parker, 2000, p 83). In Chapter 1, the conceptual utility of the 'diaspora' construct was referred to, and 'diaspora habitus' sheds additional conceptual light on some of the circulating concerns in this book. It refers, according to Parker, to the 'scheme of perception, appreciation and action which governs everyday practice in diaspora' (Parker, 2000, p 82). The 'diasporic social location adds an extra element which he [Bourdieu] cannot accommodate in his model' (Parker, 2000, p 82). It is also 'forces a closer investigation' of how 'imperial legacies structure exchanges' (Parker, 2000, p 74). Hence, 'imperial capital' is the 'accumulated historical advantage of colonial power' (Parker, 2000, p 88). Importantly, though, 'the diasporic habitus does not simply predispose those without imperial capital to a stoic and passive acceptance of the hand dealt to them' (Parker, 2000, p 85). Neither does the 'diasporic habitus' simply 'give rise to a conformism which equips people for subordination, it also offers resources between the legacies of the past, the imperatives of the present, and the possibilities of the future' (Parker, 2000, p 74).

Go (2013) argues that most commentaries on Bourdieu's work tend to locate him within the class structure of France and the milieu – or field – of the Parisian intellectual scene. It is also possible to argue that Bourdieu, along with seminal French intellectuals (such as Derrida, Lyotard and Foucault) were profoundly shaped by colonial experiences; many, in fact, spent time in overseas French colonies, and consequently their own sense of habitus evolved in this context (Ahluwalia, 2010). This, and the gradual process of decolonisation, might also explain the emancipatory dimensions to their theorisation. Perhaps when Bourdieu conceptualises habitus as lacking in permanency, when one encounters new experiences, he is drawing on his own lived experience and those of the Algerians he interacted with throughout his career as a sociologist (Go, 2013).

Given some of the concerns at the heart of *Social Work with the Black African Diaspora*, maybe the habitus of White Irish social workers might be changed because of their encounters with Black African colleagues and service users. If so, might this possibly help to dilute their dominant monocultural and ethnocentric understanding of, for example, childhood and parenting? This makes sense, considering Garrett's (2018) argument that habitus is not something 'natural' or 'inborn'; rather, it is a product of history, social experience and education. Such an interpretation also implies that one's habitus might be changed via education and reflection. This reading coheres with Bourdieu's own, which lays emphasis on the habitus being a dynamic system of dispositions with a generative capacity.

Garrett (2018) suggests that the patterning of habitus begins to coalesce in childhood and reverberates throughout life. In this context, Bourdieu acknowledges the role and function of education as a major ideological base in the construction of habitus. Habitus encompasses the way a person speaks, dresses, feels, thinks, and their response to 'authority'. The habitus that results from exposure to diverse intercultural education and experiences can be to the potential realisation of 'culturally sensitive practice' in social work. Since habitus can be changed through awareness and pedagogic effort, it could be argued that intercultural education might help to instil cultural awareness and could enhance practitioners' capacities and capabilities in working with service users from different cultures.

The concept of capital is an important component of Bourdieu's theory. Economic capital is defined as material and financial assets. Cultural capital can be defined as scarce symbolic goods, titles and skills. Social capital is defined as resources or contacts accrued through membership of various groups or networks. Lack of access to education implies limited opportunities for well-paid jobs. The resultant low income is often a barrier to accessing other resources that are determinants of basic requirements such as good health and adequate nutrition. The unequal distribution of this capital serves only to maintain the social hierarchy.

Despite being a non-economic form of capital, education provides pathways to societal domination and hierarchies based on distinct classes. Bourdieu (1986, p 471) confirms this when he suggests that social order is progressively inscribed into society's processes through institutions such as education. Credentialism is also important in postcolonial spaces when seeking out a 'better life', and this struggle to attain the 'right' credentials is, unsurprisingly, welded to social class. Nevertheless, it is important to acknowledge that not all agree with the conceptualisation of capital as articulated by Bourdieu. Yosso and Burciaga (2016), for example, suggest that there exists another form of cultural capital known as 'community cultural wealth'. For people of Black African origin, this includes an array of knowledge, skills, abilities and networks that are useful as resources not only for abstract analysis but for countering and surviving racism and discrimination. Yosso and Burciaga (2016) argue that the mainstream view of cultural capital is narrowly defined by White, middle-class values, but other forms of capital are significant. It is only through the ethical practice of listening and learning about the strengths and resources that minority ethnic individuals and communities possess that social workers from the wider community can become more attuned. There may be a 'kaleidoscope' of resources available: knowledge and understandings that have resisted historical erasure and have, often in violent and humiliating circumstances, been preserved and passed on to future generations (Yosso et al, 2016).

The relationship between habitus and Ubuntu

Perhaps *Ubuntu* helps to structure the Black African habitus and to imbue it with a certain affective and even political character? We need, therefore, to briefly explore this philosophy, particularly in light of the claim that the 'adoption of *Ubuntu* has the capacity to decolonise African social work from dominant western pedagogies' (Mugumbate, 2020, p 412; see also Mungai, 2013).

Letseka (2013), for example, illuminates how *Ubuntu* morality is anchored in the community, the family and in personhood within a South African political and cultural context. It is also a concept that demonstrably encapsulates various moral norms such as altruism, kindness, generosity, compassion, benevolence, respect and a deep concern for others. Letseka emphasises the communal character of life that still characterises much of contemporary Africa and he stresses the importance of communalism in defining people's perception of self-interest, their freedom and their place within an encompassing social whole. Furthermore, *Ubuntu* is of significance beyond continental African borders among diasporic Africans in Ireland and elsewhere. In this context, we also need to remain alert to the fact that there may be a 'tendency' to regard such a word as 'representing the same concept across all ... cultural spaces', but we might also inquire how its use could 'represent subtly different concepts in different places' (Janz, 2016, p 158).

Mugumbate and Nyanguru (2013), for example, articulate *Ubuntu* as an onto-epistemology that has been successfully applied to diverse fields including theology (Tutu, 2000) and politics (Mandela, 1994). Mandela (1994) advances the view that an individual human being belongs to the 'whole', that is, 'humanity', and that the liberation of the oppressed actually also liberates the oppressor from the inhumanity and indignity of denying others their full humanity. One of the central elements of *Ubuntu* relates to the role of the family in socialising community members in certain practical ways of thinking and acting. *Ubuntu* functions as a medium for transmitting communal values that valorise social cooperation, responsibility and imparting an interactive ethic promoting and nurturing humane relationships within the community. In summary, Letseka's arguments, supported by numerous other commentaries on Ubuntu, appear to support the notion that we might try to bring it into conceptual 'conversation' with Bourdieu's habitus formulation (Samkange and Samkange, 1980; Swanson, 2007). In this context, *Ubuntu* is frequently culturally embedded in communal experience and oral traditions and it markedly contributes to the shaping of individual life trajectories and sensibilities. Jacob Mugumbate (2020, p 418) explains that, in Zimbabwean Shona culture, *Ubuntu* is communicated in folklore (*ngano*), songs (*nziyo*), stories (*nyaya*), poems (*detembo*), teasing (*zvituko*), jokes or humour (*nyambo*), metaphor or idiom (*dimikira*) and proverbs (*tsumo*) and riddles (*zvirahwe*). *Ubuntu* also gives rise to certain ways of managing community interactions, many of which resonate with the more progressive forms of social work interventions. Again in Zimbabwe, such

> strategies of *Ubuntu* include *dare* (a groupwork strategy used for discussions) and *nhimbe* (a community strategy used for co-operative work). *Dare* is similar to sharing or yarning circles where each person gets a turn to contribute to discussions without interruption. A *nhimbe* could be used to assist one family (or person) ... or could be used for community projects. (Mugumbate, 2020, p 419)

Turning to the 'organisational studies' literature, Mbigi (1997) deploys his understanding of *Ubuntu* to suggest that 'service quality' is not only determined by what we do for the service user, but more by the 'spirit' in which the service is rendered. He suggests that *Ubuntu* values (such as collectivism, solidarity, acceptance, dignity and hospitality) are crucial. In computer science, Linux software developers, motivated by the philosophy, developed free '*Ubuntu* software', which was rooted in the idea that every computer user should have the freedom to download, run, copy, distribute, study, share, change and improve their software for any purpose without paying licensing fees. Additionally, they should be able to use their software in the language of their choice (Mugumbate and Nyanguru, 2013).

The 'value-base' of *Ubuntu* might also be conducive to that of social work practice ethics, community work and the conduct of research. For example, in gerontology within African settings, it is the responsibility of children to look after elderly members of the inner and extended family who cared for them when they were growing up. The institutionalisation of children, disabled persons, older people and offenders has not been very successful in the African setting. Perhaps this is because this form of 'processing' and 'warehousing' people rarely improves lives and is entirely alien to African ontology.

At a global and political level, it has been argued that *Ubuntu*, as an onto-epistemology, lacks aggressive, imperial, colonising and exploitative dimensions. A major criticism has been that the 'strength' of its values is also its 'weakness'. For example, openness to new ideas, welcoming strangers and treating them humanely may have contributed to Africa being more vulnerable to the colonisation that ultimately promoted disenfranchisement, culture erosion and dependence. Mugumbate and Nyanguru (2013) argue that while *Ubuntu* has been identified as the foundation for South Africa's post-Apartheid project of 'forgiveness' and 'reconciliation', it has slowed down the pace of equitable land distribution and other resources, leaving many Black South Africans, despite having an *Ubuntu*-based constitution and a welfare system, impoverished.

Other criticisms of *Ubuntu* centre on its purported failure to acknowledge the value of individual freedom, and that its ideas fit traditional, small-scale culture more than a modern, industrial society. To some, this type of criticism gels with the reading of de Sousa Santos (2012) that the logic of the dominant scale and the monoculture of the universal and the global involves designating rival realities as having relevance only to the 'particular' and the culturally and geographically specific, as discussed earlier. Metz (2011), however, offers a philosophical interpretation of *Ubuntu* that is not vulnerable to such criticisms. He constructs *Ubuntu* as moral theory grounded on Southern African worldviews suggesting a promising new conception of human dignity. According to his conception, human beings have a dignity by virtue of their capacity for community. This is understood as the combination of identifying with others and exhibiting solidarity with them, where human rights violations are egregious degradations of this capacity (Metz, 2011, p 532).

Having introduced Bourdieu and then used his work as something of a conceptual 'bridge' into *Ubuntu*, we will now begin to move beyond the European canon, to look in a little more detail at counterhegemonic epistemologies emanating from the Global South and African-America. Clearly, in drawing attention to some of the focal ideas, we cannot be exhaustive. Rather, our aim is two-fold: first, we can begin to consider if some of the writers we explore might contribute to the unravelling of Eurocentrism within social work; second the 'voices' we will hear may help us to get a better sense of some of the unquestioned onto-epistemological assumptions underpinning the professions often governing social work interactions with Black African families in Ireland.

A sociology of 'absences' and 'emergences': Boaventura de Sousa Santos

Boaventura de Sousa Santos (2014, p 238) argues that 'dominant epistemologies' have remained intent on the 'massive destruction of ways of knowing' that did not fit the dominant epistemological canon; he terms this 'epistemicide' (de Sousa Santos, 2014, p 238). Aspiring to counter-hegemonic western understandings of the world, he avows that there is a need to recognise that many emancipatory transformations in the world adhere to 'grammars and scripts other than those developed by western-centric theorising' (de Sousa Santos, 2014, p viii). Much of the 'western-centric critical tradition' positions itself as a 'vanguard theory that excels in knowing about, explaining, and guiding rather than knowing with, understanding, facilitating, sharing, and walking alongside' (de Sousa Santos, 2014, pp viii–ix). As part of a move to challenge and confront this tradition, de Sousa Santos (2014, p ix) champions and aligns himself with *teoria povera* (or poor theory): a form of 'rearguard theory' rooted in the experiences of those struggling against 'unjustly imposed marginality and inferiority, with the purpose of strengthening their resistance'. He identifies a 'ghostly relationship between theory and practice', in that there is a cleavage separating the theorists' paradigms and the quotidian struggles and resistance of many in the Global South (de Sousa Santos, 2014, p 43). The Portuguese scholar is scathing about the shallow forms of radicalism embedded within the universities of the Global North:

> In our time, genuine radicalism seems no longer possible in the global North. Those who proclaim themselves as radical thinkers are either fooling themselves or fooling someone else, since their practices are bound to contradict their theories. Most of them work in institutions such as universities that require protective hats and gloves to deal with reality. One of the tricks that western modernity plays on intellectuals is to allow them only to produce revolutionary ideas in reactionary institutions. On the other hand, those who act radically seem to be silent. Either they have nothing intelligible to say, or if they were to speak, nobody would understand them outside their circle of action, or they might even be thrown in jail or killed. (de Sousa Santos, 2014, p 3)

Consequently, a sense of 'exhaustion haunts the western, Eurocentric critical tradition. It manifests itself in a peculiar and diffuse uneasiness expressed in multiple ways: irrelevance, inadequacy, impotence, stagnation, paralysis' (de Sousa Santos, 2014, p 190). He calls, therefore, for an 'epistemological reconstruction' (de Sousa Santos, 2014, p 42). In what follows, therefore, we will briefly explore how he seeks to achieve this aim. The sociology of 'absences' and 'emergences' articulated by de Sousa Santos might potentially provide an epistemological foundation to facilitate the recognition of the presence of subjugated knowledges (de Sousa Santos, 2012). We will turn now to examine his main ideas in a little more detail.

A sociology of absences

This concept, according to de Sousa Santos (2012), pivots on an inquiry that seeks to explain that what often does not exist is actively produced as a 'non-credible' alternative to what exists. His approach aspires, therefore, to transform and bring into presence that which has been forced into absence by countering the logics and processes in which a hegemonic criterion of 'rationality' and 'efficiency' produces 'non-existence'. The author argues that 'non-existence' is generated whenever any phenomena are disqualified and rendered invisible, unintelligible or irreversibly disposable. The Portuguese scholar goes on to identify five main social forms of non-existence produced by hegemonic epistemology and rationality.

The monoculture of knowledge

Modern science and dominant cultural knowledge systems are canonically positioned as the sole criterion of truth and aesthetic quality. All that is excluded from the canon, in turn, becomes illegitimate, unrecognised and, therefore, non-existent. In this case non-existence is in the form of ignorance or being allegedly lacking in culture. For example, potential rival knowledge or practices are often dismissed as lacking academic rigour/ empirical support and so on, based on approved ethnocentric set standards. The African Charter on the Rights of the African Child, for example, is considered 'non-existent' in social work when dealing with Black African families in Ireland. This is seen in how the discourse on child protection and welfare exclusively references the 'universal' – but arguably still western-centric – UN Convention on the Rights of the Child as a normative standard for all children.

The monoculture of linear time

This is premised on the idea that time is linear, and *ahead* of time are the main countries within and 'leading' the world system. Non-existence in this case is produced by being described as 'backward' ('pre-modern', 'under-developed' and so on). Such perceptions are integral to the worldview of seminal figures within western political theory, such as Hannah Arendt (1998). For example, belief in evil spirits and witchcraft is for some Black African people still existentially meaningful, whereas White practitioners might view such beliefs as 'primitive' or 'backward'.

The monoculture of classification

This is based on the naturalisation of differences by grouping people into categories that naturalise racial classification. The inherited collective memory of historic and socially constructed notions of racial superiority functions as 'symbolic power' that presupposes that unequal relationship between Black Africans and people of European descent is merely naturally given and existing in the world. These inherited assumptions of racial superiority, despite having no proven evidence, continue to influence many White people's concept of the 'self' in relation to Black Africans and others (Ani, 1994). Social work and its agents, as products of the Euro-western socio-cultural hemisphere, risk internalising and reinforcing this inherited ideological falsehood at the collective and unconscious ethos level (Ani, 1994). Relatedly, Christian scriptures, such as the Bible, while purporting that we are all 'equal before God', ironically associate Blackness with evil and thus, for some, provide anti-Black racism with a measure of theological grounding and legitimacy (Tsri, 2016).

The logic of the dominant scale

Here, entities or realities widen their scope to the whole globe, designating rival entities as simply 'local'. That is to say, non-existence is produced through designating rival realities as having relevance only to the 'particular' and the culturally and geographically specific. The entities or realities defined as such are captured in scales that result, therefore, in their being constructed as palpably incapable of being credible alternatives to what exists globally and universally. Thus, non-western notions of epistemology and ontology deemed local, not universal/global, are marginalised as lacking credibility. Despite the increasing valorisation of philosophies such as *Ubuntu* from Southern Africa and Confucianism from Asia, these philosophies continue to be viewed, through the lens of the western canon, as exotically local and merely particular.

The logic of productivity

This is expressed through the monoculturally freighted criteria of capitalist 'productivity' and 'efficiency' privileging growth through market forces and capital accumulation. Non-existence is produced in the form of 'non-productiveness'. According to de Sousa Santos, non-productiveness is then equated with lack, sterility, and also 'laziness' and even 'professional incompetence'. Might this be related to the fact that Black and ethnic minority social workers are over-represented in 'fitness to practice' cases adjudicated on by the Social Work England regulatory authority (Samuel, 2020)?

The conceptual utility of 'sociology of absences' for our book is that it provides the space to enlarge the scope of credible experiences. We will now briefly look at the 'sociology of emergences', which may furnish a theoretical foundation to counter the 'sociology of absences'.

A sociology of emergences

The 'sociology of emergences', according to de Sousa Santos (2012, p 54), consists in 'replacing the emptiness of the future according to linear time (an emptiness that may be all or nothing) by a future of plural and concrete possibilities, utopian and realist at one time, and constructed in the present by means of activities of care'. Central here is the argument that plural 'ecologies' must replace 'monocultures'. By attempting to identify emergent signals that are disqualified exactly because they have not yet consolidated, this 'sociology of emergences' adopts a 'not yet' attitude so as to think about reality as something that does not exist, but is potentially emerging. In *Social Work with the Black African Diaspora*, we remain attentive to his dimension and sensitive to 'emergent' possibilities. In critically exploring hitherto silenced and marginalised knowledge systems and other non-western philosophies we align ourselves with the ethnical imperatives implicit in the 'sociology of emergences' approach.

The 'sociology of emergences' is analysed in the discussion of Khoo and Walsh (2016) on the 1994 Zapatistas' 'pedagogical revolution' that aimed to meaningfully address human concerns following the rejection of failed mainstream education's neoliberal agenda. It fashioned 'new ways of being' using an alternative endogenous educational paradigm generated 'from below'. Closer to home and related specifically to social work, the successful 2014 SWAN campaign against a proposed 'cheap labour' scheme for new graduates exemplified a small, concrete oppositional effort that is 'not yet' the norm but could signal future enlarged possibilities. More broadly, in order to liberate people from cultural misrecognition and economic marginalisation requires critical engagement with political and neoliberal capitalist structures. The relationship between social work and global capitalism generally, and more specifically the Irish context, is one of the recurring preoccupations in this book.

Critical race theory

CRT is another body of theory which might inform our engagement with this book's core themes. This is not to argue that such theorisation, derived from a US economic and cultural context, can be lazily cut and pasted into the Irish or, indeed, wider European scene. CRT involves the application of critical theory to 'race'-based human injustice (Matsuda et al, 1993; Milner, 2008). Solorzano (1997, p 6) defines CRT as a 'framework or set of basic perspectives, methods, and pedagogy that seeks to identify, analyse, and transform those structural and cultural aspects of society that maintain the subordination and marginalisation of people of colour'. Delgado and Stefanic (2012) posit that CRT emerged during the US civil rights movement era as part of the study and analysis of the law. The theory was founded on challenging the liberal interpretation of the law and the myriad of associated legal processes. The liberal claim, at the time, was that the law was 'objective', 'colour-blind' and 'neutral', but CRT advocates, in contrast, confronted such claims by arguing that to say the law was, for example, 'colour-blind' was tantamount to ignoring the pervasive influence of racial inequality manifestly characterising social structures and institutions.

CRT supporters continue to maintain, therefore, that perceiving the law as 'neutral' amounts to perpetuating racism, given that the legal field is a racialised zone of oppression and *producer* of authoritative pronouncements on what constitutes normativity. For example, in terms of social work in the Republic of Ireland, it has been asserted that child protection guidelines are maybe unreflexively rooted in White Irish norms (Christie, 2010). This potentially allows White Irish practitioners to defend their actions as 'lawful' against accusations of being racially biased.

In general terms, CRT is drawn from diverse disciplines including sociology, political science, feminism, postcolonial theory, law, economics and cultural studies. Gotanda (2000) argues that when one makes the conscious decision to exclude 'race' as a factor in any situation it means that, by default, its existence and powerful influence is being – paradoxically – recognised. The six main tenets of CRT can be identified as follows.

'Race' as endemic occurrence

Rather than viewing racism as 'abnormal' and 'individualistic', CRT argues that racism is an ordinary everyday occurrence for minority groups. It is so embedded in our social structures and practices that it informs and directs our thought processes, but this is rendered largely 'invisible' particularly by those accruing racial advantage. It is this mundane banality – functioning as a barely detectable background noise or hum – that perpetuates racism. Relatedly, Jones (2000) defines 'institutionalised racism' as those structures, policies, practices and norms resulting in differential access to the goods, services and opportunities of society by 'race'. Institutionalised racism is normative, sometimes legalised and often manifests as 'inherited' disadvantage. It is structural, having been absorbed into our institutions of custom, practice and law, so there need not be an identifiable offender. Indeed, 'institutionalised racism' is often evident as *inaction* in the face of need; it is also reflected in material conditions and in differential access to a range of goods and services. Here we might include, for example, a good-quality education, sound housing, gainful employment, appropriate medical facilities and clean environments.

'Race' as social construction

CRT asserts that 'race' is a socially constructed concept with no proven correspondence to any biological or genetic reality. Despite this interpretation, CRT acknowledges the meaning, implications and *force* of 'race' when it is contrived as a system of categorising people based on observable physical attributes. This construction is enabled by laws and legislation and, on occasions, supposedly 'empirically based knowledge' is used to promote and protect dominant interests. Such constructions become gradually accepted as 'common sense' – in a Gramscian sense – if not challenged. CRT also acknowledges that being White implies 'rights' and 'advantages' that make 'success' more likely for those who inhabit the category. Such 'rights', 'advantages' (and, indeed, 'entitlements' for White people who also happen to be members of the ruling class) largely go by unacknowledged. This lack of awareness reinforces a culture that espouses myths of 'meritocracy'. Within this CRT framing, 'Whiteness' can also be perceived as a type of 'property' (Harris, 1993). In Bourdieusian terms, 'Whiteness' might also be perceived as a particularly useful form of 'capital' in a racist social world.

Differential racialisation

CRT suggests that dominant social groups construct discourses that racialise certain minority groups at different times in history to suit different political, social and economic agendas. For example, it has been maintained that Asian-Americans were often poor and demonised, but after some members of this community became wealthier and powerful they began to be identified as something of a 'model' minority ethnic population (Delgado and Stephanic, 2012). Racist discourses and practices, directed particularly at Chinese-Americans, flourishing in the wake of the COVID-19 pandemic, may have altered this construction.

More pervasively, differential racial categories are used to determine who is 'in' or 'out' of the dominant group over time. The cumulative effect of 'race'-based societal stratification through institutional arrangements is that disparities are created and nurtured. These disparities further result in poor outcomes – in, for example, the areas of health, educational attainment and housing – for those situated on the lower rungs of the discursive and materially generated racialised hierarchies. 'Citizenship' and its related processes also determines access. For example, the outcome of the 2004 citizenship referendum in Ireland resulted in many Black African immigrants being denied 'Irish citizenship' for their children, irrespective of the fact that their offspring may have been born on 'Irish soil'.

Interest convergence/material determinism

CRT asserts that racism has material and psychic benefits for the dominant social group. Any progressive change to the status quo takes place, therefore, only when the interests of the dominant group converge with those of the racially oppressed. For example, in Ireland, commercial providers of DP hostels are paid an enormous amount of money. This would suggest that DP will not speedily be brought to an end if certain financial interests evidently continue to profit from it. This could also mean that if, in future, the 'business' of DP becomes unprofitable it may cease to exist or, at least, to transform in terms of how it is presently constituted. This now seems likely, following the publication of a White Paper in early 2021 (Government of Ireland, 2021). Abandoning such a no longer 'viable' business model would benefit asylum seekers in human rights terms, but it might also furnish business entities (and their political advocates) with a 'politically correct' narrative: they would, in these circumstances, appear to be spurred not by cynical financial considerations but by a (sudden) concern for 'human rights'.

Voices of the oppressed/rewriting history

Delgado (2003) argues that dominant racial social groups often construct narratives of history that distort, minimise or exclude racial minority perspectives to justify and legitimise their power. Such action has the effect of silencing alternative experiences as well as obscuring the interplay of power and oppression across time and place. In such situations, CRT advocates for the rewriting of history to encompass the perspectives of the oppressed groups (based on the reality of their lived experiences and in their own words). Providing space for such narratives contests the liberal claims of 'neutrality', 'colour-blindness' and 'universal' truths. The audibility of counter narratives gels also with the notion of inclusive 'discourse ethics', which are, on occasions, said to inform social workers' endeavours to listen to all sides' perceptions of social problems and issues (Houston, 2003). For CRT, marginalised voices/stories must be 'heard'. In child protection in Ireland and elsewhere in Europe, the 'voice' of Black African parents is often marginalised, given the cultural insularity reflected in mainstream ideas as to what constitutes 'good parenting' (Mukanjari, 2020).

CRT and intersectionality

Hutchinson (2000) suggests that CRT acknowledges the 'intersectionality' of different oppressions. The same writer warns that focusing solely on 'race', at the expense of other oppressions, risks replicating the very social exclusion that CRT aims to combat. CRT also seeks, therefore, to avoid essentialising oppressions and reducing experiences to one *entirely* determining category. Park (2005), however, argues that attention needs to be given to how racism still tends to remain the pivotal mechanism of oppression for minority ethnic groups. One must, therefore, not get lost on a 'level playing field' and equalise all oppressions, since this might perpetuate colour-blindness and aid those intent on denying the potency of historically rooted patterns of racism. Park's (2005) argument is that one can be female and disabled, yet retain advantages if one is situated in a 'White category'.

Criticism of CRT

CRT is credited with enhancing our critical consciousness by drawing extensively on interdisciplinary scholars who challenge racialised forms of hierarchy. Not only does CRT destabilise the master narratives of Eurocentric interpretations (Hylton, 2012), it also provides new narratives that enable alternative ways of thinking and reflection based on Black people telling their own 'stories' and opening avenues for possible ameliorative actions (Zuberi, 2011; Delgado and Stefancic, 2012). More saliently, CRT exposes the complicity of the law, and other fields of state operations, in the maintenance of racial hierarchy and order-making (Zuberi, 2011).

Despite these benefits, CRT can be criticised – like much of the Afrocentric theory that we will discuss in the next chapter – for being largely a product of the US experience. As a result, it may not easily apply translate to other national contexts with differing histories. Mike Cole (2009) is critical of CRT's proclivity to conflate 'race' with class in oppression discourses (see also Mills, 2009). In particular, he pointedly criticises CRT's tendency to homogenise *all* White people as occupying positions of power and 'privilege': a move which entirely ignores the lived reality of many poor Whites who have their lives distorted and wrecked by the voracious process of capital exploitation. Cole (2009, p 248) also cogently and persuasively identifies 'four significant problems' with the 'white supremacy' notion:

> The first is that it can direct attention away from modes of production; the second that it homogenizes all white people together in positions of power and privilege; the third is that it is inadequate at explaining non-colour-coded racism; and the fourth, that it is totally counter-productive as a political unifier and rallying point against racism.

Critics also point to the absence of a CRT 'road map' leading to the achievement of the desired social change. How is structural racism going to be eradicated by merely confining oneself to the CRT line of argumentation and analysis?

Critical whiteness theory

As the cultural critic Richard Dyer (1997, p 19) suggests, historical and contemporary processes of racialisation have been 'enormously, often terrifyingly, effective in unifying disparate groups of people'. In the context of critical Whiteness discourses in the US, Toni Morrison's (1992) contributions on 'Whiteness and the literary imagination' are significant. More generally, a growing literature on Whiteness has been evolving since the late 1980s and a good deal of this is, once again, derived from the US, which has, of course, a very particular history of racism (Kovel, 1988; White, 1990; Allen, 1994; 1997; Roediger, 1994; 2017; Winant, 1997; Twine and Gallagher, 2008; Low, 2009; Annamma, 2015). Within European social work there has not been the same keenness to interrogate pivotal ideas about 'Whiteness' (Gregory, 2020). However, as Hazel Carby observes, there is a need to 'think about the invention of the category' of Whiteness as well as that of Blackness and, consequently, to make 'visible what is rendered invisible when viewed as the normative state of existence; the (white) point in space from which we tend to identify difference' (in Giroux, 1997a, p 326; see also Giroux, 1997b; Bonnett, 2000).

Whiteness 'certainly carries privileges, but they are not always guaranteed', and in order to 'give back meaning to the apparent emptiness of the "white" category it is necessary to explore the specificity of white experiences' (Walter, 2001, p 6). Historically, in fact, 'some are more securely white than others', and this is reflected in the creation of people who are 'sometimes whites' (Dyer, 1997, p 4). That is to say, some, such as Irish people and Jewish people, may be 'let into whiteness under particular historical circumstances' (Dyer, 1997, p 19; Ignatiev, 1995; Garrett, 2004, Hickman et al, 2005). In short, 'Whiteness' as a category is socially constructed and contains historically shifting borders and complex internal hierarchies (Mac an Ghaill, 2002).

CWT is a further strand, or theoretical offshoot, of CRT that problematises the notion of 'Whiteness' as a 'marker' associated with White 'privilege'. Audrey Thompson (2008) posits that CWT is comprised of several theories which treat 'Whiteness' not as a biological category but as a social construction. Thus, CWT questions the 'normalisation' and 'naturalisation' of 'Whiteness'. Advocates of CWT reject the notion of 'White values' as a generic or 'colour-blind' norm and emphasise that the status of 'Whiteness' as a 'norm' is a 'privilege'. In CWT terms, 'Whiteness' is evoked as a form of 'property' conceived as conferring material and symbolic advantages to White people or those 'passing' as White. In this context, she also argues that CWT is not intent on assigning guilt but can help non-racist White people to learn how to better respond to personal and societal racism.

Thompson (2008) argues that not all who inhabit 'Whiteness' are observably 'White': hence the term 'honorary Whiteness/Whites', which suggests that 'Whiteness' can be a conferred status. 'Honorary Whites' denotes those 'deserving few' non-Whites (some Black and Brown people) to whom White-privileging mechanisms have been extended by White power structures on account of merit or otherwise. Thompson argues that, often, 'honorary Whites' enjoy White privileging mechanisms more or less 'on probation', in that they are constantly expected to demonstrate their worthiness.

This analysis also relates to a criticism of 'tokenistic' responses to racism and racial discrimination in which Black people are strategically and 'visibly' located within organisations so as to vouch for the fact that these structures are simply 'meritocratic' and contain no elements of colour or 'race' prejudice. Thompson also argues that 'honorary Whites' are disenfranchised if they jeopardise their precarious status by, for example, demonstrating significant interest in, or solidarity with, the causes and political resistance projects of other Black or Brown people. However, for a period, material advantages may accrue, such as better access to jobs, higher education and a safer neighbourhood in which to live. Charbeneau (2009, p 2) argues that CWT helps to illuminate 'behaviours that signify what it means to be White in our society', while Frankenberg (1993, p 1) suggests that White and Black people live racially structured lives. More importantly, CWT stresses that 'Whiteness has a set of linked dimensions ... racial advantage, egocentrism, and an unawareness of whiteness as "race"'.

The proponents of this theory argue that 'Whiteness' theories do not agree on a single methodology or theoretical claim. CWT is interdisciplinary in nature and this is reflected in the composition of the associated four major theoretical tendencies which coalesce around material, discursive, institutional and personal/relational forms of analysis.

Material theories of Whiteness

These disturb and problematise how White people as a social group come to enjoy advantageous access to tangible, everyday goods such as well-paying jobs, health protection, environmentally safe communities, good education and basic civil liberties Although such theories are structural in their approach, in that they prioritise targeting systemic racism, they do not ignore individual prejudice.

Discursive theories of Whiteness

These analyse how language, mass media, discourses and symbols are deployed to frame Whiteness as the *preferred normal way of being*. In this regard, the predominant image of violent Black gangsters in films perhaps helps to embed enduring perceptions of Black people – more particularly, Black *men* – as inherently prone to crime and violence. Discursive theories often identify 'binaries' that treat Blackness/Brownness as a comparative background (the melodramatic 'other') for Whiteness. This favourable framing of 'Whiteness', and all associated with it, enables it to emerge, therefore, as relatively superior. Proponents of this theoretical approach also point to the meta-narratives implicit in our mainstream discussions of 'race': for example, White/light/good vs Black/dark/evil reflect this pervasive cultural dynamic in racist societies (se also Dyer, 1997). One of the preoccupations of *Social Work with the Black African Diaspora* is to try to discern if such embedded perceptions impact on social work cross-cultural encounters.

Institutional theories of Whiteness

Such theories combine material and discursive approaches and question systems of privilege that result in negative material consequences residing in institutions such as banks, schools, universities and hospitals. Institutional theories are also concerned with strategies through which White privilege is rendered sustainable. Such theories of 'Whiteness' tend to focus on how 'regulations' or 'codes of conduct' privilege certain discourses, cultures or value systems within institutional settings. Thompson (2008) refers to examples such as protocols dictating the appropriate presentation of scholarly research and explicit (or implicit) codifications of merit, authority, legitimacy and expertise. She maintains that the consequences of these practices can be material (for example, one can be sanctioned, even dismissed, for not abiding by the approved codes), but the emphasis in institutional analyses is more on the *maintenance* of a system of symbolic privilege through exclusionary practices: for example, categorising 'dreadlocks' or other non-White hairstyles/ways of dressing as 'unprofessional' while, in truth, being aware that such 'codes' of etiquette will mostly impact on and constrain people who are Black.

Personal/relational or psychological or identity theories of Whiteness

According to Thompson (2008), such theories aspire to address the ways in which White privileging mechanisms affect how we perceive ourselves and others. Thus, this perspective is concerned with assumptions about personal development, morality and decency. The same author also acknowledges the presence of Black people who internalise White-privileging institutional norms and go on to benefit from and participate in the promotion of institutional 'Whiteness'. Some go to the extent of hating being Black and wishing they had been born White.

A number of social work research reports, in fact, indicate that some Black children internalise notions of White superiority and are alert to the attendant material privileges. These children not infrequently prefer to be fostered to White families, despite that there may be Black substitute carers available. For example, Dalikeni (2013) refers to a Black child fostered to a White family that permitted her freedom to have boyfriends, smoke and drink alcohol at an age when her biological Black African family would not have done so. This child, therefore, came to perceive her own family as 'backward' and the White family as 'cool' and ambiguously 'modern'.

Giroux's (1997a; 1997b) 'oppositional Whiteness' theory and strategy is arguably meant to assist White people, be they students/practitioners or educators, to understand the power of Whiteness, White supremacy and the historic legacy of racism. Giroux's argument is that before White people can become meaningfully anti-racist campaigners there is a need to rearticulate or reinvent 'Whiteness' in a way that enables them to be aware of and take responsibility for their privilege. This rearticulation of Whiteness, according to Giroux, starts with asking the question 'what does it means to be White?' He suggests that how that question is answered potentially opens space for some White people to critique and reject oppression inflicted in the name of Whiteness, while also providing intellectual space for an 'oppositional' White identity to emerge. This White identity, in the form of reinvented Whiteness, could potentially operate, he maintains, outside of the racial superiority/inferiority binary, while directly confronting hegemony associated with 'everyday Whiteness'. Giroux further argues that by confronting the tyranny of White supremacy, 'oppositional Whiteness' minimises the projection of guilt on the part of individual White people. This, the writer believes, is crucial in fostering a sense that it is possible for White people to be allies in coalitions seeking the obliteration of racial injustices and helps to enable true social justice through what he refers to as 'critical democracy'.

In Ireland, the notion of 'oppositional Whiteness exists in some sections of the wider society, and if this finds tangible expression it is apparent in, for example, protests against 'institutional racism' (for example, anti-DP demonstrations). At the institutional and organisational levels, significant 'oppositional Whiteness' is far less detectable. Nevertheless, perhaps the institutionalisation of 'oppositional Whiteness' within social work programmes in universities could reinvigorate more progressive projects committed to educational and organisational transformations within the sector. In Australia, for example, significant steps have been taken to try to make social work more culturally representative. Social work educators have used 'action research' methodology to examine their own teaching (Gair et al, 2003). In doing so, they became much more aware of the monoculturally biased manner of their presentation and the dominance of

White, Eurocentric cultural values and norms as the onto-epistemology underpinning their curricula. This discovery of the dominance of White monoculturalism led to an acknowledgement that social work was, indeed, 'very White'. By excluding non-western onto-epistemologies, social work education in Australia was not only disrespectful to non-western people, it was also largely *irrelevant* to a good deal of their lives and daily experiences. Gair et al (2003) maintain that if such a situation persists it could potentially lead to social work being viewed as functioning to serve the interests of White people while also working against the interests of marginalised minority ethnic populations. The utility of this contribution lies in not only exposing ethnocentric monoculturalism but also in that it illustrates the potential negative impact on social work's legitimacy in the eyes of Indigenous and minority ethnic peoples. More generally, Gair et al (2003) prompt critical reflection and they signal some necessary changes involving the movement from a monocultural onto-epistemological value base towards one that is somewhat more respectful and relevant to the non-western community's cultural values. These remedial actions taken by the, mostly White, Australian social work educators could perhaps provide important 'messages' for their colleagues in other parts of the world.

Conclusion

Later in our book, the theoretical frameworks mentioned will inform our engagement with our interview participants (see also Chapter 6). Hence, decolonisation, the work of Gramsci, Foucault, Bourdieu and de Sousa Santos will aid comprehension of some of the focal issue and themes. Added to this shifting and complex range of theories will be contributions informed by both CRT and CWT. Whiteness is, of course, a far from monolithic entity, and part of the ideological sleight of hand of White supremacists is to maintain that it and the solidarities it ought to nurture and sustain are – and or should be – indivisible. Indeed, this is the manifest move made by the Far Right in the US and elsewhere. In Chapter 6, we implicitly cut against the notion of White unanimity by including the perceptions not only of White Irish respondents: we also include White respondents originating in England, Australia and the US. Indeed, that chapter is, perhaps, the first empirical study examining Irish social work education and practice that includes include an internationally differentiated White sample.

In the next chapter, we begin to critically engage with notions connected to Afrocentricity. While largely absent within social work discourse in Ireland and other parts of Europe, it has had an impact in the US. Indeed, many of the ideas associated with this body of theory have tended to emanate from the US. While purporting to pay particular attention to Black experiences, Afrocentric thinking might be perceived has having an allure for those aiming to improve social work responses when working with the Black African diaspora. Nevertheless, as we will see, Afrocentricity theory, mired in essentialism and fastened to reductive binaries, is laden with conceptual problems and fails to furnish a compelling theoretical base for those of us intent on radically reforming social theory and practice.

Reflection and talk box 3

As we have read, there have been numerous calls to 'decolonise' academic disciplines. How might this relate to social work education?

How might a range of European thinkers continue to add to our theorisation of 'race' and racism? Perhaps consider this question in relation to Gramsci, Foucault and Bourdieu.

How useful are the work of Boaventura de Sousa Santos and his sociology of 'absences' and 'emergences'?

Why is CRT so controversial? Moreover, can CWT add to social workers' engagement with issues circulating around 'race' and racism?

4

Afrocentricity and its critics

Introduction

Afrocentricity is the label given to a range of theories that rhetorically aspire to confront the erasure and exclusion Black Africans from our historical and contemporary intellectual universe. Afrocentric theory recognises that Eurocentricity or 'Westernity' (Euro–American thought and behaviour) as a worldview not only has come to represent an expression of European culture but, despite its cultural particularity, it has become an imposed universal denigration of other worldviews. Supporters of Afrocentricity bluntly declare, therefore, that current methods of inquiry, logic and research in academia are inappropriate to study the lives and ways of being of Black African peoples.

Purporting to constitute a systematic alternative and challenge to western epistemology, Afrocentricity evolved as a theory of knowledge in the 1980s in a decidedly African-American cultural and political context, with Gilroy (1993, p 191) observing that 'Africentricity might be more properly called *Americocentricity*' (emphasis added). In this chapter we investigate primary definers of Afrocentricity such as Marimba Ani and Molefi Asante. We then look at how there have been sustained attempts to transport this body of theory into social work. Prominent here are figures such as Jerome Schiele (1996; 1997; 2017), Mekada Graham (1999; 2001) and Dumisani Thabede (2005; 2008). As alluded to at the end of the previous chapter, and despite its stridency and emphatic and declaratory style, Afrocentricity is bedevilled with problems. We will therefore briefly dwell on some of these difficulties and will conclude by introducing the more conceptually persuasive perceptions of the Beninese philosopher Paul J. Hountondji.

Yurugu: Marimba Ani

Marimba Ani's (1994) *Yurugu: A Critic of European Thought and Behaviour* is a fascinating and highly problematic contribution. Formerly known as Dona Richards, the author is an anthropologist and African Studies specialist, and her book furnishes a detailed critique of many foundational aspects of European thought and culture which are, ordinarily, insufficiently examined by those entirely constrained by the worldviews and dominant perceptions of the Global North. Eurocentrism is mostly cast in terms of power-laden binaries such as civilised/barbaric, advanced/backward, developed/

undeveloped and core/periphery. All of which imply an evolutionary schema through which societies inevitably progress. Underlying this is the White, male, western 'self' as the focal referent and superior figure (Sundberg, 2009).

In her theory of culture, Ani (1994) argues that every culture has an *Asili* (an explanatory germinal principle of being a culture), an *Utamaroho* (collective unconscious ethos) and an *Utamawazo* (epistemological definitions that account for a perspective in how a culture identifies notions of truth). The author posits that the concept of *Asili* – arguably her main focus, and a Kiswahili word – is used variously to mean beginning or origin, source, essence and, more importantly, a fundamental initiating principle. The *Asili*'s utility is that it can function as a conceptual tool for cultural analysis, mapping differences between Black African and European ethnic cultures. That is to say, the *Asili* is like a template carrying within it the pattern or archetypical model for cultural development. It embodies the 'logic' of the culture, how a culture works and the principles structuring its development.

Asili allows us to recognise culture as a basic organising mechanism that forges a group into an 'interest group' or ideological unit. *Asili* accounts for consistence and pattern in a culture, also its tenacity. It determines the cultural development, the form that a culture takes, how a culture maintains its integrity. Every culture has an *Asili* determined by the collective, fundamental nature of its members. Accordingly, the *Asili* of a culture can be identified and its inherent nature delineated. If this is the case, the concept presents us with a potentially powerful tool of explanation about the organicity, structure and development of any culture. It might allow us to explain and to see the way in which the various aspects of a culture relate and cohere. In short, *Asili*, if used critically and in conjunction with a range of other conceptual tools could potentially aid our understanding of the behaviour, thought and creative lives of a people.

The first section of *Yurugu* relates to 'Thought and Iconography' and Ani outlines the epistemological, ontological and axiological assumptions and principles grounding European thought (Ferguson, 2016). She argues that the source of Eurocentrism can be found in Plato's epistemological framework, which privileges 'reason' over 'emotion', the 'cognitive' over the 'affective' and the 'objective' over the 'subjective'. In this sense, Ani perceives the European cultural *Asili* as dominated by the concepts of separation, control and domination. Separation, for example, is manifested in splitting man/ nature, European/other, thought/emotion, spirit/matter.

The second section of her book dwells on 'Image and Consciousness' and it examines the self-image of Europeans as illustrated in their behaviour, literature and other forms of cultural expression providing ideological support for European cultural imperialism. Clearly, Ani furnishes culturally essentialist and reductive readings, but the utility of her work for *Social Work with the*

Black African Diaspora is that she provides a way to *decentre* and *deconstruct* facets of traditional western scholarship. Consequently, she arguably helps us to better comprehend the construction of Black people as 'inferior' and to recognise how Black people initially became 'otherised' within western schemes of thought and material practices. In her chapter on the European image of others, for example, Ani highlights that, while Europeans tend to view 'others' as 'irrational', 'illogical', 'uncivilised', 'primitive', 'unruly', 'lazy' and 'passive', they view themselves as antithetically superior.

More generally, *Yurugu* is a thorough critique of the historical and anthropological construction of the White supremacy which, as we have seen CRT and CWT theorists maintain, continues to resonate today. In this context, Ani also conceptualises racism as an ideological formation that influences both Blacks and Whites to believe what it actually means to be Black or to be White. In the third section of her book, she expounds on what she terms 'rhetorical ethics': for example, she illuminates how religion, in the form of Christianity, espouses humane and well-meaning statements such as one should 'pursue peace and love of one's enemies' and 'hold dear to the brotherhood of man' and so on. However, such abstractions rarely find material expression in how Europeans, propelled by rapacious processes of capital accumulation, have historically engaged with other cultures. Ani maintains, in fact, that when Christianity became institutionalised it furnished part of the assemblage of 'soft power' for European colonial and imperialist adventures. In contemporary Europe, one could argue that some elements of this form of 'rhetorical ethics' is discernible in the utterances of state and non-state actors who trumpet 'human rights', yet fail to practise them in the actual treatment of, for example, 'asylum seekers'. The Irish DP system manifestly exemplifies this dynamic (Irish Refugee Council, 2020).

In what follows we will briefly examine some of the key beliefs that Ani associates with the embedded western European worldview.

Freedom, individuality and self

Ani (1994) makes clear that a critical understanding of the European concept of 'self' enables us to better understand the ideology of individualism and the related assumed value of individual human 'freedom'. Concepts such as 'individuality' and 'freedom' tend to be prominent in White Europeans notions of value and, indeed, to contribute to bolstering the notion that their culture is superior. Consequently, 'traditional' forms of community, based on collectives that are functional to specialised ends, are not valued. Here, the concept of individual power is understood as freedom from constraining forces for one (usually, of course, a wealthy, White, European or American, male) to do whatever they might desire to advance self-interest and to promote self-actualisation. Many of the defining characteristics of this European worldview arguably reflect the imperatives of capitalism as much as any free-floating cultural system of meaning (see also Chapter 5).

Ani suggests that, within this understanding, the individual perceives that the best way to ensure survival and progression is to be competitive, to win, to get ahead and to accumulate objects of value before others do so. Ani also implies that within this European cultural framing it is not considered immoral to act in one's own interest at the expense of others. In this context, the atomised 'I' might be associated with social work conceptualisations and terminology: for example, it is central to notions of 'self-determination', 'person centred practice', 'individualised services' and 'choice' (see also Biestek (1975 [1957])). In contrast, with *Ubuntu* and similar African worldviews, the individual's obligation is to become more fully human through entering more deeply into community with others (Mugumbate, 2020). Hence, although the goal may remain one of personal fulfilment, it is arrived at via solidarity and wider group-based orientations. That is to say, an individual life project is comprehended alongside how one enters into and advances beneficial communal relationships.

Knowledge and the means of knowing

Gyekye (1995) contends that western culture has acknowledged reason and sense (rationalism and empiricism) as the main sources of knowledge. Such a stance fits in with Plato's epistemology, which postulates that to be capable of critical thought one must be independent from that which is to be known. One must be detached, uninvolved and remote. This, it is argued, allows for control of the 'self', which will no longer be influenced by emotions and context; a 'self', in short, no longer fettered, without a context and free of community constraints. Within African understanding this implies a self entirely bereft of meaning.

Relatedly, according to Ani, the way objects are created in western culture is through detaching themselves from that which they wish to know. The implied rationale is: through eliminating or gaining control of the emotions and replacing them with reason, we become thinking subjects different from the object to be studied. Through this separation of object and its relationship with context we achieve objectivity. Ani suggests that a cognitive modality which designates everything other than 'self' as an 'object' facilitates knowledge as 'control' and 'power' over the other.

Scientism, logic and de-spiritualisation/de-sacralisation

Ani argues that, within western culture, rationalistic science serves as the supreme definer deemed capable of representing the religious/spiritual attitude. The 'scientific' person is purportedly logical, detached, remote and able to control, manipulate and predict the movement of people and other objects. Ani concludes that the western cultural psyche requires the 'illusion' of a rationally ordered universe in which everything can be known. Rationalism and its ascendancy to the cultural dominant mode of European culture have devalued the spiritual dimension in human life and the universe. The universe becomes reduced to lifeless matter, with the supernatural being reduced to the natural and physical (Ani, 1994).

Ani maintains that the major reason for de-spiritualisation and de-sacralisation is that spirituality represents a constant threat to the kind of ordered system the Europeans have socially constructed; it cannot, in short, be measured or controlled as a determinant and inspiration of cultures and subsequent human action. In this context, Ani notes the relentless focus on linearity and the counting and measuring of physical reality. Relatedly, Thabede (2008) implies that materialism begins with separation of spirit and matter. When critically reviewed, Ani's arguments suggest that the Eurocentric mode of thought has produced the kind of technical and materialistic social order that currently exists in the western world. According to her understanding, it is equally apparent that this kind of social order – this form of 'rationality – has also led the world into a spate of spiritual and moral disasters. What is more, in terms of humanity's engagement with the 'natural' world, the fate of the planet has become precarious. From wildfires in Australia and the Amazon, to extremes of heat in India, to drought in East Africa, to floods in Europe, climate-induced extreme weather is already shaping human lives in adverse, even disastrous ways. By 2070, a billion people are likely to be confronted by intolerable heat (Watts, 2020). Moreover, it is the 'most vulnerable individuals and communities' who are 'disproportionately impacted by the destruction and degradation of the natural environment' (Harris and Boddy, 2017, p 337).

The role of intellectuals

Traditionally, in many non-western cultures, 'uneducated' wise old women and men ('village elders') were – and to some degree still are – valued as 'intellectuals' because of their lived, real-life experiences. Pitika Ntuli (2002, p 61) avows that the saying, 'When an old person dies it is like a library burning down', best expresses and encapsulates this sentiment. This notion might also be connected to the whole genre of what is termed 'sage philosophy' (Presbey, 2016). Articulated by the Kenyan philosopher, Henry Odera Oruka, this body of philosophy is based on the oral knowledge and reflective capacity of African 'sages'. Oruka distinguishes between 'folk-sages, who simply transmit the knowledge of the previous generations' and more critically oriented 'philosophical sages', who 'reflect on such knowledge and develop their own insights' (Dübgen and Skupien, 2019, p 5).

As for Ani, she maintains that Plato not only established a theory of humanness that valorised scientific cognition, to the exclusion of other cognitive modes, but he also established the 'academy'. She further suggests that, consistent with Plato's beliefs, there is a rooted assumption within western culture that association with 'academia' equates with 'superior reasoning capacity', 'impartiality', 'objectivity' and a 'commitment to truth'. In our contemporary times, and cutting very much against the democratising theorisation of Gramsci (Singh and Cowden, 2009), for any person to be recognised as an 'intellectual' they must be 'trained' and validated in a university (see also Chapter 3). This illustrates, for Ani, how western culture has developed Plato's 'academy' idea to influence not only European and US culture, but also cultures in the Global South.

The 'academy' mode, according to Ani, might also be considered significant within the fabric of 'social control'. 'Academia', following her line of reasoning, ensures that the ideological infrastructure remains intact. In this context, Beenash Jafri (2018) points to the neoliberalisation of the academy, characterised by the commodification of academic work, the disciplining of critical scholars, the increasing precarity of academic labour and fewer permanent positions. She argues that, while this could force many intellectuals to operate outside mainstream academia, this development potentially opens up possibilities for more transformative work free from the 'chokehold' of organisational and institutionalised neoliberal structures.

Western European culture's 'universal syntax'

Ani asserts that the *Asili*, or cultural structuring of the European thought, is determined by a 'will to dominate', conquer and control nature, the universe and all its inhabitants. She associates the notion of White Supremacism with both Platonic and Judaic influences. Plato's original theory of humanness was based on splitting humans into dichotomies of 'superior thinking/ rational beings', on the one hand, and 'emotional inferior beings', on the other. The latter was then applied – wholesale – to non-western cultures. The Judaic influence, she contends, was manifested in the notion of a few 'chosen people' leading the rest. Controversially, she states that this has been translated into the idea that a small minority (for example, Davos gathering and the like) are able to speak for rest of humanity. More pervasively, White western, male political interests continually masquerade under the guise of representing the universal human interest of all of us. She concludes that this myth of universalism has enabled western culture to impose its specific cultural particularities on the whole world. Closer to our disciplinary home, it might be contended that social work continues to mirror this practice (Midgley, 1981).

The final section of Ani's admittedly powerful contribution focuses on how 'culture' as 'ideology' is used to define social reality. Here, she draws on Foucault's work in exposing the relationship between European 'knowledge' and 'power'. Frankenberg (1997) and Nylund (2006) express similar views on the historical construction of 'White Power' and on how 'Whiteness' became an 'invisible' normative marker against which all other cultures are judged. In this context, for real equality to prevail, there is a need – as we saw in our previous chapter – to *deconstruct* and *decentre* Whiteness.

However, perhaps obscuring the real cause of the problem, Afrocentric thinkers such as Ani identify the Eurocentric worldview – and not capitalism – as the primary cause of the callous and uncaring economic and social welfare regimes existing in the US and the EU. They argue that the current welfare regimes, based on Eurocentric philosophy, have failed to achieve equity, given the lived experience of many people of non-European (*and* European) heritage. Levels of hardship and exploitation have only increased. These scholars conclude, therefore, that it is, perhaps, time to look at possible philosophical contributions from other cultures when formulating social work and social welfare policies and practices truly intent on liberating all people (European and non-European alike) from social and economic oppression that currently exists. Haug (2005, p 130) supports this perspective by arguing that the globally interconnected injustices/crises we face today can be shown to have roots in the imbalances caused by the global hegemony of western systems, structures and ideologies. She cites Einstein's famous saying: 'No problem can be solved by the same consciousness that created it.' She further argues, in the same philosophically idealistic manner, that new thinking and innovations are required to solve the problems of the world today and these cannot emanate come from those traditionally viewed as 'experts'. Rather, this must emerge from those positioned at the 'margins'.

The 'Godfather of Afrocentrism': Molefi Asante

Formerly, plain Arthur Lee Smith Jr, but rejecting his 'slave name', Molefi K. Asante is an African-American professor and philosopher based at Temple University in Philadelphia (see also Asante, 1980). Asante has been dubbed the 'leading Afrocentric spokesman in the United States today' (Walker, 2001, p xviii) and the 'Godfather of Afrocentrism' (Howe, 1998, p vi). Echoing Asante's perceptions, Graham (2001) asserts that African-centred worldviews are grounded in an understanding that Africa is an often unacknowledged source of historical beginnings and of templates for culture, belief systems, philosophies and values. Relatedly, a significant aspect of Afrocentricity is the belated reclamation of the African origins of ancient Egypt (Kemet) and the Nile Valley civilisations (see also Howe, 1998, part 2 for a summary of the flaws in this perspective). While some Black Africans, living on the continent – such as Thabede (2005; 2008) – and members of the diaspora, have embraced Afrocentrism, many remain highly sceptical. Walker (2001, p 41), for example, suggests that in 'focusing on ancient Egypt as a site of black achievement, Afrocentrists like Asante create an idealised mythic space that stands in opposition to the present grim reality of black inner-city America'.

Expressed via popular commentaries and accessible books, the prime claim of the Afrocentrists is that African-Americans might better understand themselves if they were able to nurture a more globalised Black African sense of identity and unity. More emphatically, as Asante would have it, this entails 'an uncovering of one's *true* self, it is the pinpointing of one's centre, and it is the clarity of focus through which Black people *must* see the world' (in Gilroy, 1993, p 188, emphases added). Equally important, Black Africans are positioned not as marginal figures, but as vibrant agents, actors and participants in determining their own collective destiny. This involves perceiving Europe in a particular way because, according to Asante:

> Europe is dangerous; it is five hundred years of danger for Africans – and I am not talking of physical or ecological danger (although that history is severe enough), but psychological and cultural danger. One knows, I surmise, that a people's soul is dead when it can no longer breathe its own philosophical air and when the air of another culture seems to dominate every aspect of conscious life. (In Adeleke, 2009, p 160)

Surveying the work of Asante, Anderson (2012, p 765) comments that his perspective asserts that the:

> knowledge produced by European intellectuals such as British philosopher David Hume in his essay 'Of National Character', German philosopher George Hegel in his 'Lectures on History', and US President Thomas Jefferson in his text 'Notes on Virginia' … are part of a corpus of the racist, sexist and anti-African work that form the Western Enlightenment; and are part of a large body of work that form a powerful academic, pseudo-science, and sociopolitical cultural tradition in regards to the humanity and agency of Africans, and provide the leitmotif or underlying pattern for the global formation of White supremacy.

Asante believes that to 'undo the psychological damage of Eurocentric miseducation' Black education must be 'grounded in a philosophy that affirms blacks as "active historical agents"' (Adeleke, 2009, p 89). Such an approach valorises 'stepping outside' of the historical constraints of the fixed European historicism to generate new interpretations, new criticisms and so on. Afrocentricity, therefore, entirely contests the orientation to history that is foreign to the African subject: it demands an epistemological re-location that places the critic/scholar *inside* the Black African experience. Hence, Black African ideals and values are situated at the centre of inquiry and there is an attentiveness to cultural codes, symbols, motifs and myths that bestow a particular history and a sense of place in the world arena. Within this paradigm, terms such as 'multicultural', 'inclusive' and 'ethnic minority' are interpreted as actively promoting the dominance and superiority of White people (Asante, 2006, pp 651–653). Lee (1992) argues that the application of this type of theorisation to education legitimises Black African stores of knowledge and positively exploits and scaffolds productive community and cultural practices. It can potentially extend and build upon indigenous languages, and reinforce community ties.

As we have seen, very much embedded in an American milieu, Asante is critical of African-American scholars (polemically labelling them 'enemies' of Black Africans) who use European means of research and knowing, such as empiricism, to try to understand the experience of their own culture. Asante maintains that such figures speak out of European 'centredness' instead of out of a sense of fidelity and integrity in respect of the culture of Africa. Asante (2006) maintains that many scholars of Black African origin are victims of the hegemonic influences of their teachers and are, therefore, caught in a uniquely stifling bind. He also believes, though, that many African-American scholars write not just as if they are conceptually European, they also possess a potent 'anti-African agency'.

Afrocentricity has several broad goals, including the need to expose and resist White racial domination. This goal is foundational because, as Asante sees it, people of African heritage will never thrive until they recognise that the western world examines social phenomena from only a White perspective, while actively negating African cultures. Another argument advanced for the problematising of Eurocentric thinking is an assumption of universality in European–American culture. The pervasiveness of such thinking results in the positioning of Euro-American culture at the centre of the social universe. Thus, Afrocentric theory argues that a society built upon the racist domination of other groups is incapable of developing in truly humane, pluralistic or (multi)cultural ways.

Asante argues that his theorisation is not aiming to merely usurp 'White knowledge' with 'Black knowledge'. He emphasises that what perspectives on knowledge require is a sense of their *location*. This is an orientation that refuses, therefore, the subaltern place that has frequently been conferred to

Black expression, artistic and cultural endeavour by Eurocentric scholars. Asante further argues that Black Africans might begin to regain their epistemological platforms and stand in their own cultural spaces. If they believe that their way of viewing the universe is just as valid as any other, then they will achieve the kind of transformation needed to fully participate in meaningfully multicultural societies. Without a sense of historical and cultural centredness, Black Africans may have little to contribute at the 'multicultural table' other than merely a darker version of Whiteness (Asante, 1998).

Cultural residues shaping the lifeworlds of the Black African diaspora

This reasoning implies that, even given European acculturation and an apparent rejection of African folkways, there is still a 'strong pulse' of African life beating within the habitus of an individual from Africa or possessing a sense of an African heritage. Relatedly, Ruch and Anyanwu (1981) maintain that many empirical research projects examining African culture proclaim that the African people have changed, that their traditional beliefs have collapsed and that they have become ambiguously 'modern'. These authors contend that, even in accepting that some changes have taken place, we still need to investigate what it is that subsists of the ancient beliefs *beneath* these apparent changes. Ruch and Anyanwu (1981) also point to how we often use the metaphor of biological inheritance, but do not extend it to cultural inheritance. Thus, while conceding that all cultures of the world are dynamic, and change with time, we might also equally accept that there are elements within *all* cultures that have been there, remain there and will continue to be *enduringly* present as potent residues impacting on and shaping behaviour. For example, despite the undoubted cultural diversity arising from ethnic pluralism in Africa, the Ghanaian philosopher Kwame Gyekye (1995) argues that the threads of underlying affinity exist, and this can be witnessed through the beliefs, customs, value systems and sociopolitical institutions. Rather sneeringly, Pitika Ntuli (2002, p 63) maintains that to 'touch on these issues is to compel our westernised intellectuals to experience severe conceptual violence, and yet many of them secretly subscribe to these beliefs'.

In what follows, therefore, we will briefly dwell on what might be perceived as five enduring common characteristics of African culture mentioned in the extant literature. These five components evince evidence of potent cultural residues that may well continue to shape the lifeworlds of diasporic Black Africans. Consequently, social workers and others engaging with Black African communities need to be aware of such components. Couched in more theoretical terms – and detaching this awareness from any philosophical allegiance to Afrocentric thinking – we might argue, along with Gramsci, that the five elements we briefly discuss constitute part of the 'common sense' of the Black African diaspora in Ireland and beyond (see also Chapter 3). Predating the arrival of Christianity and colonisation, specific ideas relate to belief in: ancestors and ancestral spirits; a Supreme Being and creator; witchcraft; traditional healing and medical pluralism; rites of passage and managed transitions into adulthood.

The social and cultural world of those of Black African cultural heritage is, of course, complex, and it would be foolish – and, indeed, potentially harmful and dangerous – to try to deploy reductive and stereotypical notions. Nevertheless, this matrix of beliefs has implications for social work with many people of African origin. For example, a pressing problem might be placed before a priest, one's ancestors, a traditional healer and a social worker or doctor. A person encountering difficulties in their personal and/or familial lives might seek out assistance from all of these people and an appreciation of this dimension might allow the practitioner to 'start where the client is at' psychologically. One does not have to be an Afrocentric ideologue to accept that this is a reasonable position to take.

Ancestors and ancestral spirits

According to Hammond-Tooke, ancestors are defined as the 'spirits' of the dead members of the clan or lineage (for a much more detailed exposition see Thabede, 2008). The departed occupy an important place in African religiosity and are apt to be considered part of the living family. Earhart (1993) makes the important point that Black Africans do not *worship* their ancestors, but continue to recognise them in memorial ceremonies, rites and rituals. They are regarded, in short, as a positive, constructive and creative presence as well as a source of help and guidance. In this context, the 'Ceremony of Return' (*ukubuyisa*) is performed a year after death to welcome back the deceased into the community. After *ukubuyisa*, the dead exist in our midst and are referred to as if they are visible. Ancestors are also capable of retribution if wronged or not respected and often the retribution is perceived as manifested in misfortunes. Ancestors are credited with 'curing' a wide range of illnesses when their assistance is invoked through divination by a traditional healer or spirit medium. This belief in ancestors' impact on everyday life is more likely to be prevalent among Black Africans, particularly during difficult, stressful and traumatic times.

A Supreme Being and creator

Often, Black Africans believe in the Supreme Being who created humanity, nature, the earth and the cosmos. They believe the human being has a spiritual and physical body. The spirit enters the body at birth and is released at death to join the ancestors. Black African knowledge of God predates the arrival of Christianity on the continent and is expressed not in sacred writings as in many other cultures, but in proverbs, idioms, myths and stories that are *orally* transmitted to each generation: there is no 'atheist' in traditional African culture and proverbs acknowledge that God is so self-evident that religious instruction is entirely unwarranted. Thabede (2008, p 240) maintains that different African tribes continue to have an indigenous name for the Supreme Being. The indigenous names of the Supreme Being among the African tribes in South Africa are as follows: the Xhosa – Dali or Qamatha onyawo zilengela eweni; the Zulu – Nkulunkulu or Umvelinqangi (the first to emerge); the Venda – Raluvhimba; and the Sotho, Modimo'.

This strong spiritual orientation, coupled with ancestral beliefs, can potentially enhance the will to persevere in times of difficulty and it can be a source of hope that social workers, for example, can 'tap into'. Perhaps recognition of such an orientation gels with the profession's contemporary – frequently uncritical fixation – with the notion of 'resilience' (Garrett, 2016)? Relatedly, Van der Walt (1992) argues that Christianity was strategically weakened when missionaries ignored the traditional African worldview and 'packaged' the gospel with colonialism and western culture. The same author also maintains that this produced 'a dualistic form of Christianity which prompted 'schizophrenia' in the life of the African'. This approach resulted in a 'divided soul', as the average Black African 'convert' was not wholly able to 'experience the western gospel as adequate for life'. Consequently, Van der Walt concludes, most Black African Christians, in times of need and crises (such as illness or death), often revert to their traditional faith. This notion implies that, at its deepest core, more embedded older cultural beliefs endure and remain residually blended into what Bourdieu might term the 'habitus' of the Black African (see also Chapter 3). This, perhaps, also helps to explain the contemporary emergence of Black African-instituted churches throughout the continent. Although deemed 'syncretic' and 'unorthodox', such churches highlight that in order to 'reach' the Black African one must incorporate an indigenous heritage and ethos. (In Zimbabwe, examples of such churches include those founded and owned by Guti, Makandiwa and Magaya, among others).

Witchcraft

'Western sensibility', maintains David McNally (2012, p 187), typically identifies witchcraft with evil, thereby obscuring its much more fluid meanings in many African contexts. The local words translated as 'witchcraft', or *sorcellerie* in French, do not carry a universally pejorative charge. In many African cultures, the terms used refer to extraordinary powers that can be used for either social or anti-social purposes. Traditionally, in most Black African societies, profound existential occurrences (deaths, divorces, accidents, major health problems) did not simply 'happen' but were interpreted as prompted by the intervention of witchcraft. This understanding is vital because White, western social workers engaging with Black Africans need to be aware that, occasionally, a belief in witchcraft may be significant to the worldview of some users of services (Thabede, 2008). For a person from Africa, or of African heritage, to disclose such beliefs about witchcraft requires an immensely trusting relationship with the social worker.

Garrett (2006), for example, refers to this dimension in his examination of pertinent factors connected to the death of Victoria Climbié (an Ivorian child killed by her aunt and her partner in London in 2000) and, more recently, Ndukaire (2019) discussed how beliefs about witchcraft among the Black African diaspora can shape perceptions of childhood intellectual disability. In an authoritative UK article, Briggs and Whittaker (2018) refer to how the issue was related to the death of Kristy Bamu in 2010 and a number of other children in the UK. These authors refer to 'faith-based abuse through accusations of witchcraft and spirit possession'. The issue has to be dealt with in a very sensitive way and it would, of course, be entirely wrong – and, indeed, racist – to assume that because a user of social work services happens to be Black African, then they will *inevitably* believe in the power of witches. Drawing on the research of Eleanor Stobart (2006), Briggs and Whittaker (2018, p 2161) state that 'beliefs in witchcraft and spirit possession were not confined to people of particular countries, cultures or religions'. What is more, 'there is a strong hypothesis that there is a relationship between adverse economic, social and political contexts and the perceived need for and adherence to these belief systems' (Briggs and Whittaker, 2018, p 2171). That is to say, belief systems cannot be neatly abstracted from wider global shifts taking place in the material world.

It is also important to recognise the opposition that witch-thinking has encountered *within* African societies. Many have deplored and vilified the role of the witch doctor and associated community leaders and, in this context, the comments of Fanon are illustrative:

Colonialism uses two types of indigenous collaborators to achieve its ends. First of all, there are the usual suspects: chiefs, *kaids*, and witch doctors ... [The] peasant masses, steeped in a never changing routine, continue to revere their religious leaders, descendants of illustrious families. The tribe, with one voice, embarks on the path designated by the traditional chief. Colonialism secures the services of these loyal servants by paying them a small fortune. (Fanon, 1989 [1959], pp 86–87)

Traditional healing and medical pluralism

Fanon similarly condemned the 'marabouts and witch doctors' who prevented the sick from 'consulting a physician' (Fanon, 1989 [1959], p 65). In the area of health and well-being, what we might loosely refer to as 'culturally competent practice' presupposes a modicum of understanding of the socio-cultural meaning a person or social group attaches to illness and well-being. Before the arrival of western medicine, Black Africans relied on their own indigenous traditional healing methods and processes. The belief in the effectiveness and appropriateness of practices associated with traditional healing may endure to this day. Pitika Ntuli (2002, p 59) argues that *Izangoma* and *izinyanga nezanusi* (traditional healers) who 'long resisted the fragmentation of their vision of health, who always insisted that healing involved the whole person (body, mind and spirit), are today joined by western physicians who have come to realise the wisdom of indigenous science'.

Black African traditional healers are classified into four categories: diagnosticians, healing doctors, specialists and faith healers (*n'anga* in Shona, *isangoma* in Zulu) (Sodi, 1998). They deal with a range of issues that include consultations relating to difficulties at individual, community and societal levels: for example, impotence, recurring droughts/crop failures, protection from evildoers and so on. Many South Africans, as well as many others elsewhere in Black Africa, consult traditional healers in preference to, or in conjunction with, western allopathic healthcare professionals; particularly in relation to illnesses and disorders attributed to spiritual factors, ancestor punishment and superstitious beliefs. In this context, treatment often includes use of a variety of natural substances, prayers and rituals to restore equilibrium (Ross, 2010). There remains, however, a substantial current of thought within what might be termed 'African philosophy' that continues to decry the role which the 'witchdoctor' plays. Prominent here have been figures such as the Ghanaian philosopher and public intellectual, Kwasi Wiredu, who recognises the harm prompted to individuals who may fail to seek out scientifically based medical attention (Masolo, 2016).

Rites of passage and managed transitions into adulthood

In most African cultures, the rite of passage rituals mark the end of boyhood and beginning of manhood. Girls attend initiation ceremonies at puberty that serve as a form of what might be loosely termed premarital tuition or schooling. For both boys' and girls' rites of passage, rituals function as instruction for the duties, responsibilities and requirements of adulthood. Within western cultures the process of reaching adulthood is different, and is mapped in contrasting developmental stages by figures such as Erikson, whom we mentioned earlier, and Piaget. The traditional Black African worldview, based on community cohesion and solidarity, carries with it a system of encouragement or stimuli to continue with life at points of anxiety and stress. Individuals are members of an extended family and the community/family nexus is supposed to provide psychological reinforcement in times of crisis (Mathema, 2007).

Importantly, 'rites of passage' and dominant ideas around 'transitions' might be points of tension in diasporic Black African communities such as those found in Ireland. For example, we might ponder if such rites are rooted in what some might also perceive as stifling patriarchal norms and gendered, heteronormative orders. This dimension is illustrated by the perceptions of Pitika Ntuli. An academic, sculptor and poet, he valorises traditional indigenous knowledge and traditional modes of being. Reanimating such systems and practices might, he avows, re-energise an 'African Renaissance'. Indeed, 'utilising Indigenous Knowledge Systems (IKSs)' might produce a 'counter-hegemonic tool' (Pitika Ntuli, 2002, p 53). He asserts:

> Education was also carried out through secret societies, initiation schools and through the *amaqhikiza* system – a type of mentorship programme where older girls mentored younger girls to ensure sexual abstinence until the girls were ready to take full control of their affairs … The current revival of *ukuhlolwa kwezintombi*, the so-called 'virginity testing' in KwaZulu-Natal, seeks to achieve the goal of purity in the context of the spread of HIV/AIDS. The debate that attends this revival needs to be seen in its proper perspective, both from those who oppose it – mainly westernised Africans and westerners who read their own fantasies into it – and those who seek to instil a new sense of morality into our youth.

Clearly, this 'new sense of morality' is likely to be contested by some Black Africans who may well perceive this component of the 'African Renaissance' as a new form of 'police order' that can only serve the interests of powerful men (Rancière, 1999 [1995]). A number of the 'most prominent post-colonial mechanisms for instituting control over women's bodies are associated with customary law and practices' (Lewis, 2011, p 212). Many may well object to being allotted and locked into stultifying societal and familial roles that they despise. Nevertheless, it remains important to be aware that these ideas, such as those promoted by Pitika Ntuli, may have currency within Black African diasporic cultures. More generally, we are living through a period in which appeals to nationalism and reclamation of a supposedly unsullied and 'purer' past has political and cultural potency.

Taking Afrocentric theory into social work: Jerome Schiele, Mekada Graham and Dumisani Thabede

Despite some of the criticisms, already alluded to and to be returned to shortly, a number of educators have tried to inject Afrocentric theory into social work's academic discourse (see also Mullings et al, 2021; Obasi, 2021). Prominent here have been the contributions, from the 1990s onwards, of Jerome H. Schiele in the US and Mekada J. Graham, based initially in England, but later in the US. Here, we will briefly discuss, first, the former's article in the *Journal of Black Studies* (Schiele, 1997; see also Schiele, 1996; 2017), and then the latter's intervention in the UK social work's flagship, the *British Journal of Social Work*, on the cusp of our present century (Graham, 1999). We are not suggesting that these authors are the only ones to seek to make connections between Afrocentricity and social work, but they are two of the most lucid advocates of the need for productive dialogue between this theorisation and social work teaching and praxis. Finally in this section, we will draw attention to the guidelines for social work casework that have been articulated by Dumisani Thabede (2005). His contribution is significant, because – unlike Schiele and Graham – is he an Afrocentrist who is actually residing in continental Africa.

Like a good many of the contributions hingeing on Afrocentricity, Schiele's work is firmly located in a US context and there is little focus on Africa as such. He remarks, however, that 'African Americans have held on to *some* of the values, psychobehavioral patterns, and ethos of traditional, West African culture' (Schiele, 1997, p 285, emphasis added). He does not, though, interrogate the scale and constitution of such West African cultural residues. Nor are his readers prompted to inquire how and in what ways the culture of contemporary African-Americans might depart from that of people born, raised and presently living in Africa. Issues pertaining to class, and how the imperatives of capital accumulation structure and inflect life choices, are largely omitted within the analysis of Schiele and most others identifying with Afrocentric thought. Similarly, issues related to patriarchal dominance are, if not reaffirmed, then evaded. This failure to 'confront asymmetrical power relations outside of a cultural critique of Eurocentric racism within existing capitalist society is a serious weakness of Afrocentricity' (Akinyela, 1995, p 28; see also Akinyele and Aldridge, 2003). Still, perhaps some of the criticisms that Schiele levels at US social work education resonate today in and beyond the US.

Schiele's (1997, p 817) focal assertion is that 'African American social workers' need to 'examine honestly' the extent to which they are 'incarcerated within Eurocentric social work and social science models' (Schiele, 1997, p 817). In the second decade of the 21st century, African-Americans constitute over a fifth of the US social work workforce, but, referring to his own professional formation as a social worker, Schiele notes that one of the consistent and disturbing features of my undergraduate and graduate training was the pervasiveness of academic theories that emerged from people who were not members of my cultural group. Regardless of the course, the textbooks used and theories discussed were almost exclusively written and developed by White people, especially White men. (Schiele, 1997, p 800)

Despite social work's 'fanfare about equality and social justice', its actual focus remained insular and simply reflected and affirmed 'the knowledge hegemony of White intellectuals', even if occasionally these 'intellectuals were women' (Schiele, 1997, p 281).

Crucially, therefore, the central task of Afrocentric social workers becomes one of challenging and deconstructing the 'Eurocentric knowledge hegemony that permeates social work education and on which social work practice is heavily based' (Schiele, 1997, p 282). Two 'fundamental problems' are apparent in the US social work profession. First is the fact that the 'theories and paradigms undergirding social work practice models' are embedded in a Eurocentric worldview predicated on the geohistorical, political/economic and philosophical traditions of Europe. This worldview 'highlights a linear, individualistic, materialistic, and rationalistic understanding of human beings and reality' (Schiele, 1997, p 282). Schiele (1997, p 282) maintains that if such models

reject linear logic, as is the case with the ecological perspective, there is still a tendency to focus on (a) the individual as a sort of isolated, autonomous entity (even if the interaction between the individual and the social environment is acknowledged) and (b) material expressions of reality that underscore sensory perception as the exclusive or primary means of determining whether something exists.

A second problem for African–Americans is that alternative approaches supposedly tailored to address some of their concerns are inadequate. Here Schiele specifically identifies 'ethnic sensitive' and 'cross–cultural social work practice' models that were evolving at the time he was writing (Devore and Schlesinger, 1991). These perspectives, supposedly dealing with some of the gaps in Eurocentric theorisation and confronting racism, emphasised: how 'racial discrimination' had 'blocked opportunities' for African-Americans and other people of colour; how social workers should become more sensitised to the 'cultural values and nuances' of a service user who was not from the same 'racial/ethnic group' as themselves; how social workers should become more attuned to their 'biases and preconceptions' when working with someone from a another 'racial/ethnic group'.

While acknowledging the potential gains that these ameliorative approaches might confer, Schiele argues that the Afrocentric paradigm furnishes a robust approach that might truly begin to grapple with some of the issues that confront African-Americans. The three-fold foundational 'assumptions' of Afrocentricity are, he argues, that

- individual identity is conceived as a collective identity;
- the spiritual aspect of humans is just as legitimate as the material component;
- the affective approach to knowledge is epistemologically valid.

In amplifying the first assumption, Schiele (1997, pp 285–286) suggests that

> Afrocentric social work views identity as akin to a spider web. If you think of a spider web, you know that it is made up of a series of interdependent strands of fibre, and if you touch one strand or component, the entire web shakes. In other words, one cannot affect one part without affecting the others. The focus on a collective identity is supported by a traditional African belief that there is no perceptual separation between an individual and others … Although people may be at different positions on the spider web, each with her or his own unique vantage point and individual expression, the common factor that binds them together is the web or the core ethos of a group.

Articulating the second constituting component of Afrocentric social work, Schiele (1997, p 810) charges that 'extreme materialism' results in a 'society in which material objects become primary in the person's life and in which spiritual oneness of all things and people is denied'. Relatedly, this type of society is one which is fragmented, dilutes social cohesion and is inhabited by atomised individuals. All of this contributes to an 'emphasis on difference and exclusion rather than on similarity and inclusion' (Schiele, 1997, p 810).

Turning to the third ingredient that imbues Afrocentric social work, Schiele (1997, p 813) briefly dwells on the vital importance of practitioners' developing affective professional relationships in their everyday work and encounters with service users. Informed by the Afrocentric worldview, more efforts should be made to establish and nurture 'an emotional connection between the helper and the helped that equally acknowledges the viewpoints of both in defining and understanding the problem at hand' (Schiele, 1997, p 813). Schiele (1997, p 813) discerns that his ideas might be frowned upon within the mainstream of US social work education – and even be viewed as heretical – because of rooted and insular notions of 'professionalism'. (Indeed, it is reasonable to suggest that his emphasis on relationships within social work might be viewed as somewhat subversive, given that it ran counter to the 'electronic turn' – and a fixation with e-working and the widespread use e-templates dictating workflows – which was to characterise social work from the following decade [Garrett, 2005]).

Schiele also proposed that particular strategies might be pursued in order to achieve more cultural pluralism within the wider society. Arguably entirely failing to get to the root of the problem – the divisive racial order that capitalism promotes – he rather timidly suggested that there might be an increased number of people from 'historically oppressed groups' becoming elected officials. Additionally, there might be a growth in schools and businesses owned by such groups. Finally – and, we have seen, central to his argument – is the idea that there should be a more diverse multicultural educational curriculum (Schiele, 1997, p 811). Schiele's view on addressing ongoing coloniality in the wider society appears to be shared by others who argue that while working toward decoloniality is an imperative, a more narrow interpretation, as it relates to the decoloniality of a curriculum as a potential for change, is problematic. They suggest that there is a risk that focusing on epistemic decoloniality alone, while ignoring the material realities of ongoing coloniality in *all* spheres of society, would lead to the perpetuation of the very structures of oppression and injustice mentioned earlier (see, for example, Patel, 2014).

Significantly, although she was still located in England in the 1990s, the literature on which Mekada Graham (1999) drew was also mostly US based, and Asante featured prominently. In terms of her lexicon and conceptualisation, 'African and black' were 'terms used interchangeably' to refer to 'people of Africa and of African descent throughout the world' (Graham, 1999, p 251). Quoting Nobles, she stated that 'Afrocentric', 'Africentric' or 'African-centred' were 'interchangeable terms representing the concept which categorises a quality of thought and practice which is rooted in the cultural image and interest of African people and which represents and reflects the life experiences, history and traditions of African people as the centre of analyses' (in Graham, 1999, p 257).

Graham (1999) dwelt on how the ethnocentric ethos of social work education, based on European historical and cultural development, impacted on practice with Black African families. The author argued that social work interventions with such families had resulted in controversy, disquiet and conflict for many years. There was a manifest 'over-representation' of Black children in state institutions that primarily had a control function and an 'under-representation' in preventative and supportive services. Within the sphere of mental health services, Black adults have been disproportionally targeted for harsh and coercive interventions (Littlewood and Lipsedge, 1997; Metzl, 2010). Overall, the research evidence suggested that, beyond these factors, 'institutional racism' and the punitive impact of the 'welfare' system contributed to social work operating mostly *against* the interests of Black people.

Graham's (1999) core argument was that there was a clear lack of fit between the profession's ethical claims, reflected in the foundational values and how social work was actually experienced by Black families. The lofty professional aspirations included a commitment to equality, social justice and the promotion of human rights. This formed an integral part, as we have observed earlier, of the profession's rhetorical 'mission' to uphold the dignity and worth of *all* people. This encompassed, one would have thought, responding to the unique social needs of Black families through sensitive and ameliorative interventions. However, Graham illuminated a focal paradox: while the value base of social work emanated from a belief in the inherent worth and dignity of all people and the repudiation of all forms of negative discrimination, these well-meaning principles rarely found actual expression in everyday interventions. More fundamentally, the monocultural hegemony of social work's knowledge base continued to bolster cultural oppression.

Like Schiele, Graham (1999, p 256) maintained that this 'existing knowledge base for social work' emerged from 'epistemologies that are an expression of European historical and cultural development'. Echoing the African-American educator, she also asserted that the African-centred worldview challenged social work to 'expand its philosophical and intellectual base to embrace humanity'. What is more, it would be beneficially therapeutic if 'African people' could be freed from the 'domination of the Eurocentric worldview' over their 'psyche', given that this might 'open the way for the transformation, creativity and unlimited potential that is embedded within authenticity' (Graham, 1999, pp 252–253).

Despite failing to convincingly define and unpack how this 'authenticity' might be constituted, Graham moved on, in a similar way to Schiele, to question emergent social work paradigms that purported to meaningfully address the situation of Black and other minority ethnic people: namely, 'anti-discriminatory practice (ADP) (which now incorporates anti-racist practice) in the UK and ethnic sensitive social work practice' in the US (Graham, 1999, p 253). Although not furnishing evidence to support such an emphatic statement, Graham was scathing about the UK model, which supported 'institutional and cultural racism at all levels' (Graham, 1999, p 253). Largely portrayed as, at best, an opportunistic, sterile and tokenistic endeavour, ADP was comprehended as an exercise in 'damage limitation', which might also be interpreted as pernicious insofar as it functioned to obscure and 'mask more fundamental theoretical deficits inherent within the ethnocentric nature of social work' (Graham, 1999, p 254).

In drawing attention to the Afrocentric theoretical alternative, Graham lumped together a range of theorists whose work cannot, in truth, be convincingly viewed as sharing Afrocentric perceptions of the world. For example, the more Marxist-inflected work of Frantz Fanon and Walter Rodney cannot be comfortably placed in the same conceptual hat as that of the anti-Marxists Asante and Marcus Garvey.

Graham (1999, p 258) informed her readers that the African-centred worldview

> begins with a holistic conception of the human condition which spans the cosmological (an aspect of philosophy that considers the nature and structure of the universe), ontological (the essence of all things), and axiological (an area of philosophy that considers the nature of values and value preferences in a culture). African-centred philosophy is a holistic system based upon values and ways of living which are reinforced through rituals – music, dance, storytelling, proverbs, metaphors – and the promoting of family – rites of passage, naming ceremonies, child rearing, birth, death, elderhood – and values of governance.

Drawing on the writings of Asante and others, Graham then identified five components that, when looked at as a totality, constituted the principles and values underpinning this worldview. These relate to:

- the interconnectedness of all things;
- the spiritual nature of human beings;
- collective/individual identity and the collective/inclusive nature of family structure;
- oneness of mind, body and spirit;
- the value of interpersonal relationship (Graham, 1999, p 258).

According to Graham, social work and associated forms of intervention in the lives of Black children and their families might be enhanced if these were meaningfully inflected with the perceptions of the Afrocentrist theorists. In this context, perhaps one of the most informative parts of her article was that which focused on and undermined social workers' use of the 'therapeutic tool of the ecomap', which, she cogently maintained, often entirely failed to capture the complex and lived reality of Black families and the network of cousins and other family members lying beyond western notions of the 'extended family' (Graham, 1999, p 262).

Graham (1999, p 261) also laid emphasis on the 'Rites of Passage' programmes for young Black people. Although she failed to mention it, such programmes, borrowed from Africa and run by one of us (Washington) during his time in the US, are mostly concerned with the life trajectories and outcomes of African-American boys and young men (see, for example, Harvey and Rauch, 1997). This gendered dimension aside, Graham argued that these endeavours are imbued with *Nguzo Saba*. This is a Swahili phrase meaning seven principles identified as: *Umoja* (unity), *Kujichagulia* (self), *Ujima* (collective work), *Ujamaa* (cooperative economics), *Nia* (purpose), *Kuumba* (creativity) and *Imani* (faith). Strikingly, viewed together they can been interpreted as a cluster of keywords in tune with mainstream neoliberal values, given the associated focus on positivity, self-help and resilience (Gilroy, 2013). However, paradoxically, such words may also hint at notions and practices rooted in collective unity and cooperative work antithetical to neoliberal nostrums. Indeed, farming, fishing and house building co-ops are still found in parts of present-day Africa and *all* in the community share in the success of such businesses.

Located in South Africa, Dumisani Thabede (2008) asserts that, although the colonisation and vilification of Africa by Europeans and Arabs changed Africa in so many ways, the philosophical integrity of traditional Africa survived. Advocates of Afrocentricity refuse to accept that Eurocentric theories alone, reflecting notions of human behaviour entirely developed in Anglo-American cultures, can provide a universal explanation of human behaviour across *all* peoples and *all* cultures. Most Black Africans have adopted a bi-cultural stance incorporating elements of both western and African cultures (Thabede, 2008). So, it can be safely concluded that the contemporary African worldview, while still retaining elements of traditional African culture, has also incorporated some elements of Euro-western culture. That is to say, it is a hybrid incorporating traditional precolonial culture and modern western cultural influences. Adopting this bi-cultural stance, one could argue, has allowed Africans to survive in a world dominated by Anglo-American cultural hegemony underpinned by capitalist imperatives. It would, though, appear that many Europeans may not be aware of this bi-culturalism, in that they assume that the Black Africans have abandoned their cultures wholesale for the 'superior' western one which now equates to a global 'benchmark' (Ruch and Anyanwu, 1981; Thabede, 2005; 2008).

Given the diversity of African cultures, it is often argued that it is nearly impossible to come up with a rigid 'checklist' as to what constitute African belief systems. This is on account of the fact that the African diaspora is in a process of 'integration' – inevitably leaving behind elements and transforming and adapting/rejecting elements of traditional cultural beliefs; in this sense, Eurocentric worldviews are subject to being challenged and changed. It can still occasionally risk appearing that some foreign observers, and indeed some Africans, have been misled into thinking that Africans have entirely absorbed European and American cultures wholesale, even to the point of totally disregarding their own (Thabede, 2005; 2008).

Thabede (2005, pp 201–203) refers to at least a dozen factors needing to be taken into account when social workers are engaging and interacting with Black Africans (see for more detail, Thabede, 2005, pp 2001–2003). If, according to Thabede, in the process of engagement with the service user the caseworker's worldview clashes with that of the service user, it is the caseworker's worldview that may have to yield, since the user of services is always an 'expert' on what constitutes their problems. This may be problematic in western practice situations in which practitioners have been socialised into having their credentialised 'expertise', 'authority' (and resources of 'symbolic capital') recognised and valorised.

Critiques of Afrocentric theory

Returning to what we might loosely call 'Afrocentric ideology' at the heart of much of this thinking, it is not difficult to assemble a critique. The reading of African cultures in reductive and there is also a complex dialectical engagement with 'common sense': on the one hand, constructing it, and on the other, aiming to amplify it as *natural* and existing since time immemorial in folklore, rituals and communal ways of being. In the 1990s, Makungu M. Akinyela (1995) pointedly claimed that in providing a critique of White racist ideology, the Afrocentrists seem to be carving out a comfortable and acceptable Afrocentric niche for themselves in established Eurocentric academia. In a withering contribution, Akinyela (1995, pp 29–31) powerfully confronted the worldview of figures such as Asante and their proclivity to lend their support to African despots:

> Little or no mention is made in Afrocentric writing of the role of the ancient African peasantry and the labourers who actually constructed the ancient monuments of Kemet, Ethiopia, and Great Zimbabwe ... It is probably no coincidence that Afrocentrists and cultural nationalists in the United States have often been the most vocal supporters of dictators like Mobutu in Zaire, Amin in Uganda, Burnham in Guyana, the Duvaliers in Haiti, and many other despots who have exploited and oppressed Africans for their own ends. All of these men have done so while supposedly promoting 'traditional' African customs and culture.

Afrocentricity has, to be sure, attracted a welter of criticism with prominent sceptics including Howe (1998), Walker (2001) and Adeleke (2009). The proponents of this body of theory, often aimed at African-Americans with only very basic formal education, have been criticised for lacking robust and scholarly rigour. The African-American educator Tunde Adeleke (2009, p 122) maintains that even 'among Afrocentric or "Africancentric" scholars, there is now a growing concern over the absolutist stance of Asante and Marimba on the subject of identity'. Adeleke (2009, pp 101–102) further argues that Asante's contributions 'underscore the depth and ubiquitous nature of the Pan-African ethos; however ... though psychologically therapeutic ... Asante's "African perspective" sustains a romanticized, abstract, and idealized Africa and emphasizes a nonexistent harmony and consensus'.

Another African-American scholar, Clarence E. Walker (2001, p xix), characterises Asante's prime text *Afrocentricity* as operating as a 'form of cultural recuperation, Afrocentrism heals and restores black psyches wounded and disoriented by centuries of Eurocentric historical presumption and arrogance'. It is a 'self-help book or psychological primer' that, when 'placed in the broader context of the contemporary recovery movement', can only be regarded as 'banal' (Walker, 2001, p 78). In this context, core facets of Asante's oeuvre can be situated within US identity politics and its affective vibe, with the 'godfather's' contributions being not unreasonably perceived as having a deep affinity with what Furedi (2004) calls 'therapy culture'. Stephen Howe (1998, p 108) identifies the 'unacknowledged but intense North American parochialism' that frequently lies at the core of Afrocentric theorisation. For example, Ani appears to be 'quite uninterested in Africa itself' (Howe, 1998, p 248). Within this discourse, there is a 'dismissal of the whole notion of proof as Eurocentric and the substitution for it of an ill-defined concept of "soul as method"' (Howe, 1998, p 233). *The Journal of Black Studies* is apt, moreover, to slide into a 'mixture of New Age and ethnophilosophical mysticism' (Howe, 1998, p 246).

In terms of the concerns of *Social Work with the Black African Diaspora*, a striking dimension of the debate that has ensued relating to Afrocentricity is the fact that it is, as mentioned, very much shaped by a US political and cultural milieu. In an early and incisive critique of Afrocentric thinking, Manning Marable (1993, pp 118–119) usefully historicised the evolution of this corpus of ideas. He suggested that Asante's writings fulfilled a significant role for the African-American intelligentsia and the associated new African-American upper middle class who were keen to find ways of expressing themselves through the 'prism of race, while rationalising its relatively privileged class position' (Marable, 1993, pp 118–119). Indeed, allowing the discursive space for more scholarly and meaningful forms of Afrocentrism, he argued that 'vulgar Afrocentrism was the perfect social theory for the upwardly mobile Black petty bourgeoisie. It gave them a vague sense of ethnic superiority and cultural originality, without requiring hard critical study of historical realities' (Marable, 1993, p 121). Hence, Afrocentrism tended to be a discourse that merely looked to a 'romantic, mythical reconstruction of yesterday to find some understanding for the cultural basis of today's racial and class challenges' largely prompted by the 'vast structure of power and privilege which characterises the political economy of post-industrial, capitalist America' (Marable, 1993, p 127).

In truth, the utility of Afrocentricity in an Irish context is limited. Asante, and similar figures, are dismissive of ideas about hybridity that are so central to the lived experience of all diasporic peoples. Thus, Afrocentric scholars, including Asante and Ani, simply 'proclaim the centrality of Africa to the construction of black American identity and insist upon identifying black Americans as quintessentially Africans' (Adeleke, 2009, p 26). Asante, for example, simply 'rejects any notion of difference' between continental

Africans and Black people in the US (Adeleke, 2009, p 96). As for himself, he never felt 'two warring souls in one dark body', nor any conflict over his sense of identity (Adeleke, 2009, p 91). Such a strident attitude would seem to have little utility for a social worker working with a youngster growing up in north Dublin who was born in the outskirts of Harare. The lived experience of one of us (Washington) as a continental and diasporic Black African reflects some of the complexities that the Afrocentricity advocates risk screening out. While he has adapted or rejected some elements of his traditional cultural beliefs, he has not entirely rejected his more 'traditional' cultural beliefs.

In contrast, Asante, and those sharing his perceptions, appear to inhabit a world in which individuals are encased in notions of identity that are binary, flat and aridly reductive. Asante, in 'groping for some timeless "essence"', detects 'little or no difference between a poor Zimbabwean peasant woman and a rich male Barbados banker' (Lemelle, 1993, p 103). Meanwhile, Ani's *Yurugu* has the 'dubious merit of carrying its relentless pursuit' of racialised thinking to 'logical conclusions within its own structure, by having two separate Bibliographies and Indexes – one for "Africans", one for others' (Howe, 1998, p 247). This problem is connected to the fact that these writers promote a simplistic, insular, static and prescriptive understanding of culture. Among others, Howe (1998, p 71) identifies how Afrocentric writers express 'vehement hostility to Islam'. Anti-Semitism is also a detectable current within particular corners of Afrocentrism. Furthermore, there is a tendency to tumble into thinking structured around conspiracy theories; for example, Ani amplifies the idea that AIDS is a 'deliberately created disease, a genocidal plot against Africans' (Howe, 1998, p 248).

What we also find in the work of Asante and those adopting similar approaches is a certain intolerance to those who refuse the call to fit into what we might term a 'pure' African identity. This might also be related to the 'facile yet pervasive assumptions that "feminism," often viewed as a single (and moreover western) movement or school of thought, is a *Fremdkörper*, a foreign import' on the continent of Africa (Du Toit and Coetzee, 2016, p 333). In the US, Barbara Ransby and Tracye Matthews (1993) furnished a scathing rebuttal of some of Afrocentrism's focal patriarchal ideas in the earlier 1990s. This critique forms part of a wider and fascinating examination of the 'visible resurgence of various forms of Black cultural resurgence' occurring during the period of the Reagan and Bush presidencies in the US over the period 1980–93 (Ransby and Matthews, 1993, p 57). While acknowledging that Afrocentrism contained 'an oppositional edge which offers respite from the oppressive realities of daily life in a hostile dominant culture', they wrote that it still amounted to a 'very male-centred definition of the problems confronting the Black community and proposes pseudo-solutions which further marginalise and denigrate Black women. A masculinised vision of Black empowerment and liberation resonates through the literature on Afrocentrism' (Ransby and Matthews, 1993, p 57). They continued:

> The classless African past we are told to revere and recreate is one in which there is little conflict, less struggle and no diversity. It is not a dynamic past, but a static one which belies the vast, rich and deeply contested political and cultural terrain of the African continent. It is not insignificant that the great African past which we are told we need to recreate is also a patriarchal past in which men were men and women knew their respective place … [M]ale-headed nuclear families are synonymous with strong functional families. Those who reject the prescribed gender roles are dismissed as inauthentic and/or Eurocentric. (Ransby and Matthews, 1993, p 59)

Convincingly, Ransby and Matthews (1993, p 59) also identified how a good deal of this theory mirrored the thinking of the Reaganite Right wing, and similar tendencies in the Democrats, in appearing to argue that 'main problems confronting the African-American community and diaspora at this historical juncture are internal to the Black community itself. The problems are defined as cultural, behavioural and psychological, not as political, economic or structural'. More recently, Sarah Balakrishnan (2020, p 79), a scholar much in sympathy with aspects of Afrocentrism, concedes that in 'identifying race as the paramount form of oppression, Afrocentrists gave little attention to the intersectional ways that categories like gender and class changed experiences of discrimination'. Indeed, this seems to be not simply an enormous theoretical lacuna. Rather, the Afrocentric project to erase patriarchy and class exploitation as legitimate targets of inquiry is one of the prime constituting elements of this defective paradigm.

Very much associated with Afrocentricity, Victor Oguejiofor Okafor (1991, p 255) boldly asserts:

> One of the institutions of the African culture that has stood the test of time is the family. This suggests that, generally speaking, the African male and *his* female experience a more harmonious relationship than their western counterparts, despite the relative affluence of the West. The crumbling state of the family institution in the West testifies to this. In order to save the African family, African families must guard against cultural aggression. Africa must guard against the set of western values, practices, and sexual habits which negates the family institution. (Emphasis added)

As for Asante, his essentialist, intolerant and insular construction of 'African' is evinced by the jibe that the British historian and cultural critic, Paul Gilroy, has a 'serious problem of racial identity ... He can't decide whether he's black or British' (in Walker, 2001, p 80) – a remark prompted merely because Gilroy (1993) is better attuned to some of the sociological complexities associated with questions of 'race', ethnicity and identity. African–American feminists have also produced intellectually richer accounts of racism and its intersection with gender and class exploitation than have the ideologues of Afrocentricity (Collins and Bilge, 2016).

The policing of African identity and the delineation of what constitutes an appropriate form of Black identity becomes stark and disturbing when Asante addresses questions of male sexuality:

> The rise of homosexuality in the African–American male's psyche is real and complicated. An Afrocentric perspective recognises its existence but homosexuality cannot be condoned or accepted as good for the national development of a strong people. It can be and must be tolerated until such time as our families and schools are engaged in Afrocentric instructions for males. The time has come for us to redeem our manhood through planned Afrocentric action. All brothers who are homosexuals should know that they too can become committed to the collective will. It means the submergence of their own wills into the collective will of our people. (Asante in Walker, 2001, p 122)

As Walker (2001, p 80) observes, in its efforts to 'centre' Black Americans and to improve their 'self-esteem', Afrocentrism has, in fact, 'conjured up a host of demons. These "others" include Europe, Jews, gay people, and Blacks who do not share the Afrocentric worldview, to name only a few'. As a powerful counterblast to such homophobia, a demand for 'total liberation' was published, in Nairobi in Kenya in 2010, by a network of African LGBTI (lesbian, gay, bisexual, trans and intersex) activists (see also Tamale, 2011, p 182).

Against binaries and supposedly homogeneous cultures: Paul J. Hountondji

Paul J. Hountondji's work is vital to the theoretical orientation of *Social Work with the Black African Diaspora* because he functions as a potent counterweight to, as we have seen, some of the more extreme currents identified with Afrocentricity. These contend that all Black African people, living on the continent or part of the diaspora, are bound by the same *Volksgeist* or inner spirit. In contrast, the Beninese philosopher is scathing of focal aspects of the thinking of figures who promote an unsullied, nostalgic, deeply retrogressive depiction of indigenous philosophical 'traditions' and an uncritical valorisation of folklore. According to his reasoning, figures such as Asante (although not one of his targets) are conservative, backward looking and misleading, given their portrayal of African culture. Hountondji's contributions strongly argue for more critical and pluralistic accounts of culture and, because of this, he can aid our understanding of how social workers might more fruitfully engage with the Black African diaspora in Ireland and elsewhere. For readers new to Hountondji, his classic book is *African Philosophy: Myth and Philosophy* (Hountondji, 1996 [1976]). An invaluable and accessible commentary on his work is provided by Franziska Dübgen and Stefan Skupien (2019).

Hountondji takes a 'firm stand against intellectual self-imprisonment' promoted by the notion that all the peoples of African unanimously agree on what constitutes appropriate ways to think and act (Hountondji, 1996 [1976], p viii). For him, the pressing need is to 'acknowledge Africans' freedom of thought' and to eliminate all 'sorts of essentialist and particularistic doctrines' (Hountondji, 1996 [1976], p viii): just the sort of 'doctrines' that were to be promoted, in fact, from the 1980s by the primarily US-based guardians of African identity, the Afrocentrists. Hountondji's contributions are directly opposed to their reasoning because, as he states plainly, of the 'extreme complexity of the intellectual, cultural, political, economic, and social life' on the vast African continent (Hountondji, 1996 [1976], p xi). It is entirely misguided, therefore, for Afrocentric authors to attempt to delineate and map the boundaries of the thinkable or for them to dismiss theorists and philosophers merely because they are located within the European canon. Hountondji (1996 [1976], p xii) takes aim at the 'ideologists of African identity' and maintains that the 'realm of the thinkable is immense. Why should we exclude the works of western philosophers or forbid Africans to appropriate them while westerners still have the right to extend their curiosity to all continents and cultures without renouncing or losing their identity?' (Hountondji, 1996 [1976], p xi).

This perception is entirely aligned with the position (in drawing on figures such as Gramsci, Foucault and Bourdieu) in this book. In order to be able to free, people need to try to think and act in ways that disentangle themselves them from the stereotypes of the 'ideologists'. So as to be open to the 'richness of African traditions, there is a need to *impoverish* resolutely the concept of Africa, to *free* it from all connotations' (Hountondji, 1996 [1976], p xii, original emphases).

On first reading, such comments might appear to be helpful in combating the African cultural identity police, but they risk appearing to merely operate at the level of theoretical abstraction. However, Hountondji's perceptions can have practical consequences and inform how we might begin to think about social work with diasporic Black African children and families. For example, it is our experience that the dominant and mainstream view is that Black African parents are unduly punitive with their children and are likely to over-chastise. Such views – which probably give rise to the disproportionately high number of African families in contact with child protection social workers and the courts – are founded upon concepts and connotations of Africans that may not actually be rooted in facts pertaining to *particular* and *specific* families. There are a range of approaches to parenting among Black African families in Ireland, just like there are a range of approaches among indigenous Irish families (see also AFRUCA, 2018). The task of progressive and dissenting forms of social work becomes, therefore, one of dismantling false dichotomies, and with a view to promoting awareness of the internal dialectics of cultural difference. In what follows, in order to explore the conceptual richness and utility of Hountondji's work, we will give a little more attention to his work.

As a critical intellectual, Hountondji is resolutely opposed to claims that African people all unanimously hold identical belief systems and values. As we have seen, this idea characterises the views of many of those who promote Afrocentricity. Hountondji locates the source of much of this thinking with European colonisers and missionaries who attempted to map a specific form of African consciousness and way of life and who stressed how different these were to those of European settlers. The work of Belgian missionary Placide Frans Tempels (1906–77) is analysed in some detail by Hountondji because his presentation of Bantu culture was immensely influential in this regard. Importantly, Tempels' perspective was welcomed by many African intellectuals because it was interpreted as furnishing a fresh account of indigenous life and culture. Tempels was significant also in that he appeared to stress how the lives and belief systems of Africans were unlike those of Europeans, rather than being of less worth. In this sense, he seemed to break free from the dominant perspectives that emphasised how the lives, culture and belief systems of Africans were inherently inferior. In short, Tempels' work appeared to erode a core idea of the colonial system – that it was possible to establish a hierarchy of cultures that invariably viewed European cultural and mores as superior. His *Bantu Philosophy* (Tempels (1969 [1959]), although still deeply racialised and still promoting the objectification of Black Africans, might even *seem* to be a 'positive appraisal' and rehabilitation of their primitive life and local forms of knowledge and understanding (Dübgen and Skupien, 2019, p 2).

Hountondji views *Bantu Philosophy* as a prime example of 'ethnophilosophy' and he identifies similar reductive approaches to life and culture in the work of indigenous figures such as the Rwandan priest and philosopher Alexis Kagame (1902–81). In this context, Hountondji demonstrates the 'lines of continuity between colonial anthropological research on non-western contexts, with their racist underpinnings, and the ethnophilosophical research of his contemporaries' (Dübgen and Skupien, 2019, p 11). This critique of Hountondji stretches beyond the fields of philosophy and anthropology in that he identifies similar problems in politics. Thus, Kwame Nkrumah's (1909–72) ideas on African 'Consciencism' are subjected to a good deal of critical scrutiny (Hountondji, 1996 [1976], ch 7). Similarly, concepts circulating around Négritude, for a time popular in the fields of the arts and literature, are perceived as inherently problematic. Underpinning these critiques of cultural essentialism, which give rise to identity politics, is Hountondji's intellectual refusal to accept the core notion that there are modes of being and associated practices that can be easily defined as 'African'. Rather, his philosophical aspiration is to promote critical and creative forms of reflection on questions of identity. As he maintains, the search for

> identity remains irrepressible. But people will themselves realise at some point that the identity they are looking for is not as simple as they thought … [the] search for identity in my view is surely legitimate and necessary. But finally, our identity is not behind us, it is ahead of us, depending on the future we want to build for ourselves here and now. (Hountondji in Dübgen and Skupien, 2019, p 176)

Hountondji is deeply worried, therefore, about ideas aiming to curtail and shackle individuals and to enforce particular templates of what is thought to constitute a proper 'African'. This is a topic that preoccupied Fanon (2004 [1961], p 103) during the final years of his life when he identified how the nationalist bourgeoisie in the new nations of Africa were constructing forms of hegemonic power that were beginning to drift from 'nationalism to ultra-nationalism, chauvinism, and racism'. As Dübgen and Skupien (2019, p 50) aptly point out, Hountondji's philosophy reminds us that ethnophilosophy and its political and cultural derivatives 'tends to be a discourse of power and group domination over minority positions, having dangerous political implications. It can be abused as a weapon of the conservatives and traditionalists'. Since African societies are 'marked by high social inequalities, they can never be reduced to one collective thought' and series of culturally appropriate practices (Dübgen and Skupien, 2019, p 67).

If we locate Hountondji's concerns in a contemporary context, for example, we might refer to the situation in Ghana where community and social centres for the LGBTI community are being closed, with reports indicating that 'Ghana's National Coalition for *Proper* Human Sexual Rights and Family Values has … ramped up threats against sexual minorities … including proposing conversion therapy' (Parveen and Akinwotu, 2021, emphasis added). Bringing Hountondji's perspective closer to social work with the Black African diaspora, we might similarly wonder if ethnophilosophy, never named as such, haunts social work practitioner engagement with Black African families in Ireland and elsewhere; are exchanges imbued by White practitioners' unreflective view that Black

Table 4.1: 'Culture' as a weapon in the colonial/postcolonial era

'First order' ethnocentrism (Hountondji, 2000)	A product of cultural imperialism during the period of colonialism and neo-colonialism.
	Attempts to impose the culture and worldview of the colonised onto the colonised.
	Integral here is the 'message' that the colonisers' culture is superior to that of the subjugated, colonised population and that it represents human 'progress'.
'Defensive' or 'second order' ethnocentrism (Hountondji, 2000)	A form of culture essentialism that may help nationalist forces to forge resistance and collective opposition to the rule of the colonisers.
	Identifiable in Ireland prior to independence in 1922 and, particularly following the Second World War, nurtured in African states seeking independence.
	Cultural nationalism risks promoting an excessive and uncritical valorisation of a purportedly homogeneous 'national' culture and a dismissal of all those facets of culture associated with the coloniser.
	Can be used to promote the culturally 'authentic', 'appropriate' or 'proper' identities to discipline and quell internal opponents and to subdue minorities within the 'space' of the nation.
	Can be used as a 'screen discourse' (Bourdieu and Wacquant, 2001) to shore up tradition and to divert attention from equalities rooted in class, gender and other intersectional considerations both during the struggle for independence and afterwards. Becomes, therefore, antithetical to political, social and economic liberation.

Africans have a particular way of being and that, say, their style of parenting is always the same and undifferentiated merely because they are categorised as 'Black African'? Albeit perhaps implicitly, are interventions posited on the denial of heterogeneity within the 'Black African' category? How, we might inquire, can a person's geographical point of origin or complex cultural heritage dictate and truly determine a particular cultural practice such as parenting? We will, of course, return to examine some of these themes in the next two chapters. Presently, the key point, as Hountondji's philosophy recognises, is that there are invariably internal contradictions, a plurality of positions and minority standpoints within every group and cultural system. As we can see from Table 4.1, in colonised societies, culture can also function as a weapon that can be used to sustain ('first order' ethnocentrism) or challenge the hegemonic power of the ruling power ('defensive' or 'second order' ethnocentrism). As Hountondji's contribution remind us, however, even the latter, more resistant form of ethnocentrism can become something of a straitjacket that limits human potential. Relating this to Afrocentricity, the same criticism can be applied. That is to say, what might appear to be a body of theory beneficially promoting Black African consciousness in the face of White and Eurocentric domination can also become a project that risks stultifying and limiting the multifarious ways in which one can live one's life as a Black African.

Hountondji (2000, p 8) writes of the importance of listening for 'murmurs' or quiet sounds that risk remaining unheard when culture is perceived as a unified whole or when only the dominant currents are audible. This occurs, he asserts, when there is a lack of attentiveness to the 'internal pluralism of African cultures, the inner tensions that make them living cultures, just as unbalanced and therefore, just as dynamic, just as bound to change as any other culture in the world'. Greater attention should, therefore, be paid to what lies 'beyond the norms and social practices usually held as characteristic of a given culture, to the wide range of marginal practices and norms' (Hountondji, 2000, p 9). Very much in tune with the best of social work practice, intent on listening to marginalised and quiet voices, he asks how 'can we best recognise, behind the brouhaha of the dominant culture, the stifled voices that tell another story?' (Hountondji, 2000, p 9). More generally, beyond the façade of what might appear, or be trumpeted, as a unified culture there is likely to be internal diversity and pluralism. 'Africanness' – along with ideas pertaining to 'Westernness' – cannot be 'fixed once and for all' because they are essentially open, plurivocal and contradictory' (Hountondji, 1996 [1976], p 177). Such an unpacking of 'culture' and 'heritage' runs, as we have seen, entirely counter to the essentialism we find with the Afrocentrists. Hountondji's perceptions are also fundamentally opposed to the notion that there is a 'clash of cultures' between the West and the rest, as is proposed by neo-conservative thinkers and right-wing populists (Dübgen and Skupien, 2019). In recognising the instability and contestations that occur within culture and civil society, Hountondji develops a perspective that has more affinities with Gramsci (see also Chapter 3).

Hountondji's articulation of questions pivoting on culture becomes potentially helpful as we begin to think more deeply about how social work engages with notions of 'difference'. As he maintains, 'culture stagnates if it holds on to a narrowly defined, homogenous form of identity that musealises culture, and that it prospers if it endures internal plurality and controversy' (Dübgen and Skupien, 2019, p 144). Especially useful, perhaps, are his views on cultural pluralism (Table 4.2).

For us, it is a social worker's ethical duty to confront simplified notions of culture and to be constantly alert to what is occurring at the dissenting edges of supposedly unified cultures. In this sense, Hountondji's recognition of the importance of internal cultural pluralism, and his criticism of the pluralism of alterity, is significant. What is more, his ideas are resolutely at odds with reductive, nativist and exclusionary constructions of 'cultural identity' that presently haunt the globe.

Table 4.2: Hountondji and cultural pluralism

Forms of cultural pluralism	Characteristics of approach
Pluralism of alterity	Simplifies cultures by amplifying a false image of seemingly entirely divergent practices, values and norms separate – for example the 'host community' – from the 'migrant or diasporic community'. Both cultures viewed as containing people who entirely broadly share the same approach to life and human interactions.
Internal pluralism	Recognises that differences may exist between the 'host community' and 'migrant or diasporic community', but acknowledges the internal dynamics of cultures. Dismisses the notion that a clear separation exists. Cultural heterogeneity, opposed to fundamentalist evocations, is to be encouraged because the internal dynamics of cultures are positive features that have the potential to trigger beneficial and progressive social change.

Commentating on Hountondji's perspective, Dübgen and Skupien (2019, p 137) observe that in speaking about culture we should 'understand it as (1) historical; (2) contested; and (3) as embedded in power relations'. The task, therefore, becomes one of 'analysing culture as a contingent and changing system of human interaction that is always entangled with other "cultures", which, themselves, are internally fragmented. In this sense, speaking of culture always remains precarious, because it never fully grasps the phenomenon in question' (Dübgen and Skupien, 2019, pp 137–138). Hence, if we truly take into account Hountondji theorisation, it is easy to see that there are considerable risks in social workers and others locating people in 'boxes' (perhaps indicating 'minority ethnic' or even 'Black African') and then proceeding to ascribe certain norms and a way of life that may be reflective only of dominant cultural patterns and mores. Black Africans, in fact, have the same right as Europeans to perceive their culture as dynamic and in flux. Just like Europe, Africa cannot be viewed as static, unified and only producing 'traditional' patterns of thinking and behaviour. The civilisation of Africa, like that 'tiny corner of the earth which is called Europe', is 'not a closed system in which one can enclose oneself or let oneself be enclosed' (Hountondji, 1973, p 108).

If Hountondji does recognise something that can be loosely referred to as 'African philosophy' it is constituted in a way that is very different to the ethnophilosophers and those who now promote Afrocentricity. His favoured approach is one that seeks to remain sensitive to complexity:

The problem today is that, in the context of colonial domination, we have to a large extent internalised the discourse of our former masters on our cultures, their denigrating views on African ways of life and modes of thought. As a consequence, we were and are still tempted to undervalue our own heritage, including the immense legacy of indigenous knowledge. At the same time, however, we must be warned against the opposite danger. We have sometimes been, and may still be tempted to overvalue our heritage, by way of reaction against the first prejudice. We will then tend to deny any difference between indigenous and scientific knowledge, and will adopt a nationalist or populist stance. (Hountondji, 1983, p 25)

This statement is also important because it makes it clear that Hountondji does not, as some of his critics charge, dismiss local knowledge. His main assertion is that such knowledge needs to be assessed 'according to its ability to advance the emancipation and positive social transformation of the people concerned' (Dübgen and Skupien, 2019, p 50). Indeed, in his contributions following the publication of *African Philosophy*, initially in France in the mid-1970s, he has seemed much more enthusiastic about the role that, what he terms 'endogenous knowledge' can play in beneficially transforming social life. He is also very much attuned to how the Global North continues to channel and exploit African knowledge and expertise in ways that colonial powers exploited the continent for raw materials during the so-called 'golden age' of imperialism (Hountondji, 1995).

Conclusion

We hope that this chapter prompts much reflection. We have examined a good deal of material that is ordinarily omitted when issues pertaining to the Black African diaspora are discussed. As is manifested in our critical engagement, we view Afrocentric perspectives as providing an interesting and contentious body of theory, but reject its foundational assumptions and social and political agendas. Within this corpus, it is also easy to discern aspects that are deeply troubling and that aim to curtail certain ways of thinking and of being. A whiff of authoritarianism characterises the contributions of Asante and some of his followers.

We have emphasised that there may be significant cultural elements, relating to the lived experience of Black Africans, that are distinctive, and these should not be neglected by those providing or associated with social work. In this context, we drew attention to what may be five enduring common characteristics of Black African culture. We also critically examined writers (such as Jerome Schiele, Mekada Graham and Dumisani Thabede) whose contributions have tried to reorient social work in a way that is congruent with the ideologues of Afrocentric theory. Having criticised these endeavours, we then rounded off the chapter by highlighting the work of Paul J. Hountondji and showed how his lucidly insightful and pluralistic perceptions of culture and identity are far more compelling than those of the Afrocentrists.

Still, there may be elements of Afrocentric thinking that we can distinguish from the more 'vulgar' variant identified by Manning Marable. Sarah Balakrishnan (2020, pp 71–72) suggests that whereas the term *Afrocentricity* denotes a movement in the US academy in the 1980s to pursue liberation through African thought and practices, what we may call *Afrocentrism* refers to a long narrative tradition regarding history and Africa – one that has been a grassroots political language among Black communities for generations (Balakrishnan, 2020, pp 71–72, emphasis added). Relatedly, in certain social work practice situations it might be useful utilise *Afrocentrism* to adopt forms of 'defensive' or 'second order' ethnocentrism (Hountondji, 2000) when working with marginalised members of the Black African diaspora. In Ireland, for example, various community support and development programmes have been eliminated on account of neoliberal 'austerity' measures. In the wake of this, and informed by some of the precepts of Afrocentrism, one of us (Washington) has been involved in initiating new forms of community participation in the US and Ireland (see also Mungai, 2013).

Indeed, as we argued earlier, none of the ideas we have explored in this chapter should be perceived as a mere abstraction, because the theory relates in complex ways to the work undertaken 'on the ground' with members of the Black African diaspora. In the next chapter, therefore, we will begin to narrow our lens and entirely concentrate on Ireland. What is the character of social work? What are the hegemonic economic and social imperatives? How is the notion of 'multicultural' constructed and managed? What are some of the key considerations impacting on social work with the children and families of the Black African diaspora? These are just a few of the questions we will pose in Chapter 5.

Reflection and talk box 4

The work of Marimba Ani and Molefi Asante has been particularly influential in the US. What are your perceptions of their contributions?

How should social work assessments address issues related to the spiritual beliefs of the Black African diaspora?

How convincing and successful have been the attempts to locate Afrocentrism at the heart of social work with Black people?

Paul J. Hountondji has a very different approach to philosophy and politics. Do you find his perspective more persuasive than that of the Afrocentrists?

5

Social work in neoliberal, 'multicultural' Ireland

Introduction

In the previous four chapters of the book we have largely directed a wide-angle lens at a range of issues pertaining to questions of 'race', racism and cultural identity and the Black African diaspora. In this chapter we begin to narrow the focus much more specifically onto Ireland. This is not, of course, to imply that our discussion will solely be of interest to readers based in Ireland. Readers located elsewhere will be readily able to make connections with what is occurring, in relation to issues pertaining to social work and 'race', closer to home.

After briefly discussing social work in Ireland, we hone in on neoliberalism. This dimension is immensely important because social work with the Black African diaspora cannot be detached from the wider, exploitative dynamics that are integral to all capitalist societies. This point needs to be stressed, because many contributions that examine issues of 'race', racism and cultural identity tend to float free from material moorings and occlude any, or adequate, reference to the encompassing imperatives of capital accumulation that help to construct and shape how 'race' and racism is lived and experienced. Following our discussion on neoliberalism, we revisit the subject of multiculturalism in Ireland, which we initially engaged with in Chapter 1. We then concentrate on a number of themes specifically attached to the Black African diaspora and social work, especially as this relates to the children and families practice arena.

Social work in Ireland

Socialist aspirations were a key element of the project for national freedom, but the new Irish state that emerged in 1922 was firmly embedded in a corrosively conservative form of hegemonic power (Coquelin, 2005; see also Lloyd, 1999). Within this new order, elite groups were hesitant to embrace social work because it was viewed, especially by senior figures within the Roman Catholic Church, as a harbinger of secularism and modernity. Perhaps more specifically, they were fearful about what they perceived as social workers' potential capacity to interfere in, even to disrupt, the 'private' sphere of family. Far from coincidentally, of course, most of these potential interferers were also female. Perhaps also, the idea persisted that social work was irredeemably 'protestant' and ran counter to the 'Catholic' ethos of the newly founded state.

In the first two decades of the current century a good deal of discussion relating to child abuse has centred on historical instances where the perpetrators have been priests and members of religious orders (Garrett, 2013). Much of the focus has been on Industrial Schools and similar institutions that held the 'troublesome' children of the urban and agrarian poor (Commission to Inquire into Child Abuse, 2009). Although it was mostly disregarded by the state, there was a constant flow of knowledge about the harm occurring in such places (Tyrrell, 2006). Dissenting and oppositional voices faced considerable, often insurmountable obstacles because of the power of the Church and the social standing and status of priests, nuns and other associated religious figures.

In official circles, poor families were regarded with contempt, and from the early years of the new state the 'impoverished child was viewed as a burden' (Holohan, 2011, p 188). Furthermore, they were apt to be viewed as potentially contaminating the hegemonic Irish Republican ideal of petty bourgeois civility and propriety. This is significant not only because of what it tells us about state responses to children and families in the past; it also provides an optic through which contemporary ways of relating to children and families, by social workers and other professions, can be assessed and understood. Garrett (2017), for example, draws parallels between how 'unmarried mothers' were treated in the 20th century and how asylum seekers are responded to by the state in our current century, with both groups being stigmatised, held in quasi-confinement and prevented from enjoying 'parity of participation' with others in civic and community life (see also Fraser, 2013, p 193). Indeed, as Gramsci's theorisation constantly reminds us, a hegemonic apparatus and power structure always needs its vilified pariahs and outsiders, in order consolidate its rule over a particular social formation (Garrett, 2018, ch 6).

Rather than creating a Northern European-style welfare state, in Ireland there developed a 'mixed economy of welfare' influenced by Catholic conservatism, economic underdevelopment and a postcolonial culture. Echoing Tom Inglis (1998), Vesna Malešević (2019) argues that this involvement of the Church in the running of education, health and welfare resulted in a 'moral monopoly' that extended into both the institutional and individual spheres of life. It also meant that one particular religion was favoured over others and patriarchal social values were valorised over and above a politics of 'equality'. For Malešević (2019), the influence of the Church began to wane in the early 21st century only on account of secularising tendencies of that period spurred social changes and prompted a significant erosion of the institution's social status and political 'reach'. Although the most recent Census reports that 75% of Irish people still claim to be 'Roman Catholic', it is now accepted that the Church's hegemony over much of the 'social' sphere is punctured, since it is no longer regarded as holding a monopoly on 'truth' (Malešević, 2019). As mentioned, the clerical sexual abuse scandals further places the Church/state relationship under strain (Garrett, 2012). However – and significantly – a mixed economy of welfare and residual Catholic influences continue to adversely impact on and shape education and health.

The position of social workers and the associated social professions, in general, is best understood within a context of rapidly changing social, economic and political environments (Christie, 2005). The 'Celtic Tiger' years of the 1990s, in which the Irish economy grew more quickly than most others in Europe, resulted in a large increase in the number of social workers. This increase started from a relatively low base, and Ireland continues to spend the lowest amount on social protection as compared to other EU countries, that is, as a percentage of gross domestic product (GDP) and gross national product. When the economy was expanding, the government actually reduced the percentage of GDP spent on social welfare. Nonetheless, during the period of the 'Celtic Tiger', a neoliberalised and restructured economy also attracted many immigrants from countries whose social and cultural practices were often dissimilar to those in the Republic. The resultant 'diversity' meant that social workers had to work with service users and colleagues from Africa and Asia whose ethnic cultures occasionally had little in common with their own European ethnicity or its systems.

Turning to our present conjuncture, Irish social work is situated within a western socio-cultural and political framework and, to a large degree, it resembles – in its modalities and thematic preoccupations – countries such as the UK. Relatedly, social work education and training is similar to that found in most western countries. Prior to 2014, social work within the state sector was administratively situated within the Health Service Executive (HSE). It is not clear whether, in 2014, the establishment of the Tusla (the Child and Family Agency) was merely a part of the state's wider 'reforming' of social work services due to neoliberal 'austerity' measures or whether the idea originated internally within the professional field. Irrespective of the main driver, Christie (2005) argues that a complex mixture of success and failure across a range of welfare services led to a fragmented social work and social care system based on a pattern of uneven progress and development. This he attributes to tension between neoliberal and social democratic ideologies at government policy-making levels.

The professional training protocols on 'fitness to practice' are regulated by a quango called CORU, which is derived from the Irish word, *coir* meaning fair, just and proper. Significantly, CORU's 'Social Workers Registration

Board Code of Professional Conduct and Ethics' (CORU, 2019) entirely omits reference to the profession safeguarding and promoting 'human rights'. This appears rather extraordinary, given that the IFSW definition of social work situates the aspiration to safeguard and promote human rights as central. As the IFSW (2014) maintains:

> Social work is a practice-based profession and an academic discipline that promotes social change and development, social cohesion, and the empowerment and liberation of people. Principles of social justice, human rights, collective responsibility and respect for diversities are central to social work. Underpinned by theories of social work, social sciences, humanities and indigenous knowledges, social work engages people and structures to address life challenges and enhance wellbeing. The above definition may be amplified at national and/or regional levels.

The British Association of Social Workers' (BASW, 2016) 'Code of Ethics for Social Work: Statement of Principles' refers to the phrase 'human rights' on 16 occasions in a document of 16 pages. We can only assume that CORU is concerned that social workers may deploy a 'human rights' discourse to try to defend the rights of service users faced with debilitating neoliberal cuts to services. Hence, the easiest (and crassest) thing to do was merely to delete the worrisome phrase. In this context, we will say a little more about neoliberalism because, as stated earlier, it serves to structure approaches to social work and adversely impacts on the lives of Black African and other minority ethnic users of social work services.

Neoliberalism

Globally, capitalism continues to provide the material base, and it conditions perceptions of, and responses to, an array of other issues and preoccupations. In much of Europe, North America and the Global South, neoliberalism has been dominant since the late 1970s. With the fall of the USSR and its satellites, this model became more globally entrenched, even emboldened. In short, neoliberalism has been deemed the most adequate way to organise capitalism by the global ruling class in order to extract and maximise the volume of surplus value garnered from those compelled to sell their labour power to those owning – or acting in line with the imperatives of those owning – the means of production and distribution. In short, neoliberalism is the dominant regime of capital accumulation, and its associated ideological 'truths' constitute, to differing degrees, the hegemonic and governing ethic that coerces and cajoles subordinate populations in market-centred societies. In this sense, for decades, neoliberalism has been ascendant as the default logic that prioritises a narrow economic rationality in all sectors of society: at the collective level of state policy making as well as the personal level of individual choice making (Brown, 2015). Neoliberalism promotes, therefore, a market-centred society, and disciplines people to be compliant in adhering to its strictures, incentivising market-consistent behaviour and punishing people when they fail to comply (Schram and Pavlovskaya, 2017, p i). In this context, Cahill (2011, p 479) defines neoliberalism as the sum of a political rationality that organises the way in which we think and act and it transforms the relations between the state, the market and citizens.

With the financial 'crash' of 2007/2008, we witnessed how the ruling class also possesses its own ideological and material 'flexibility'. In the US alone, the Federal Reserve pumped between $19 trillion and $29 trillion into the financial system to rescue the banks. Such massive bailouts by states, often referred to as quantitative easing, fly in the face of neoliberal tenets rhetorically founded on the need to 'roll back the state'. A not dissimilar scale of intervention to shore up the capitalist system is apparent in the response to the COVID-19 crisis (Brenner, 2020; Aradau and Tazzioli, 2021). Hence, it should be highlighted that the loyalty of the ruling class is not to neoliberalism per se; rather, its loyalty is vested in capital. So, post-pandemic (or even during an extended period of COVID-19-related emergency), the neoliberal model may morph into something else that is better able to serve the needs of capital. Following Gramsci, we can maintain that we are living during a period when the 'old is dying and the new cannot be born' (Gramsci in Hoare and Nowell Smith, 2005, pp 275–276). We are at an 'interregnum' in which the course of history is manifestly uncertain.

Currently, our ability to respond to the COVID-19 pandemic has been hampered because, after years of neoliberal capitalism, social and state institutions in most parts of the world have been hollowed out and are ill-equipped to deal with a global pandemic, despite such a possible event having been signalled for decades (Harvey, 2020). Restructuring, reorganising and centralising capital to the disadvantage of the majority of the world's inhabitants, neoliberalism has produced an enormous cleavage between the super-rich and the rest. As the rich get richer, more than half of the world's population lives on 'between $2 and $10 a day' (Oxfam, 2018, p 12). This is precisely the state of affairs that Marx predicted when he wrote *Capital*. There are 'now 2,043 dollar billionaires worldwide … 82% of all of the growth in global wealth in the last year went to the top 1%, whereas the bottom 50% saw no increase at all' (Oxfam, 2018, p 8). For many at the economic apex, the pandemic has massively inflated their wealth. The US-based Institute for Policy Studies (2020, p 1), for example, reports that between 1 January 2020 and 10 April 2020, 34 of the nation's 170 wealthiest billionaires saw their wealth increase by tens of millions of dollars. The 'wealth surge' of Jeff

Bezos, of Amazon, is 'unprecedented in modern financial history' in that his 'fortune had increased by an estimated $25 billion since January 1, 2020'.

In drawing readers' attention to these figures, the aim is not to imply that the Fordist period, stretching approximately from the end of the Second World War until the late 1970s, was an unequivocally 'golden era' in the West (Bohrer, 2019). It is to recognise that this era of assembly-line, factory-based production may have accrued, for some, relatively high wages (that is to say, a decrease in the rate of exploitation) and more benign welfare systems. It was a period also characterised by the continued exploitation of workers' labour power and by racist and patriarchal forms of domination. Furthermore, Fordist regimes financed social entitlements in the West by continually exploiting the mass of people in the Global South.

Within the hegemonic neoliberal framing, individual citizens are constructed as 'social entrepreneurs' and rational 'consumers' able to exercise 'self-care' through responsible choice making about care providers/services. Citizens' access and entitlement to basic social welfare protection is made conditional on fulfilling a variety of tasks such as attending parenting classes, job-seeking workshops and so on. For social work agencies and practitioners, the application of a 'business model' to public administration and service provision is saturated in New Public Management ideology. White et al (2008) argue that the ascendancy of neoliberalism has increased the tension between standardisation and meaningful responsiveness through increased 'form-filling' and use of centrally devised electronic templates. They also maintain that such templates perform 'double duty' by recording service-user information and measuring practitioner performance.

Although neoliberal approaches purportedly enhance 'transparency' and 'efficiency' and promote 'equal treatment', they are rightly criticised for aridly routinising practices at the expense of 'client voice'. Matarese and Caswell (2018) argue that casework under the neoliberal (not so) 'new managerialism' privileges form-driven interactions that provide limited space for service-user narratives and extended participation. A welter of research studies point to the loss of the social work 'relationship' and practitioner 'stress' and 'burn out' (Unison, 2019).

Neoliberal Ireland

In Ireland, neoliberalism has assumed a hybrid or mixed form, borrowing 'elements of US neoliberalism, such as public–private partnerships, privatisation of public services, low corporate and individual taxation, low level of government expenditures on social programmes and light regulation of the financial system ... It also incorporates aspects of European social welfarism' (Mercille, 2014, p 82; see also Allen, 2007; 2012; Phelan, 2007). Kitchin et al (2012, p 1306) observe that Irish neoliberalism is frequently 'ideologically concealed, piecemeal, serendipitous, pragmatic, and commonsensical. Successive Irish governments have never had an explicit neoliberal ideology (apart from a small number of influential ministers) ... Ideology thus remains largely hidden in the apparatus of Irish politics. Its presence is barely articulated and often invisible'. Hence, 'new policies and programmes' tend to be 'folded into the entrenched apparatus of a short-termist political culture shadowed by low-level clientelism, cronyism, and localism' (Kitchin et al, 2012, p 1307).

The embeddedness of 'neoliberal rationality' (Brown, 2015) shapes the everyday aspects of life and social interactions, given that on 'trains and buses, and sometimes in hospitals and universities too', we have become customers, not passengers, patients or students. In all these instances, a 'specific activity and relationship is erased by a general relationship of buying and selling that is given precedence over it' (Massey, 2015, p 24). Writing in Ireland, Marnie Holborow (2015) highlights how neoliberal economics have found key supporters within the universities, which are increasingly modelled on corporate businesses. Affirming the values of the market, academic institutions amplify and mimic private sector practices underpinned by notions of performance, customer, enterprise and entrepreneurship (Holborow, 2015, ch 6). More pervasively, and driven by a new 'comprador class' of chief-executive-style chancellors and presidents, there is now relentless competition relating to world table leagues, research funding, securing the 'best' academics, erecting state-of-the-art buildings and so on (Byrne, 2017, p 113).

Oxfam Ireland (2021) report:

> Mirroring this global inequality trend, Ireland's own nine billionaires saw their fortunes increase by €3.28 billion since March − a tenth of which would pay for a Covid-19 vaccine for every person in the Republic of Ireland. Meanwhile, essential workers − such as our carers and supermarket and factory workers − cared for our vulnerable and kept our food supplies running throughout the pandemic − quite often on minimum or low-paid wages.

This is the overarching context in which social work (both in practice and within the classroom) often seems to prefer to 'help' the 'disadvantaged' fit into their allotted places within the fabric of neoliberal capitalism. Analytically and practically, the task of confronting the source of this 'disadvantage' − the capitalist class − tends to be rendered obscure, even 'non-existent'.

In 2007, more than 200 asylum seekers went on hunger strike for two days at the Knockalishsheen accommodation centre located on the border of Limerick and Clare (see also Baker, 2021). One of the residents, originally from Iran, told journalists: 'People outside the walls of Knockalisheen don't know how we live. It's a prison. Animals should live here, not humans. It should be destroyed. The minds of the managers are not to open to us' (*The Irish Times*, 30 January, 2007, p 2 ; see also Garrett, 2007). The same news item referred to a letter that the residents had sent to the Department of Justice referring to a whole series of petty humiliations and degradations: 'In meals we find foreign objects such as hair strands, broken plastic shards, rough particles of shells ... Only one toilet roll is given out once a week, which is not enough because before the week runs out it finishes. Then we have to wait till the next date of supply' (*The Irish Times*, 30 January, 2007, p 2).

Not all provision for asylum seekers is as woefully bad as the situation described. Yet such circumstances are entirely calamitous for those compelled to reside in such places. More pervasively, neoliberal approaches to housing provision have prompted a crisis (Hearne, 2020). During the early months of the global pandemic there were a 'record 10,000 people in Ireland without a home, among them almost 4000 children' (Coulter and Reynolds, 2020, p 68). Black people are especially adversely impacted because of discrimination in the rental housing market (Gusciute, 2021; see also Gusciute et al, 2020). The point to emphasise is that this situation would be entirely avoidable if the needs of the mass of the people were placed before the imperatives of capital.

Significantly, an enormous social and economic cleavage separates lives and experiences. For example, while, as we have observed, asylum seekers are often treated like 'animals', many of the nation's wealthy are able to actually coddle and lavish money on the animals they keep as pets. Worth quoting at length, a feature writer in *The Irish Times* gushes:

> Designer dog bowls, coats and collars are only at entry level to a whole new world of pooch pampering ... Irish dog owners ... trading up or doing a big refurbishment are factoring in luxuries such as underfloor heating in outdoor kennels, dog bed shelves integrated into the designer kitchen, and even dedicated showers in the utility room to facilitate regular grooming and dialling down of the doggy smell ... A luxury shower or wet room is another popular request [explained the owner of a bespoke joinery and kitchen company] ... At its most basic, this usually features a ceramic shower base and a hand-held shower-head with a niche or shelf for grooming products. Some are as sleek as their owners' wet rooms and have stone-panelled sides. An off-the-shelf option is the Vasca by Italian outfitters Nic Design. It comes in a range of cool colours from the sunshine yellow pictured to soft greens and teal blues (from €4,900). (Gallagher, 2020)

The same article included photographs of items that other wealthy dog owners might purchase for their pet. Prominent here were a 'Tibetan sheepskin bench' (€904) and a 'velvet-lined Louis XIV-style dog bed' (from €395).

Such patterns of grossly conspicuous consumption appear to reprise the circumstances of the second half of the 19th century that led Marx to identify and castigate 'over-consumption', 'insane consumption' and a 'turn toward the monstrous and the bizarre' (Marx, 1981 [1857–58], p 434). As Marx noted, the capital accumulation process is an 'endless process' with capital constantly crashing through what have previously been seen as its limits, or what we might dub 'no-go-areas'.

> The only utility whatsoever which an object can have for capital can be to preserve or increase it … It is therefore inherent in its nature constantly to drive beyond its own barrier … Thus, growing wealthy is an end in itself. The goal-determining activity of capital can only be that of growing wealthier, i.e. of magnification, of increasing itself. (Marx, 1981 [1857–58], p 270)

This dynamic has been pronounced during the neoliberal period in Ireland and elsewhere, with capital violating and relentlessly aspiring to push beyond what was formerly viewed as publicly and ethically unacceptable. As a result, many goods and resources have increasingly become commodified. Kieran Allen (2020, p 24) trenchantly observes that, like much else in Ireland, 'asylum seekers have been turned into a commodity to be used by business to make a profit'. We would also add that this development provides a case study of the entanglement of 'race' and profit within what we termed earlier as the capitalist racial state (see also Chapter 2). Companies who have been paid millions of euros to hold, surveil and manage the bodies of Black and minority people, and to boost the coffers of their chief executive officers and shareholders

> include Mosney Holdings PLC which received fees of over €8 million in 2018 for 600 asylum seekers. The Barlow Group received over €7 million in 2017 for operating centres in Cork and Waterford. Millstreet Equestrian Services which has over 500 asylum seekers in Cork and Waterford, received payments of €6.53 million. Aramark's Campbell Catering LTD received €5.89 million for operating State-owned direct provision centres at Knockalisheen, Co. Clare, Co. Cork and Co. Meath where over 825 asylum seekers are accommodated. (Allen, 2020, p 42)

In February 2021, the Irish government announced its plans to end DP (Government of Ireland, 2021). This is not scheduled to occur until 2024. Even if this actually happens – and it is not guaranteed, given the Irish government's dismal track record of policy implementation – the system will have been in place for almost a quarter of a century. Meanwhile, the lower echelons of the labour market have become, in recent years, filled by floating populations of poorly paid migrant workers who have undertaken a large proportion of DDD (Dirty, Dangerous and Demanding) and CCC (Caring, Cooking and Cleaning) jobs.

Social work and social care provide examples of sectors in which there have been consistent attempts to privatise services so as to prise them open for profit and shareholder enrichment. In the years leading up to the COVID-19 pandemic, 'venture capitalists and vulture funds' began to view the Irish care sector as 'sexy' and ripe for exploitation (Keena, 2015, p 5). By the summer of 2020, this 'sexy' sector was transmogrifying into a vast mortuary, given that Ireland had one of the highest rates of COVID-19 deaths in care homes in the world (Cullen, 2020; see also Allen, 2020; Mercille and O'Neill, 2020). The fragmented and inadequate health service has unsurprisingly been subject to enormous pressures. As Coulter and Reynolds (2020, p 73) spell out:

> The cuts to funding and personnel that occurred during the austerity era ensured that the (two-tier, semi-privatised) Irish health system was poorly prepared. The shortages of essential equipment were especially glaring in a country that hosts the overseas headquarters of nine of the ten largest pharmaceutical companies in the world – the authorities had to scavenge for Personal and Protective Equipment (PPE).

Relating to provision for children in contact with social workers, Branigan and Madden (2020), in their review of the residential costs being incurred by Tusla, illuminate a growing reliance on the private sector. There were '483 children in residential care at end 2019, across all service types' and '56% (or 272) were in private residential care; 27% (or 128) were in Tusla-owned residential centres; and 17% (or 83) were in voluntary centres' (Branigan and Madden 2020, p 34). Additionally, the authors advise that the

> greatest changes in residential care costs in recent years have been observed within privately-owned centres. The total cost of residential care rose between the years 2016 and 2019, from approximately €152 million in 2016 to almost €193 million by year end 2019. However, '87% of this cost increase occurred within private service provision. This compares to just 2% attributable to Tusla-owned services, or 4% and 7% for voluntary and administrative costs respectively. (Branigan and Madden 2020, p 48)

Colluding with colonialism and morphing into 'multiculturalism'?

Ireland cannot be wholly absolved of involvement in colonisation (see also Chapter 3). Following the Act of Union of 1801, it was part of the 'metropolitan core of the British Empire, albeit not straightforwardly so'

(Howe, 2003). Irish people, both Catholic and Protestant, from the north and south, were involved in the 'business and workings of empire as merchants, soldiers, administrators, doctors, missionaries, and educators' (Crosbie, 2009, pp 965–966). Nonetheless, because Irish nationalism was generally

> equated with anti-imperialism, the role that Ireland played in the empire (and conversely the role that the empire played in Irish history) has been largely ignored. Throughout the twentieth century, Irish historians and historians of Ireland alike sought to produce narratives that traced the historical course of the nation from the onset of colonialism through to independence, virtually ignoring Ireland's substantial in involvement *in* the empire. (Crosbie, 2009, p 966)

In his fascinating excavation of the role played by Irish scientists in the East India Company, Barry Crosbie (2009, p 986) concludes that they were only a 'part of emerging late nineteenth-century Irish professional networks that viewed the empire as a legitimate sphere for work and as an arena in which they could prosper'.

Although a deep interrogation of this dimension lies beyond the scope of this book, the Irish also played comparable roles in 'British Africa'. As functionaries of the British Empire, 'substantial numbers of Irish and Anglo-Irish people engaged in the slave trade and were actively involved in projects of colonial expansion ... one third of all colonial governors in South Africa in the eighteenth century were either Irish or Anglo-Irish' (Aniagolu, 1997, pp 45–46). Chichi Aniagolu (1997, p 46) comments that there is

> little evidence that they identified more with the indigenous population than with the colonising British. On the contrary, they appear to have supported the latter in their colonial drive and lent their services wherever they were required. It was these very Christian evangelists, particularly in their travels into the bush, who first made Africans aware of the colonial attitudes toward them and their culture.

In the Cape Colony in the 1830s, for example, Wexford-born Bishop Griffith opposed White Catholics cohabiting with Black people. Into the next century, and as recent as 1959, then *Taoiseach* [prime minister] Sean Lemass told *Dail Eireann* [the Irish parliament] that his Fianna Fail government entertained 'nothing but friendly sentiments' for apartheid South Africa (in Aniagolu, 1997, p 48). In short, Ireland remained situated within a western European socio-cultural context marinated in historical notions of western racial and cultural superiority (McClintock, 1995; Ohlmeyer, 2020). In the international arena, and especially, in the US following the unsuccessful Easter Rising of 1916 in Ireland, bourgeois nationalists frequently constructed their argument for independence in terms of the sheer unfairness of a 'White nation' not been allowed to manage its own affairs (Walsh, 2016). It seemed that access to their stock of White 'cultural capital' and its associated range of White privileges was being ignored by their racial kinfolk (see also Chapter 3).

In a significant comment, in February 2021, the president of Ireland conceded:

> We also must acknowledge that the British found willing agents of Empire among the native Irish from the earliest days of conquest. While many were drawn through economic necessity, it cannot be denied, that both at home in Ireland, and throughout the expanding Empire, some Irishmen became even enthusiastic accomplices to the excesses, cruelty and hubris of colonialism. (Higgins, 2021; see also O'Sullivan, 2021)

The state is also, in contemporary geopolitical terms, through NATO's so-called 'Partnership for Peace', embedded in neocolonial practices; relatedly, Irish troops have been stationed in countries such as Afghanistan in the Global South. The Irish state has also provided authorisation for US military flights to regularly 'stopover' at Shannon airport in the west of the country. None of this is to crudely argue that Eurocentric, colonising and racist practices in Ireland merely replicate those in, say, the UK. Rather, it is to propose that in every country in the Global North, racism evolves in ways that are conditioned by particular and specific histories. More generally, it might still be suggested that in Ireland 'Whiteness' continues to be central to the hegemonic construction of national identity. This deeply racialised sense of identity is naturalised and relentlessly (re)constitutes itself by constructing a margin. When this plays out in social work such an ideological orientation is, of course, entirely at odds with the profession's rhetorical egalitarian claims.

Fanning (2002) argues that nationalism and Roman Catholic religiosity continue to shape how the Irish view themselves through a nativist lens and to structure who they construct and perceive as outsiders. This aspect also shapes the 'race' thinking that is frequently integral to social policy making. Fanning also draws on literature sources to evoke public perceptions. He refers, for example, to the recollections of the popular historian and commentator, Tim Pat Coogan, who recollects:

> We were brought up believing that Africans as a class were much in need of the civilising influences of the Irish religions as parched earth was of water. It was an image propagated by missionary magazines with their pictures of a big beaming Irish priest, generally robed in

white, surrounded by a group of adoring chubby little black children. (In Fanning, 2002, p 16)

Fanning (2002, p 16) also refers to a passage in a Clare Boylan novel from the late 1980s in order to underscore his analysis of the roots of Irish people's often paternalistic understanding of Black people:

The Irish have always had an intense sentimental preoccupation with distant pagans. There was no tradition of nursery stories. Instead, it was the dusky heathen that stirred the infants' imagination. There was a romance in these stories but terror too, for the missionary fell prey to foul disease, to the leopard's tooth, and the cannibal's pot. Children loved to hear such stories and were schooled early to sacrifice for God's unchosen. 'Penny for the black baby' was the first phrase learned. There was as much pleasure in putting a penny in the mission box, with its nodding black head on top as it was on spending it on an orange.

The same author also reminds his readers about the ill-treatment of Jewish people in 1904 in Limerick and he explores responses to Hungarian refugees in the 1950s and, more contemporaneously, the situation of Irish Travellers. This provides an analytical platform for him to look at the plight of refugees and 'asylum seekers' in contemporary Ireland.

Located in the UK, Gurnam Singh (2020, pp 23–24) observes that on account of the genocide perpetrated against Jewish people and other groups in 'the name of "race"', international organisations, especially UNESCO, began in the postwar period to 'establish the principle of "multiculturalism" as a means of combating the lingering effects of scientific racism' (Singh, 2020, pp 23–24). This ambiguous concept generates criticisms from the political Right and Left. A decade ago, the UK prime minister David Cameron called for a 'much more active, muscular liberalism'. He went on: 'we have allowed the weakening of *our* collective identity. Under the doctrine of state multiculturalism, we have encouraged different cultures to live separate lives, apart from each other and apart from the mainstream … We've even tolerated these segregated communities behaving in ways that run completely counter to *our* values' (Cameron, 2011, emphases added).

A subsequent administration led by Boris Johnson has been manifestly multicultural, with prominent roles government held by Kwasi Kwarteng (formerly of Eton College and Cambridge University, but the son of parents from Ghana), Rishi Sunak and Priti Patel. These have fitted comfortably and helped to shape and define deeply retrogressive and nationalistic political programmes. This agenda, which rhetorically celebrates a measure of 'diversity' and meritocracy while dismantling social protections, might be understood in the context of what Nancy Fraser (2016, p 113) terms 'progressive' neoliberalism. It also gels with Fraser's assessment that mainstream 'multiculturalism' and its 'affirmative strategies' aim to correct some of the 'inequitable outcomes of social arrangements without disturbing the underlying social structures that generate them' (Fraser, 2003, p 74).

Reflecting some of these complexities and tensions, Ireland's *Tánaiste* [Deputy Prime Minister] at the time of writing is Leo Varadkar. Gay and of partly Indian heritage, he embodies the new 'multicultural' Ireland that the governing class likes to present to the world and the global markets. This new image is often burnished in comparison to the images evoked of a supposedly brutal and bygone Ireland that is featured in the many reports highlighting the historic abuses in institutional settings that have been published this century. However, Varadkar – for many a symbol of the 'new' Ireland – is, as Colin Coulter and John Reynolds (2020 p 77) sharply conclude, a 'true believer in the neoliberal project'. They continue:

> While he has been keen to maintain a rather more benign public persona during the COVID-19 crisis, there have been moments when the mask has slipped. In early April, Varadkar could not resist the temptation to recycle hearsay that some low-paid workers were, allegedly, abusing the coronavirus welfare arrangements. Two months later, he acted on that prejudice when he cut the pandemic unemployment payment available to part-time workers by 40%.

At the level of policy rhetoric, Irish governments remain keen to espouse a 'third way' response to migration, 'race' and ethnicity (Lentin and Titley, 2011). Appearing to straddle French 'assimilationism' and British 'multiculturalism', this has focused on 'interculturism'. Such an approach ostensibly informed Ireland's first targeted migrant integration strategy statement, *Migration Nation* (Office of the Minister for Integration, 2008). In practice, there has been a 'fairly unreconstructed assimilationism' (Munck, 2011, p 4). Conceptually and politically, this discourse can be connected to the more pervasive and problematic Europe-wide conceptualisation of 'social exclusion', where the overarching imperative is one of social cohesion rather than social justice.

Formally, Ireland has 'strong equality legislation' (Council of Europe, 2013, p 6). Nevertheless, a number of 'austerity' related cuts have diluted the state's ability to meaningfully address discrimination. The National Consultative Committee on Racism and Interculturalism ceased to operate in 2008 and the National Action Plan against Racism was not renewed. More generally, the 'entire architecture of public and statutory bodies established or supported to promote equality, monitor progress, enhance awareness and develop innovative practice has been restructured, closed down, subjected to drastic budget cuts or partially absorbed' into other departments (Barry and Conroy,

2012, pp 17–18). This combination of budget cuts and inertia conveys the impression that tackling discrimination is a 'luxury' or an 'add on' to a properly functioning state, and that anti-discriminatory policy and practice can be relinquished in times of economic retrenchment. Many migrant advocacy groups undertaking vital work have to rely on philanthropic foundations – particularly the US-based Atlantic Philanthropies – to be able undertake and publish research (NASC, 2013).

Survey data reveals a 'high level of "liberal" attitudes towards immigration but that seems to be time-bound and conditional'. At key junctures, such as the 2004 Citizenship Referendum, Irish public opinion retreated into 'nationalist if not nativist tropes' (Munck, 2011, p 14). That referendum resulted in an amendment to the constitution that provided that children born on the island of Ireland to parents who were both non-nationals would no longer have an automatic and constitutional right to Irish citizenship. For Munck (2011, p 4), it 'served to reaffirm "blood and belonging" notions of the Irish nation'.

According to Fanning (2011), emerging social-spatial segregation relating to Black African settlement patterns in Ireland reflects class inequalities rather than a previous history of ethnic segregation as is the case in most European states. The Economic and Social Research Institute (2018) suggests that, despite improvement in the economy, Black Africans have not benefited in terms of employment outcomes nationally. According to the report, Black African nationals have much lower employment and activity rates than other immigrant groups. The report reveals that the employment rate of Africans is 45%, compared to an average of 70% for non-Irish White nationals.

Civil society and the Black African diaspora

The Immigrant Council of Ireland is an independent human rights organisation and law centre established in 2001. It aids people of migrant background to improve and protect their rights. Its vision is of a fair society that respects human rights and diversity, making it possible for all people to fulfil their potential. Its focus is on:

• fostering public debate on immigration and integration;
• working on immigration reform and advocacy as an independent law centre;
• supporting the most vulnerable migrants, including victims of trafficking, so they can live lives free from oppression;
• tackling racism and promoting the participation and representation of migrants in Irish life.

The scope of its undertaking has expanded to include immigration reform, consultancy for EU projects, research and influencing Ireland's approach to immigration as well as monitoring and reporting racist incidents. The current changes in the sphere of 'integration' could arguably be attributed to some of the programmes highlighted earlier. There have been campaigns from some NGOs and other civic groups working collaboratively to highlight policy shortcomings. The 'integration remit' has also been extended to small ethnic minority-led organisations at the community level. This could either be praised as a 'bottom up approach' to integration or be condemned as merely another neoliberal mechanism of outsourcing a traditional state function.

Due to institutional and structural factors, Black Africans are still likely to be viewed as 'outsiders', but this has not discouraged forms activism against injustices. The African Cultural Project is a minority ethnic-led organisation aiming to 'tell the African story' to a largely Irish-based audience. Its primary objective is to provide information on Africa that is currently unavailable through the conventional sources most people in Ireland would turn to. According to its web page, since its establishment, the African Cultural Project has been coordinating a multidisciplinary programme of cultural and educational events featuring Africa's rich and diverse cultural traditions in collaboration with major institutions. Founded on the UNESCO teaching guidelines, its flagship initiative, Africa in the Irish Classroom, is a curriculum support programme aimed at first- and second-level pupils.

Other emerging organisations include African Social Workers Ireland (ASWI) and the African Scholars' Association. The former aims to ensure that issues related to their community receive attention, and here Black African knowledge can be deployed as a resource. The latter is more concerned with providing a forum for African scholars to engage in the exchanges that are vital if we are to adequately respond to contemporary issues affecting Africa and Africans. The African and Migrant Women's Network's (AkiDwA) aim is to integrate members into Ireland's changing ethno-racial and migratory realities by becoming involved in coalitions, alliances and organisations in Ireland and beyond (De Tona and Lentin, 2011). Another well-known example is the 'new community partnership' that has a strategic partnership with Tusla and other state agencies. Critiques of both AkiDwA and the 'new community partnership' that have emerged from other migrant-led organisations operating without state funding have questioned the ability of such organisations to confront the state and its institutions about policy shortcomings. While the activism of migrant-led organisations continues to 'make a difference', their efforts still need to be complemented by statutory social service provision. The existence of all these organisations suggests, despite ongoing concerns about unequal and racialised treatment and violation of human rights, a vibrant activist culture among the Black African diaspora in Ireland (Lentin and Moreo, 2012).

New social media platforms contain possibilities for the democratisation of power by providing a space for alternative views of the world among the

Black African diaspora. Potentially, social media may also become a space for subjugated epistemologies to be expressed. It is, of course, recognised that capitalist media conglomerates largely own newer forms of media and this limits the opportunities to forge counter-hegemonic perspectives. Still, this is a 'field' of media operations where there may be scope for the Black African diaspora – along with socially progressive social workers, educators and users of services – to dissent from the entrenched dispositions of dominant neoliberal cultures currently sustained by 'traditional' mainstream structures and institutions.

In the ghetto? Disciplining Black African social work students

Importantly, there also exist a number of other groups, often operating 'below the radar', that specifically support and provide mutual aid to Black African social work students, and this helps them to survive college and fieldwork placements (Adeleye et al, 2020). From Ireland and beyond, emerging, scattered evidence indicates that Black African students are more likely to be assessed as 'failing' placements than their White counterparts (Razack, 2001; Wiebe, 2010; Tedem, 2014; Soper et al, 2016; Srikanthan, 2019). Anecdotally, discussion taking place among the diaspora in Ireland suggests that the experience of Black African students at predominantly 'White universities' is often one entailing their having to avoid 'making waves' that would lead to victimisation (and possible expulsion). Some suggest that they had to repeat 'failed' practice placements after they had been 'matched' with White practice teachers who either misunderstood them culturally or were simply prejudiced towards them. This situation is often made worse because of the patronising and managerial 'leadership' style anecdotally associated with certain directors of Irish postgraduate social work programmes.

In the UK, Bartoli et al (2008) highlight that practice learning poses different challenges for Black African students. More specifically, their study suggests that Black African students were more likely to fail their practice learning module or have serious concerns raised about them by their practice teachers/assessors. Some of the factors attributed to their difficulties include:

- gender roles and expectations based on cultural and traditional norms;
- financial pressures and difficulties;
- health-related problems impacting on placement competency and continuation;
- homesickness and culture shock;
- lack of practice experience based on unfamiliarity with UK welfare state and systems;

- cultural diversity and its impact on social work practice and decision making;
- students' motivation to study social work and preconceived ideas of the profession;
- the experience of individual and institutional racism (Bartoli et al, 2008, p 80).

Culturally based values indicate that Black African students' adaptation to UK social work could be challenging. For example, one of the Black African students stated that it is 'culturally taboo' for her to 'interrogate someone about their family' (Bartoli et al, 2008, p 83). This dimension clearly has implications for social work assessments, particularly inquiries into allegations of familial abuse. Questions relating to authority with Black African students may also be complex, given that certain cultural norms, instilled within the Black African home, may stress that one should demonstrate deference to those in 'authority' (including academic tutors and team managers). This may be further compounded by the deference often expected from women steeped in patriarchal ideology and relations of domination. Bartoli et al (2008, p 84) suggest that Black African students may, in fact, face additional adjustments, compared to their White counterparts, in order to 'succeed' on their social work courses. Such adjustments might be required on the part of social work education providers too: there should be a 'two-way street' approach with the student and teaching staff aspiring to recalibrate their approaches (Bartoli et al, 2008, p 88).

More recent data makes it apparent that the specific problems encountered do not end at the point of registration. In the UK, Skills for Care (2021) undertook a survey of Newly Qualified Social Worker (NQSW) registration and outcome data for 2018–19. It reveals that while 26% of the total number of NQSWs registered are from Black and minority ethnic backgrounds, they account for 53% of the total fails. By comparison, the 60% of NQSWs identifying as White account for 47% of the total fails. Not unreasonably, Skills for Care (2021) concede that this is a 'very concerning initial finding, which places a responsibility on all those involved with the Assessed and Supported Year in Employment (ASYE) to identify areas of inequality and to find ways of addressing them'.

The notion of social work education being a 'journey' is useful in highlighting that while the destination remains the same for all students, the Black African students may be starting from a 'different place' and their 'route' may be 'less travelled' (Bartoli et al, 2008; see also Ní Chonaill, 2021). This 'journey' rarely has the 'short cuts' that White students – and especially middle-class ones freighted with economic and cultural capital – can avail themselves of while at university. This understanding is particularly useful for those of us in Ireland, with an unpublished MA thesis by Odirih (2019) dwelling on issues relating to the disproportionate numbers of Black African social work students failing placements or 'dropping out' completely. Their reasons mostly centre on perceived racism and, on occasions, the culturally superior disposition of predominantly middle-class White practice teachers. Surveying the entire the Irish universities sector, Bríd Ní Chonaill (2021, pp 50–51) notes that the Equal Status Acts 2000–18 prohibit educational establishments from

> discriminating on nine grounds, including race. More recently, Section 42 of the Irish Human Rights and Equality Commission Act 2014 introduced a legal obligation, the Public Sector Equality and Human Rights Duty, on public bodies to 'eliminate discrimination', 'promote equality' and 'protect the human rights of its members, staff and the persons to whom it provides services', in this case students.

There has been a manifest 'dearth of data on racial inequality and a lack of focus on the outcomes of Black students' (Ní Chonaill, 2021, p 51).

Legal frameworks, guidance and protocols

The United Nations Declaration on Human Rights (UNDHR) has been incorporated into EU legislation and the EU Court of Human Rights with Protocol 12, specifically, referencing cultural minorities. Article 21 mentions the right to access public services; Article 23 refers to the right to work; and Article 25 highlights the right to adequate standards of health and well-being. The Declaration on the Rights of Persons Belonging to National or Ethnic, Religious and Linguistic Minorities, adopted in 1992, relates to the rights of persons belonging to national, ethnic, religious and linguistic minorities. The fact that these rights exist but do not find practical expression in many western contexts highlights evident limitations. This suggests that the enjoyment of such rights, or the extent to which minorities can express their respective cultures, is dependent on the tolerance and generosity of the 'host' state.

At the supranational level, the major historical critique of the UNDHR was from the counter-declaration by the Anthropological Association of America (1947) which warned that the UNDHR was an attempt to impose western hegemony over the people of the world though universalising western values as 'human rights'. The counter-declaration is rarely mentioned these days. The issue of human rights' legitimacy and their global validity is, of course, enmeshed in the classic conflict of universalism and cultural relativity. However, there is clearly some conceptual and practice convergence between human rights and social work's rhetorical aspirations to create humane and sensitive treatment for all, regardless of cultural diversity.

In December 2019, the United Nations Committee on the Elimination of Racial Discrimination (CERD) expressed concern about reports from Ireland indicating that 'people of African descent are disadvantaged and discriminated in every aspect of life, including employment and education, on a daily basis, and that there has been a high level of racist hate crimes committed especially against people of a sub-Saharan African background' (CERD, 2019, p 5). Turning to a range of measures required to address this situation, the Committee's recommendations highlighted the need for the Irish state to

- take effective measures, including special measures, to address all forms of discrimination against people of African descent, particularly in employment and education sectors;
- take effective measures to combat stereotypes of people of African descent, including education about their history and culture;
- take effective measures to prevent racist hate crime against people of African descent and ensure that all cases of such a crime are thoroughly investigated, perpetrators are sanctioned and victims are provided with effective remedies.

Legislation against such racially motivated hate crime may be more likely follow the publication of a report from the 'independent' Anti-Racism Committee in November 2020 (Department of Children, Equality, Disability, Integration and Youth, 2020).

More generally, the country's domestic immigration law is contained in a variety of primary and legislative acts that are interpreted and expanded by the courts through case law. The main relevant legislation includes: the Refugee Act 1996; the Illegal Immigrants (Trafficking Act) 2000; the Immigration Act 2004; and the various Employment Permits Acts 2003–14.

In recent years, state sanctioned poverty and economic hardship have also become fused with the callous operational consequences of the 'habitual residence condition' (HRC) – preventing access to public funds introduced under the Social Welfare (Miscellaneous Provisions) Act 2004 and schedules accompanying the Act. The legislation lays down that:

It shall be presumed, until the contrary is shown, that a person is not habitually resident in the State at the date of the making of the application concerned unless he has been present in the State or any other part of the Common Travel Area for a continuous period of two years ending on that date ... [T]he Common Travel Area means the United Kingdom of Great Britain and Northern Ireland, the Channel Islands and the Isle of Man.

The Act was amended and the 'two-year rule' no longer applies. The term 'habitually resident' is not defined in Irish law, but section 30 of the Social Welfare and Pensions Act 2007 lists five criteria to be taken into consideration when assessing whether a person is 'habitually resident'. These include the length and continuity of residence in the state or in any other country, the length and purpose of any absence from the state, the nature and pattern of the person's employment, the person's main centre of interest and the future intentions of the person concerned which appear from all the circumstances.

Harmon and Garrett (2015) illuminate the ambiguity and inconsistent interpretation of the five criteria which subject to the analysis, assessment and discretionary powers of a statutorily appointed Deciding Officer who deems the person 'habitually resident' or not. In this context, Harmon and Garrett (2015) particularly focus on the fifth criterion, regarding future intentions, arguing that this is open to subjective and highly inconsistent and, seemingly, capricious interpretation. These authors also highlight that while the HRC can be applied to anyone, it disproportionately affects migrants as it may be difficult to prove that their 'main centre of interest' is in Ireland if their families are outside the state. As for Irish Travellers, their nomadic culture means that they may also have difficulty satisfying all of the five criteria.

Interestingly, while the HRC's stringent restrictions affect those seeking to access the welfare 'safety net' in Ireland, the same restrictions do not apply to people from the EU10 countries accessing the labour market. This possibly explains Allen's (2007) assertion that the state's policy was to ease labour mobility during the 'economic boom' period to enable migrant workers to enter so long as they did not become a 'burden' on the state. The assumption, in official circles, that migrant workers would simply travel to Ireland to work and return to their home countries was also highlighted by Boucher (2008).

Underpinned theoretically by Badiou's (2008) 'one world' politics, Harmon and Garrett (2015) also incorporated a small-scale study in two cities to discover the attitude and response of Irish social workers to this policy. The study focused on themes relating to: inequality of access to the welfare 'safety net'; ambivalent social work attitudes towards the HRC; the role of practitioners in opposing the HRC; the personal cost of challenging the inflexible operation of the HRC; bureaucracy and the HRC.

More generally, Harmon and Garrett (2015) highlight the consequent dilemmas arising from the practitioners' ambivalent positioning. This is a direct product of balancing the demands accruing from their being state agents and ethical imperatives compelling them to respond to families 'in need'. To what extent are the practitioner's attitudes shaped by their agency or organisation's culture? Can social work organisations be capable of oppression, albeit sometimes even unconsciously? These all are questions we will return to in the next chapter.

As regards the general health and well-being of immigrants, the policy promulgated to purportedly address their needs was the Intercultural Health Strategy (2007–12). This was introduced to comply with international treaty obligations requiring nation-states to enact programmes that met the unique requirements of minority ethnic communities, given that the 'one size fits all' approach was ill-judged in various situations. Bojarczuk et al (2015) focus on the barriers that minority ethnic people face on account of inequalities in the area of mental health services. Ethnic minorities participating in this study, including Black Africans, drew on their own lived experiences to demonstrate the impact of a wide variety of social determinants on the mental health of the communities in which they live. Factors such as discrimination, racism, unemployment, social exclusion, culture and language differences negatively influenced their mental health. In short, the findings demonstrate that Ireland's minority ethnic communities experience multiple forms of disadvantage and disempowerment that 'incubate' mental ill-health. Alert to the potential potency of a community development approach, the report highlights the fact that community participation is vital in addressing identified 'barriers'.

While calling for such 'barriers' impeding access to mental health services for minority ethnic groups to be lifted, Bojarczuk et al (2015, pp 29–30) reasonably propose a more encompassing approach, with 'cultural competency training' incorporating issues related to:

- pre-migration factors;
- migration experience;
- settlement and integration process in the new country;
- trauma;
- language and communication ability;
- symptom expressions;
- changes in gender roles;
- intergenerational issues;
- economic distress and employment situation;
- marginalisation;
- resilience;
- intersectionality of identities that come into play;
- racism;
- support networks.

Relatedly, the lack of a common language has often caused misunderstanding and difficulties for White practitioners when working with minority ethnic children and their families. Language is, of course, not only a neutral message-delivery system, it is intertwined with the relations of power, and these shape micro-encounters involving social workers. Alexander et al (2004) also observe that low levels of language proficiency can adversely impact on access to social services. What is more, Bourdieu's (1991) theorisation of capital suggests that immigrants acquisition of proficiency in the 'host' country's language can have an enormously important impact on life chances (see also Chapter 3).

In recent years, translation and interpreting services have been widely used. Research carried out in both Norway and England exposes the limitations inherent in such services when working with minority ethnic children and their families. Fifty-three social workers interviewed pointed out that the lack of a common language and interpretation-related issues were a routine difficulty in their work with ethnic minority families. Kriz and Skivenes (2010) rightly maintain that the interaction between the communicative agents involves more than a mere exchange of words. The findings confirm that the use of translators and interpreters reduces the quality and extent of information practitioners receive from ethnic minority users of services. There are, in short, distortions – over words, meanings and intentions – resulting in communication insecurity for both social workers and minority ethnic families.

Concerns over confidentiality can contribute to a loss of trust and undermine the relationships so essential in social work practice. Such findings are also consistent with other studies on English child protection networks and on decision-making processes more generally (Reder and Duncan, 2003). To counter the limitations inherent in the use of translators and interpreters, some ethnic minority communities use their children as language and cultural brokers. This is because children are frequently able to acculturate more rapidly through school and play. While having children serve as translators and interpreters is normal in most African immigrant communities, it is a controversial issue in some western jurisdictions and fraught with practical and ethical problems.

Internationally, as well as in Ireland, 'host' countries have variously made provision for professional translation and interpreting services. Waters and Jimenez (2005) observe that failure to recognise language rights does not always reflect lack of political will. Rather, most 'host' countries lack the requisite institutional infrastructures or a supply of the necessary language skills to cater for new demands. Rarely has it has been proposed that social workers, as part of their 'cultural competence' training, might learn one of the major languages in which many minority ethnic minorities would probably be proficient, such as French, Portuguese or Spanish.

Children, child welfare, child protection and the Black African diaspora

The United Nations Convention on the Rights of the Child (CRC), very much like the UNDHR, has been targeted for criticism by some for being a western construct designed to universalise or globalise western notions of childhood. Kaime (2009) argues that the wider adoption of the CRC did not stop African governments from promulgating their own children's rights for the continent. The author argues that many African states felt the CRC did not adequately address many Afro-specific concerns, including:

- the plight of children then living under apartheid;
- harm caused to the African girl child such as forced marriages and female genital mutilation;
- the African conceptions of the community's duties and responsibilities and the role and responsibilities of the extended family in the upbringing of children;
- the duties and responsibilities of the child towards their family and community.

Viljoen (1998) attributes the 'non-inclusion' of Black African concerns in the CRC to the under-representation of Black African states at the time of drafting.

In Ireland, Kilkelly (2000) observes that the CRC provides a baseline for analysing policy and practice for children, including asylum seekers. She suggests that the treatment of ethnic minority children results from insufficient care and attention being paid to their human rights. Observations by Christie (2010) on Black African children living in DP having unmet needs suggest that they palpably do not enjoy equal rights with other children. Placing children 'in care' is another sphere in which one could argue that the rights of the Black African children are not respected. While the CRC emphasises that in providing such 'alternative' care, consideration should be given to the child's ethnic and cultural identity and any such placement should reflect the said considerations, this does not seem to be the case in Ireland in many instances. Relatedly, the recommendation by the CRC to allocate the resources necessary to maintain the quality of healthcare services that meet the needs of the children, especially refugees' and asylum seekers' children, has still to be implemented.

The underlying principle of the Child Care Act (as amended variously over the years) is not only to foster closer cooperation between and among statutory and non-statutory agencies but also to ensure and affirm the importance of child welfare while having due regard to the rights and duties of parents. In the case of unaccompanied minors arriving on Irish soil, the

Act empowers state agencies to assume their legal guardianship. The Children First Act 2015 was enacted in November 2015 and commenced in full in December 2017, and it places a number of statutory obligations on specific groups of professionals and on particular organisations providing services to children. The provisions of the Act seek to: raise awareness of child abuse and neglect; provide for mandatory reporting by key professionals; improve child safeguarding arrangements in organisations providing services to children; provide for cooperation and information sharing between agencies when Tusla is undertaking child protection. Importantly, this Act also contains a provision that removes the 'defence' of reasonable chastisement. The Children First Act 2015 operates alongside the existing non-statutory obligations provided for in *Children First: National Guidance for the Protection and Welfare of Children*, introduced in 2017 (Department of Children and Youth Affairs, 2017). Revised over the years, there are many criticisms of these guidelines. Christie (2010), for example, in analysing how minority ethnic groups are represented, argues that identification of 'special needs' pivots on the dominance of White 'Irishness' as the unquestioned 'universal norm' against which all childcare practices are judged. Writing a decade into the new century, the same author also argued that 'race' remains 'unnamed' in post 'Celtic Tiger' child protection discourse within the state. For example, under the 'emotional abuse' category in Children First Guidance, racism is not even mentioned. This is a palpably a glaring omission and renders invisible the lived experience of many minority ethnic children and their families. Additionally, there remain concerns that there is more emphasis on child protection and on looking out for abuse than there is on preventative support and the material welfare of the child.

Launched at the century's commencement, the National Children's Strategy (NCS) aims to develop and implement policies to improve quality of life for children in Ireland. The strategy particularly focuses on children needing additional support and, in this vein, minority ethnic children should receive the same care and protection as any other child in the state, but in a way that respects their culture. The NCS states that children from minority ethnic communities have 'special needs' that should be met. These 'special needs', identified with those seen as culturally different, have largely remained unnamed and unrecognised in research, policies and social work practice (Christie, 2010).

The National Standards for Foster Care, introduced in 2013, recommend that, whenever possible, children are placed with carers from their own cultural, ethnic and religious background. In situations where this is not possible, the Standards state that foster carers should be supported to enable the children to develop a positive understanding of their cultural origins and background. In some quarters, Tusla's policy to promote the culture and identity of every child in care has been described as inadequate, and the agency stands accused of not having done enough to recruit a genuinely culturally diverse group of foster carers. As we will see, some of these issues relate to the work of Ireland-based Black African social work practitioner and academic Colletta Dalikeni.

Black African asylum-seeking families and child protection social workers

Set against a background of Ireland becoming an increasingly multicultural society since the mid-1990s, Dalikeni (2013; 2021) examined the experiences of White Irish social workers and asylum-seeking families. She interviewed ten social workers and ten Black African asylum-seeking parents/guardians, along with a sample of closed case files. Her investigations took place in 2006–07 as part of a wider PhD project.

Mistrust between social workers and service users was viewed as attributable to: unfamiliarity with each other's cultures; culturally influenced communication methods and styles; ethnocentric assumptions of social workers relating to age assessments; misplaced assumptions of the universal application of child development theories in informing understanding in terms of normative indicators such as level of maturity, appearance and behaviours/acting. For example, describing her experience and concerns about the difference between child-rearing practices among the Black African families and those of Irish families, one of the social workers confided: 'I watch how they lift their children. It's very aggressive, the movements in the African families are rough and it's just how they go on. With Irish families if they are rough with a child you know that is not always how they go on' (in Dalikeni, 2021, p 13). Evoking her interaction with her social worker, a mother recounted:

> 'I can remember one day the social worker said she had come to talk to me about how I handle my child. My mother handled me that way when I was growing up, is there anything wrong with me? Why do they think their way is the only way? I am not going to break my daughter's arm, I love her but no, for the social workers they don't see it that way, they said I was rough.' (In Dalikeni, 2021, p 13)

Often, White Irish social workers were inclined to believe that members of Black African families were lying because they did not make eye contact:

> 'The social worker always insisted in me looking at them when I was talking to her. She would always say, "Look at me when you are talking". I used to feel frightened by this because in my country you don't look at people in authority when they are speaking to you. For

the children when they are speaking to an adult they sit down or kneel and speak without looking at the adults in the eye. It is considered rude in my culture to look at the adult or stand while you are talking to them. I tried to explain this to the social worker, but she kept saying "it's okay, you are in Ireland now".' (In Dalikeni, 2021, p 14)

If Black African parents did not kiss their children and show demonstrable affection, this tended to be viewed as indicating a lack of appropriate bonding. A mother, referred to as Nada, reported:

> 'This is another thing the social workers used to tell me, that I don't tell Justine I love her. I said I am sorry, I don't tell my children I love you. But the way my mother showed me she loved me was by providing for me. That's the same way I show Justine and all my children that I love them. The social workers started coaching me as if I was baby. They were saying things to me as if they were talking to a 10-year-old … they treated me as if I could not think. I often thought they were only treating me this way because I was Black. I do not know if they would have treated a White person in the same way.' (In Dalikeni, 2021, pp 14–15)

One of us (Washington) has witnessed how some NGO 'support' groups and social workers, dispatched as part of 'integration programmes' to provide information, literally 'lecture' Black African and Syrian families on the 'dos' and 'don'ts' of parenting in Ireland in a manner that is highly paternalistic and deeply disrespectful. Oftentimes, there is also a lack of dialogue about different styles of parenting and why certain parenting methods might be considered inappropriate in a new context.

Dalikeni (2021, p 15) concludes that most of the Black African families in her study argued that

> affection or providing comfort by hugging their children, as in the case of Nada mentioned earlier, was not 'normal' practice in their cultures. Parents who did not hug their children during parenting assessment, however, were reportedly considered 'cold' and unemotional by some social workers, who then questioned the strength of the parent's bond with the child.

Founded on unconscious ethnocentric orientations and the procedural and forensic nature of the child's protection, this approach has shaped assessments in circumstances where children were allegedly left 'home alone' by parents (Dalikeni, 2021, pp 15–16).

Frequently, within the confines of a capitalist racial state, it is also difficult for Black African families to differentiate between the probing approach of the state immigration officer and that of the state social worker (Lentin, 2007; see also Chapter 2). As for actual immigration officers, the social workers in Dalikeni's research felt that they and their processes were not only child unfriendly and inhumane, they also lacked transparency. For example, social workers referred to the case of an 11-year-old subjected to interrogation as if they were an adult in a criminal court proceeding. Practitioners also referred to the harsh nature of immigration officers' interventions by highlighting an incident where a breast-feeding mother had her baby taken away from her and placed into state care. This was to avoid the baby being detained together with the mother (who had to be detained pending deportation). With regard to transparency, Dalikeni's social work respondents felt that they were not given professional courtesy and recognition by immigration officers, as they were often not informed in advance about the progression of the cases of people alongside whom they were working. In some instances, they learned only very much later that a service user had either been deported or granted permission to reside in the state or had been moved elsewhere. Such practices furnished evidence, in fact, of the rhetorically valorised 'interagency collaboration' being entirely disregarded.

Relatedly, Dalikeni examined how issues of cultural relativism exercised social workers. Generally, practitioner respondents assessed families according to 'Irish norms and standards'. There was no evidence of any attempt, on the part of social workers, to consider cultural differences and the potential impact of these on assessments and on other kinds of intervention with these families. Dalikeni contended that culture impinged on communication and interaction, resulting in misunderstanding. In short – even if often unacknowledged – it was an important and influential factor. Her contributions confirm that unresolved cultural differences constitute a major a source of misunderstanding and point of disagreement between Black African families and social workers. This often functions to strain relationships between the two parties, to the extent of impeding the evolution of more culturally responsive and effective service provision.

Issues specific to asylum-seeking families, impacting significantly on parenting and 'outcomes' for children, which were largely unaddressed by social workers, included the emotional and psychological consequences of living in DP, forced institutional dependency, enforced idleness, poverty, lack of independence and prolonged periods of insecurity and anxiety while waiting for asylum applications to be processed. Narratives of racism experienced by asylum-seeking families are plentiful in Dalikeni's investigations: often these relate to racial 'micro-aggressions' in the wider community and in terms of their interactions with social workers and related professionals. Racism in the wider community was evidenced in their experiencing verbal abuse in public spaces and in neighbourhoods adjacent to the DP centres. Perceived instances of racism were reported in interactions with social workers where asylum-seeking families felt misunderstood or there was 'misrecognition' of their parenting styles or other instances of cultural misunderstanding. Often, some asylum-seeking families attributed mistreatment to the colour of their skin.

Using the Biographic Narrative Interpretive Method, Dalikeni's important work is, perhaps, the first of its kind in this field in Ireland. It highlights the need for appropriate and ongoing, critically imbued and structurally aware 'cultural competence' training for social workers (see also Chapter 2). It is unclear if such training can be operationalised and rendered meaningful. Would it lead to perspective alteration or change in entrenched ethnocentric dispositions, attitudes and practice habits? There is no doubt that her findings illustrate the complexity of social work practice in this area and the need for a coherent strategy for practice in child protection and work, more broadly, with a diverse community of children and families. Such a strategy would have to be centred on the child as well as the cultural setting in which the child is reared and it would need to critically engage with the conflicted practitioner role of care and control in mediating between the state and the family.

Social work's institutional 'inertia'?

Relatedly, writing over ten years ago, it was avowed that the evolution of

> specific texts on working with refugees and asylum seekers and the inclusion of equality and human rights on social work courses have not translated into visible anti-racist or anti-oppressive policies or practices in social work ... The lack of attention to cultural differences in child protection guidelines and child welfare legislation is one tangible example of a *continuing inertia*. (Walsh et al, 2010, p 1984, emphases added)

Strikingly, this critical reference to 'inertia' echoes Frantz Fanon's disapproval of mainstream psychiatric practices in which one the 'difficulties encountered in the exercise of a profession' is 'habit' and 'gestures' following 'other gestures without novelty' (Fanon, 2018 [1953–56], p 338).

Significantly, the 'inertia', troubling Trish Walsh and her colleagues may contribute to the disproportionately high number of children from minority ethnic communities taken into care in Ireland (Child Care Law Reporting Project, 2015). Black African families are

> about seven times more likely to face child protection proceedings than are indigenous Irish people, and this figure is likely to be greater if the

'mixed' category includes one African parent, as we have observed it often does. Eastern Europeans are about 1.5 times as likely as Irish people to face the child care courts. (Child Care Law Reporting Project, 2015, p 14)

This over-representation of Black African service users in many 'social problem' categories generates much disquiet and controversy and has, in some quarters, not unreasonably prompted a questioning of social work's ethical commitment to repudiate 'discrimination' and 'oppression' and to uphold the 'dignity' and 'worth' of every person (see, for example, Onyejelem, 2017). Such concerns echo, in complex ways, those of US scholars and commentators who point to the fact that African-American children and their families are disproportionately targeted by child protection services (Roberts, 2014; Lash, 2017; Dettlaff et al, 2020). Discussing a not dissimilar situation in the UK, relating to the experience of Nigerian parents, Cynthia Okpokiri (2021) refers to the fears of such parents being caught 'parenting-while-Black'. Literature from Canada similarly reveals that Black parents feel that their parenting practices are unfairly targeted by child welfare agencies and this contributes to the over-representation of Black children in the care system (Adjei and Minka, 2018).

A Toronto-based study highlights how Black parenting experiences are shaped and influenced by cultural knowledge and the perceived racism in Canada, but the relevant agencies barely consider such factors in their engagements with Black families. Worse, most respondents had negative perceptions of agency staff as people who disunited families and racially targeted Black families (Adjei and Minka, 2018). Hidden within the rhetorical claims of culturally universal legislation and standard practice models was a White, western standard of parenting that placed Black (and indigenous families) at risk of being identified as 'defective' or 'problematic'. Adjei and Minka (2018) recommend that child welfare agencies in Canada should take the necessary steps to understand the complex cultural contexts of parenting. This would involve their engaging with Black parents in a more positive way in the child protection process, and one practical outcome might be that more Black children would remain, safely, at home. The study further argues that, even where protective out-of-home care is the preferred plan, child welfare agencies are urged to develop strategies to make better use of the potential that birth parents possess to enhance the lives of their children. Perhaps in Ireland there are emerging signs of a greater interest in social work's positioning and the appropriateness (or otherwise) of its intervention strategies when working with those who are not only visibly different but who also may have culturally distinct worldviews and belief systems. The setting up of ASWI reflects some of the evolving concerns about the inadequacy of current mainstream responses. The launch of the Irish

Association of Social Workers' (IASW) 'Anti-Racism Strategy' in February 2021, which we will refer to again in Chapter 7, might herald a progressive departure (IASW, 2021).

Conclusion

As mentioned earlier, our intention in this chapter has been to focus on a range of contextual factors related to social work with the Black African diaspora in Ireland. In the book's penultimate chapter we aim to again narrow our focus in that we provide a ground-level account. More specifically, we will 'listen' to the kaleidoscope of views and perceptions of social workers and social work educators as they talk expansively about a range of issues that lie at the heart of this book.

Reflection and talk box 5

'The struggle against racism is inseparable from the struggle against neoliberal capitalism.' Discuss this assertion.

Why does it appear that Black social work students and newly qualified Black practitioners are confronted by particular difficulties in the workplace?

What specific issues need to be addressed when seeking to improve social work services for the children of the Black African diaspora?

Social work is a profession rhetorically committed to addressing 'human rights' deficits. Is this evidenced in the activity of practitioners with those whom states classify as 'asylum seekers'?

6

'When in Rome, you do as the Romans do'? Social work with the Black African diaspora

Introduction

The differently socially constructed social worlds of practitioners and educators are the focal interest of this empirical chapter and we investigate their day-to-day engagement with the challenges, ethical dilemmas and opportunities arising as they work alongside and support Black African service users and students. The four themes, examined to different degrees with the two groups, are:

- social work education and theoretical perspectives;
- praxis;
- organisational structures within the capitalist racial state;
- neoliberalism.

Engaging with the research participants

Our decision to adopt a qualitative research approach lies in the fact that it facilitates the exploration of human experiences in personal and social contexts (Gelling, 2015). Qualitative approaches involve immersion in the everyday life of individuals, groups, societies and organisations, giving us a measure of access to the lived experiences of respondents so as to better understand how meanings are socially and culturally constructed. In this sense, qualitative methods continually lay emphasis on the words expressed rather than quantification in the collection and analysis of data (Bryman, 2012). The limitations of qualitative research relate to the frequently small-sized samples and related criticisms dwelling on the low statistical power that such sampling techniques possess in respect of generalisability to a larger population (Maruyama and Ryan, 2014).

Our sample was purposive in that those interviewed are a population of significance integral to the study: they met the main selection criteria, requiring practitioners to be qualified and CORU registered, with a minimum of six months' experience working with members of the Black African diaspora. The social workers' experience of working with Black

African families actually ranged from six months to over 20 years. Over 30 social workers expressed an interest in being interviewed, and those not interviewed had either just qualified or had not worked with Black African service users. The practitioner sample also took account of the urban/rural divide, which is still significant in Ireland. The major practice domains (such as child protection, medical social work, primary care, housing welfare, mental health and probation services) were also represented in the sample to try to capture any differences in the challenges experienced by social workers within their specific practice domain (see also Appendix). The criterion for social work educators was that they had taught Black African students and/or had research interests pertaining to the Black African diaspora in Ireland.

A short, semi-structured questionnaire formed the basis of the interviews featured in this chapter. As mentioned earlier, this had four components based on the overlapping themes derived from deep engagement with the relevant conceptual and policy literature we have referred to in the previous chapters. None of the respondents was involved in the thematic construction of the questionnaire, nor in the formulation of particular questions. Prior to the interviews it was mailed to them to provide them with an opportunity to look at the questions and locate the interviews within the context of the larger research project that forms the basis of this book.

Importantly, the semi-structured questionnaire was not used in a rigid or restrictive way and it provided space for the interviewees to talk expansively about what *they* perceived as the significant issues. Tailored to their specific roles, slightly different interview schedules were used with the educators and practitioners, but both addressed the four main topics identified earlier. We remained open to the emergence of new topics unrelated or tangentially related to these main topics.

The interviews were far from standardised and there was no aspiration to 'hide behind the question–answer format, the apparatus of the interview machine' (Denzin, 2001, p 30). Rather, the methodological position adopted was that each interview was 'literally an *inter view*, an inter-change of views between two persons conversing about a theme of mutual interest' (Kvale, 1996, p 14, original emphases). In this context, the metaphors of 'miner' and 'traveller' have been usefully deployed to evoke contrasting approaches to interviews:

The two metaphors – of the interviewer as a miner and a traveller – represent different concepts of knowledge formation … In a broad sense, the miner metaphor pictures a common understanding in modern social sciences of knowledge as 'given'. The traveller metaphor refers to [an] understanding that involves a conversational approach to social research. The miner metaphor brings interviews into the vicinity of human engineering; the traveller metaphor into the vicinity of the humanities and art. (Kvale, 1996, p 5)

Pierre Bourdieu also furnishes an articulation of the research ethic that was aspired to in the interviews (see also Appendix). Thus, there was recognition that each interview was a social relationship. Important here was a commitment to 'active and methodical listening' as opposed to 'half-understanding' based on a 'distracted and routinised attention' (Bourdieu in Bourdieu et al, 2002, pp 609, 614).

The individual one-to-one interviews took place prior to the onset of the COVID-19 pandemic and its related physical distancing measures. Occurring between May 2017 and March 2018, they were conducted in person and face to face. Unlike surveys and questionnaires, such encounters furnish opportunities to build rapport with respondents and enable more complex issues to be covered through prompting and probing. Rather than having the respondents answer 'yes' or 'no', the interviews required the respondents to answer the questions more extensively, and facial responses were also gauged and assessed. The use of semi-structured interviews also provided for flexibility so that, as the interview progressed, questions could be slightly rephrased to suit tone and body language and to respond to visual cues, such as when the respondents shook their head from side to side, suggesting disagreement, before a question was even completely asked.

The interviews were audio recorded and this also served to minimise disruptions associated with note taking. Pile (1990, p 217) maintains that a verbatim report is the only way to attain full analysis. This recording enabled a re-listening of the interviews and, occasionally, additional clarification was sought from a respondent, following a re-listening. The main shortcoming with audio recording is that it does not, of course, capture non-verbal communication. It is acknowledged that 'transcription cannot capture the rhythm and tempo of the spoken word … It is clear that even the most literal form of redaction (the simplest punctuation, the placing of a comma, for example, can determine the whole sense of a phrase) represents a *translation* or even an interpretation' (Bourdieu in Bourdieu et al, 2002, pp 612, 621, original emphasis). That is to say, reporting interviews, as we do in this chapter, is a 'way of writing the world', not of providing 'a mirror of the so-called external world, nor is it a window into the inner life' of those interviewed (Denzin, 2001, p 25). No computer software package was used to aid the analysis of the audio-recorded interviews. Copies of the transcripts were sent to all the respondents to enable them to check that they agreed that their comments had been accurately rendered.

In what follows, no information is provided on the areas of Ireland in which the respondents are located. Similarly, the workplaces where they are situated are not provided for readers. This approach perhaps detracts from the significance of the specific context or milieu in which they are based and it might also blur the importance of the matrix of relationships in which they are locally embedded. However, it is also clearly important to safeguard the respondents' right *not* to be identified. In this context, the respondents were asked to decide on their preferred alternative names. (All the research participants availed themselves of this option.) This was connected to two factors. First, issuing the invitation reflected a desire to develop a 'partnership' approach within the dyadic research encounter. Second, introducing pseudonyms was regarded as preferable to deploying arid descriptors such as 'Ms X' or 'Respondent 12' and so on. Using an actual name, albeit a pseudonym, is much more evocative for the reader and imbues the responses with a 'warmer' and more human 'vibe'. One minor point: throughout the book we have tended to prefer the phrase 'service user'. Most of the practitioners interviewed used the term 'client', and we have chosen not to alter this to 'service user'.

We were struck by the highly reflective and nuanced responses of the respondents. However, the small group whose voices we will 'hear' is not, of course, representative of *all* social work educators and practitioners in Ireland. The interviews that are at the core of the chapter are therefore best interpreted as an exploratory venture providing a platform for additional research initiatives that could focus on a much larger group of respondents. Nonetheless, the views of those interviewed do provide further insights into the themes that have been the preoccupations of this book.

The research respondents, disguised by their alternative names, are featured in Table 6.1 and Table 6.2. It is recognised that female practitioners comprise the great majority of the global social work workforce. In the Republic of Ireland, 80% of social workers are female (Gartland, 2016). The respondents are approximately half female and half male. Twenty-one respondents comprise the sample: 17 social work practitioners and 4 social work educators. All the latter group identify as White Irish and, in respect of the 17 practitioners, 9 identify as White, with 8 identifying themselves as part of the Black African diaspora in Ireland. Three of the White practitioners would not identify as Irish: Jack is Australian, Jamie hails from the US and Meg is English.

The social work practitioners

Social work education and theoretical perspectives

All the White Irish-trained social workers believed their education had manifestly failed to equip them deal with 'issues' of 'race' and ethnicity when working with members of the Black African diaspora in Ireland. Most pointed out that their education had given them the impression that what they were taught had universal application. Their encounters

Table 6.1: The seventeen social work practitioners

Alternative name/gender	'Race'/ethnicity	Approximate age
Alice (F)	White Irish	60s
Alison (F)	White Irish	50s
Anne (F)	White Irish	30s
Breck (M)	Black African	30s
Eddie (M)	Black African	30s
Grace (F)	Black African	20s
Jack (M)	White Australian	30s
Jamie (M)	White US	40s
Maguire (M)	White Irish	50s
Maria (F)	White Irish	20s
Marko (M)	Black African	30s
Meg (F)	White English	40s
Rese (F)	Black African	50s
Roti (F)	Black African	40s
Trio (F)	Black African	30s
Vito (M)	Black African	50s
Wayne (M)	White Irish	40s

Table 6.2: The four social work educators

Alternative name/gender	'Race'/ethnicity	Approximate age
Kim (F)	White Irish	Early 40s
Michael (M)	White Irish	Late 40s
Thomas (M)	White Irish	60s
Tina (F)	White Irish	50s

with Black African service users exposed the limitations of their social work education and training at various levels. Alice, a White Irish–trained respondent, commented:

'While there was some exposure to theoretical perspectives, such as critical theory, feminist approaches and postmodern approaches (often from the writings of Michel Foucault on subjugated epistemologies etc.), no explicit attempt was made to critically link such theoretical perspectives to experiences such as colonisation, and how this colonisation (evidenced in epistemologies and methodologies in research and practice) plays out in the construction of social work as a profession and in the co-construction of the personal and professional identities of White, western social workers. Explicit consciousness of such issues was left up to the optional reading of the individual student and practitioner.'

One of the Black African respondents, Breck, commented on his experience as follows:

'I do not feel that my social work training equipped me in any way to deal with issues related to "race" and ethnicity: for example with Black African clients. I completed my social work training at X University in Ireland in 1993. Back in the day we did not cover anything in relation to ethnicity on the course. Maybe they do now, but not in my day! For my MA in Social Work, though, I decided to focus my research on a comparative study of social work training in Ireland and in my home country in Africa. I guess I was curious about differences and/or similarities in the education of social workers in my home country and in Ireland. Even there they did not teach anything about ethnicity and working with Black African clients: maybe they didn't need to because they are in Africa? I am not sure, but it just wasn't on the curriculum. What I found, though, was that the modules taught in my country mirrored my social work training in Ireland. What equipped me to work with Black African clients really was not my social work training, but rather my own knowledge and experience of being a Black African.'

A White practitioner, Alison, avowed:

'There was an implied universalism in the curricula and, from what our lecturers said, I was led to believe what we learned could be applied to *any* client. In my first professional encounters with Black African families, however, I discovered that not to be the case: there were essential differences with Irish culture especially in terms of how mental health is conceptualised and experienced. There was also no emphasis in our education that social work is a *political* activity, given its relationship with the state and the clients. A basic grasp and interest of politics is important when working with immigrants as all supports and services relating to them involve *implementing political decisions disguised as policy*. Most of us graduated with no interest in politics. Even social policy was taught as an add-on and it mostly dwelt on social welfare entitlements for our "traditional clients".' (Original emphases)

The Black African respondents, mostly from former English colonies, reported that they had a good working knowledge of western European culture and norms, on account of their colonial experience and education. They felt that they had an 'advantage', in fact, in that they were well versed in their own Black African cultures as well as western social norms and practices: perhaps they had 'double vision' (see also the Appendix). Breck noted that equality and respect for cultural difference in Ireland mostly referred to the Travelling community and people who identified as gay and lesbian.

'I trained as a social worker in Zim [Zimbabwe] and I relocated to work in Ireland. There was no difference in the education. I hit the ground running. In Ireland, however, the teaching somehow steered clear of racial and ethnic inequality as it related to Black people and instead focused mostly on Travellers and gay people.'

Another Black African respondent, Eddie, added:

'Although they teach equality, treating people equally etc., when you look at how equality is taught, it's from a very narrow, liberal perspective. I felt that there was an unconscious awareness among some of our professors that some of what they were teaching was replete with racist assumptions. However, I then came to realise that even the supposedly enlightened professors themselves were products of the same Irish society socialised in historical and contemporary assumptions of racial superiority prevalent in much of the Euro-western cultural hemisphere of which Ireland is a part.'

Anne, a White respondent having been trained beyond Ireland, offered a different view:

'I completed my education in Australia and cultural competency, cultural awareness and critical theories were a very significant part of the learning. Much of the knowledge regarding "race" was focused on the First Nation/aboriginal people. It led me to understand that not all western theories could be applied across practice areas, especially with Non-Whites. On placement, there were specific [assessed] pieces to complete regarding how to practise social work in a culturally safe and appropriate way. Although there was nothing specific to Black African clients, I was exposed to learning about critical multiculturism, critical race theory, critical whiteness theory and I undertook fieldwork with non-White clients. That kind of learning awakened in me what it meant to be "White": through critical self-reflexivity I was able to become culturally "sober".'

Nearly all of these respondents had encountered the 'cultural competence' concept, referred to in Chapter 2, and they had a 'general idea' as to what it was, but there were sharp differences about it. It also emerged that most of the respondents tended to define the concept at the 'individual' practitioner level, while acknowledging that it needed to be supported at 'organisational' and 'sociopolitical' levels. For example, many of the respondents remarked, in similar ways, that upon returning to work after attending 'cultural competence' workshops they found no structures available to support and embed the idea. In short, while one-day workshops 'raised their awareness', they felt that such training did very little to actually 'translate' that 'awareness' into meaningfully effective and better 'cross-cultural' social work interactions. A White Irish respondent, Alice, powerfully confided:

'I abhor the term "cultural competence" as it appears to suggest that history and culture can be reduced to a technical function which can then be taught to those in power so that they can be "politically correct" when it comes to working with culturally different clients. I know that I will never understand what it means to be a Black African because first "Black African" is also a construction which is blind to differences in ethnicity and culture in the vast expanse that is Africa. Second, it recreates the notion that a White, western professional can, with some adjustments, work with any group without first seriously addressing the profession's own history and culture. This is not possible in my opinion.'

Rese, a Black respondent, added:

'I think it [cultural competence] also involves having an understanding how being from a different culture affects service delivery to those who are culturally different. So, when I say "cultural competence" has different components or "arms and legs", I mean that both the social worker and the organisation they work for must buy into working in a culturally competent way because if there is no management support or organisational support the idea of "cultural competence" won't work. Staff require organisational support to develop and support policies that are geared to promoting "cultural competence".'

Anne was dismissive of the proliferating 'cultural competence' workshops:

'We are told that to be culturally competent at the individual practitioner levels then you must have knowledge, skills and the right attitude. Given that no foreign cultural knowledge is taught in our courses and my attitude is shaped by negative stereotypes of Blacks from childhood, education and media images, you tell me how do I acquire the required knowledge and attitude? I know you will say "oh they now have cultural competency courses". I can tell you there is no way one can attend a one-day workshop and suddenly become proficient in "cultural competence"; it is all so tokenistic. The question that needs to be asked is this: "have situations of cultural misunderstanding been reduced in interactions with Black African families because of the one-day workshops on 'cultural competence'"?' Of course not. It must be an embedded enduring part of your psyche/mentality. I do not think most of us are "culturally competent" even after attending the one-day workshops!'

Maria, a White Irish respondent who trained outside Ireland, reported:

'In my training "cultural competence" began with self-awareness and awareness of one's own Whiteness, privileges, biases etc. "Cultural competency" was focused on creating a "safe space" for one's culture to be acknowledged, expressed and explored. Often the conversation shifts the power balance of the relationship and the client will begin to discuss oppression and marginalisation of the culture/ "race". Yes, culture-grams were used when I practised overseas. I have yet to come across these in use in Ireland. Were they useful? Yes, in capturing some socio-cultural experiences that could not be captured by traditional family assessment tools. However, I do not think their use – alone – will make one "culturally competent".'

Jamie, a White male practitioner originally from North America, commented:

'My long experience in North America had erroneously led me to believe that it was now accepted and common practice in most of the developed world, including Ireland, that one cannot faithfully practise social work with multicultural clients without a truthful account of the history of social work's complicity in the colonial project. For some in the Americas it often helps to induce a certain guilt on the part of some practitioners. Appreciation of "race"/ethnic difference sensitively can only come from an appreciation of equal recognition or other ethnic cultural lens.'

Another White respondent, Jack, shared his experience of barriers to 'cultural competence':

'There are many identified barriers to developing "culturally competent" practitioners and organisations ... From my experience the barriers include: lack of funding for additional staff for community outreach, lack of applications from culturally diverse professionals, lack of knowledge about diverse cultures, and culture groups not being served sensitively, failure to prioritise "cultural competence" and to budget for it. Also having staff who are not comfortable with cultural diversity or who do not value cultural awareness and who stereotype culturally diverse individuals.'

As we can begin to discern, there were also different opinions on the utility and effectiveness of the various 'cultural competence' models: for example, the use of culture-grams and information guides. It was felt that some of the models, such as the information guides, tended to stereotype people and were, therefore, unacceptable in social work. Others insisted they found such models useful for their practice and dismissed 'stereotyping' argument as too 'academic' and not grounded in the realities of 'practice situations'. As an example, those familiar with culture-grams argued that they helped them to avoid stereotyping and generalising families from the same cultures. As for information guides, some argued that, in practice, knowing the basic 'dos' and 'don'ts' in respect of a specific cultural group (and sometimes relying on cultural mediators) could determine the success of an 'intervention'.

Most respondents reported not having heard of or used culture-grams, information guides and other culturally specific assessment models mentioned. Nearly all the Black African social workers felt that they benefited from a broader knowledge base underpinning both western and Black African families' worldviews. This, they claimed, enabled them to intervene 'unaided by models': rather, they relied on a more spontaneous humanistic spirit when they provided social work services. They also warned against the dangers of relying on tools such as 'information and culture guides', and the case of Victoria Climbié was mentioned in this context. In this tragic instance, a social worker, perhaps having their perceptions informed by such 'guides', falsely understood that the child's behaviour and cowed and subservient disposition were 'typical' of a Black African child interacting with an adult carer (Garrett, 2006).

Rese, a Black practitioner, felt that if only White practitioners 'gave up' their false, inherited notions of racial superiority there would be no need for them to require 'cultural competency' models. Such practitioners need to be 'humble enough' to recognise what Black people, around the world, have achieved. She also argued that it was a 'typical White' response to now want to 'study how to be competent' with Black people. Moreover, this risked objectifying Black people. In this context, she drew attention to the work of Kumagai and Lympson (2009):

"'Cultural competence" is not a static requirement to be checked off. It is something beyond the somewhat rigid categories of knowledge, skills, and attitudes. [Rather it refers to] the continuous refinement and fostering of a type of thinking and knowing, a critical consciousness of self, others and the world … critical consciousness posits that the thinking subject does not exist in isolation, but rather in relationship to others in the world. The development of critical consciousness involves a reflective awareness of the differences in power and privilege and the inequities that are embedded in social relationships and the fostering of a reorientation of perspective towards a commitment to social justice.'

When it was put to Rese that some of her social work colleagues did not think that the majority of practitioners were 'culturally competent', she replied:

'I agree that there is a huge difference between being able to define "cultural competency" from textbook definitions and actually knowing how to decipher, for example, culturally appropriate eye contact, the distance you stand from a person, nonverbal communication and non-western verbal communication styles etc. when someone who is not from your culture and does not speak English is in front of your face shouting, gesticulating etc. From my experience, knowledge on its own is not enough, that's why the information guides on certain ethnic minorities, and practice guidelines, have largely not been effective. One has to spend some time with the client group or use home visits to learn to unlearn White habits of privilege that often act as barrier to bi-cultural knowledge.'

Vito, a Black African, differed slightly:

'Although I consider myself generally bi-cultural in that I can speak English and can relate to my White Irish clients, I concede there are some aspects of their culture that I do not consider myself competent to understand or make sense of. For example, when I asked one of my White clients why they came to me for even minor things that their brothers/sisters or extended family members could assist them with, the client told me they did not want to dependent on other family members, and in any case every family member is often busy minding their own business!'

Nearly all respondents reported 'gaps' in what they were taught in college and what they encountered in their social work practice. One of the White respondents, hinting at what Chris Jones (1996) identifies as a certain 'anti-intellectualism' present in social work practice *and* social work education, stated:

'I found to my amazement, and my cost, that few if any of my student colleagues had any knowledge of what Lucy Irigaray called the "master narrative of western thought" ... that is philosophy from the conventional White male perspective. Being as how they had no formation whatsoever in philosophy of any hue, they could hardly be held responsible for being naive in relation to such issues as colonisation, epistemologies, the construction of professional social work and its subsequent development. I also found that most of my lecturers had little or no knowledge of, and less interest in, these issues. When I tried to raise these issues, I was considered, "arrogant" ... "too intellectual" ... to be a social worker by some, if not most of, those who taught me and at best a bore by my student colleagues. To survive I ceased to talk about these issues.'

Eddie, a Black African discussing the 'gap' between practice and education, added:

'There is no attempt to anchor the ethical principles taught on indigenous knowledge systems and culture e.g. *Ubuntu* [see also Chapter 3]. The ethical humanist principles of social work are presented in academia in a manner that appears to suggest that they are foreign concepts and yet these are part of the African way of life. For example, the way human rights are taught in western communities suggest the westerners have *discovered* some invention, yet every culture has always had its own notions of human dignity and rights. It is also evident that people from different cultures tend to observe and uphold those notions of human dignity and rights that are sanctioned by their respective cultures. Also, the contradictions in theories such as postmodernism when applied to ethnic minorities are not explicitly explained, e.g. how the theory supports the notion of multiple truths, whilst at the same time negating the particularity of collective historical lived experiences often reflected in ethnic minorities who see their cultures as boundaries of resistance to foreign cultural impositions.'

Reflecting on what she was taught – and not taught – at university, Anne, a White social worker, responded:

'There was nothing specific to each "race" or nationality as such in areas such as bereavement support or supporting mental health recovery. In theory you got the impression what was taught in college had a *universal* application, yet when you get into practice the differences and inadequacies of what is taught in terms of how cultural differences impact social work is like day and night. Being taught that we need to treat all people equally and bracket our own prejudices is easier said than done when you have been brought up in a society where Black Africans and other minority groups have been constructed as inferior and that mentality is reinforced by some biblical scriptures where Blackness is equated to the Devil ... plus media images of negative stories from Africa.'

Alison, a White female social worker who had worked in England in the 1980s, drew on her own experience as a victim of anti-Irish racism to observe:

'Back in college we were taught to bracket our feelings, prejudices etc. However, considering how, as an Irish person, I had suffered racism and other forms of humiliation from the generality of English people, I honestly found it difficult to bracket out feelings of hatred and prejudice against English clients that I came across in my work. So yes, the gaps are there between theory and practice. In relation to my work with Black African clients and colleagues, my earlier experiences as a "victim" of racism have helped me appreciate their predicament and relate better with them because I once was in a similar position at some point in my life.' (See also Garrett, 1998; 2004)

Grace, a Black African social worker, provided the following summary:

'Current education is incapable of teaching White students to unlearn or to even disturb their inherited entrenched conventional ignorance of the impact of their White-supremacy [conditioned] upbringing! How else could it [social work education] do so, when it is the product of, and dominated by, one ethnocentric worldview purporting to speak for all?'

Black and White respondents confirmed the very low numbers of Black African students being accepted onto social work courses. The most common response was that of Breck, who had previously been a social work student in a university outside of Dublin:

'Students? 99% White indigenous Irish with sometimes 1% Black African. Some years they do not even take any Black Africans. Staff? Mainly Irish, few Europeans (with a better understanding of issues of ethnicity and "race"). In my postgraduate course in Ireland I was the only "foreign-born" and the rest were Irish.'

Anne, who trained overseas, illuminated a very different picture in that the cultural composition of teaching staff was very diverse: "Staff members were Australian, English and Aboriginal … The students were from UK, Ireland, Australia, Vietnam, Singapore, China and Africa."

Praxis

Turning to practice-related issues, all the respondents reported that their 'race'/ethnicity was a significant factor impacting on the work they undertook from day to day. For example, Alison had the following view:

'I am Irish, White, female, able bodied, heterosexual, middle class, Christian and educated in a Eurocentric way. The profession I practise is western in orientation [and] has its cultural history and perhaps unconscious. These all play out in all my interactions with clients: how else could it be? It is not, in my opinion, a matter of delineating how this affects my work and thus ridding myself of it. [This is] an impossibility! But it's more about becoming aware and reflective of where this impinges negatively in my work with service users.'

Reflecting on her work, Trio commented:

'As a Black African, my ethnicity is significant when I encounter Black African clients in that I can relate to the experiences and circumstances that underpin their worldview and I can also understand the experience and conditions which some of my clients would have gone through in their countries of origin. Issues related to mental health and bereavement support and post-hospitalisation discharge planning are some areas which would not make sense to my White Irish colleagues. Most of the times they end up consulting me in such situations.'

Another Black African female respondent, Rese, gave this response:

'I am conscious that my cultural background influences the way I see the presenting problem. I don't really think I can separate that from myself … it's part of who I am. I must, therefore, be conscious of how this can influence my work positively or negatively. My cultural background is the lens through which I see the world. It is important in social work, though, for me to see acknowledge other lenses through which people see their world. When I work with Irish families, I find that they are quite receptive, they don't think I know about Ireland, so they like to tell me stuff. There are things they tell me that they probably wouldn't tell an Irish social worker because they think they are educating me on things I ought to know. I find that helps me to build relationships and it's a good entry point into getting to know a family.'

A White respondent, Maria, observed:

'In my experience, "use of self" and "self-awareness" is most important here. I have a responsibility as a social worker to practise in way where my cultural and ethnic background are undoubtedly present, yet are managed through the relationship. During my training, acknowledging the "personal self" in the "professional self" was significant. Also, accepting one's own cultural identity in a bid to acknowledge and accept the culture of others.'

Dynamics pertaining to 'race' and ethnicity did not, though, simply operate at an abstract level, because they helped to shape social work assessments and related forms of intervention. Eddie, a Black African respondent, argued: "Yes, I think African ethnicity is a significant factor in assessment and interventions ... an assessment that does not consider a person's ethnicity misses a major part of who the person is and, I think, you miss the specific issues that affect ethnic minorities." Maria, a White Irish respondent, added:

'Despite limited exposure to Black African clients, I always consider ethnicity as a factor when completing any social work assessment. I try and acknowledge culture and diversity where possible and do this in a culturally sensitive way. I usually start by confessing my lack of knowledge about their culture and cultural practices and let them know if I said or did anything that they may consider rude or insensitive they should understand that it is not intentional. In other words, I cover myself by apologising in advance for my ignorance, real or perceived. I am also aware the Black African clients are also, perhaps, ignorant about some of our White western ways of knowing and doing things. So, any cultural misunderstanding can be a clash of ignorance from both parties.'

As for 'cultural misunderstandings', looking at this issue from a Black African perspective, Eddie was alert to a whole range of issues:

'The ones most cited are different understandings of childhood, childrearing/child protection, and gender roles, the role of social services/social workers and homosexuality/sexual roles. Greeting and showing affection is another area of great difference. Hugging and kissing is mostly a western way. There have been situations suggesting some White social workers thought Black African mothers did not love their children or had bonding problems because they did not hug or kiss them in public! There are also differences in deciphering what eye contact means in different cultures, e.g. in western cultures if you do not look the person you are talking to in the eye, you are generally believed to be lying. Surprisingly, in most Black African cultures sustained eye contact is considered confrontational. There are also differences in death and bereavement rituals and the conceptualisation of health and well-being: especially in relation to mental health. There are other noted cultural differences relating to keeping pets.' (See also the discussion on Dalikeni's work in Chapter 5)

Turning to intersectional considerations, Alison, a White Irish respondent, observed:

'I have been influenced the work of Toni Morrison in *Beloved* and by bell hooks directly in terms of social work practice where the issues of gender and "race" interact. These writers again awaken, for this reader, the price paid by women of Black African origin for dominant White male western discourses and epistemologies.'

Vito, a Black male social worker, commented on the theme of cultural differences as follows:

'The meaning of confidentiality can be different in different cultures. Given that Black Africans are generally from a community-based society, perhaps their view of confidentiality tends to be less individualistic compared to western views? I have no doubt that knowing such cultural differences can be very helpful in assessments and interventions. This brings me to issues of applying White values in formulating practice guidelines with Black people. It does not work, as values tend to be context specific and are open to different interpretations.'

Maria, a White female social worker, shared her experiences of the cultural differences impinging on fostering services:

'I learn a lot about cultural differences when fostering Black children with White families. The idea of a pet as a friend is very un-African and pets are never allowed to live inside the house near humans … How does all this affect social work assessments and interventions? There been some instances where White families who kept pets, such as snakes and owls, would not understand why Black African children were reluctant to be fostered with such families. White families did not realise that in most traditional Black African belief systems snakes, owls and such other pets are associated with witchcraft.'

Organisational structures within the capitalist racial state

Perhaps unsurprisingly, DP − responsible for prompting and sustaining mental health problems − was often mentioned by the respondents as one of the prime organisational mechanisms illuminating the crass and harmful functioning of the capitalist racial state (see also Chapters 3 and 5). Relatedly, asylum seekers not being able to work was viewed as a major obstacle impeding their participation. Additionally, the HRC was a prominent issue, as were difficulties in accessing suitable housing (see also Chapters 1 and 5). A range of other structural or systemic issues were highlighted as blighting the lives of many Black African and other minority ethnic people in contact with social work services. Marko, a Black African respondent, maintained:

'Children without "refugee" status leave care and live in DP and are not eligible for aftercare support and do not receive state funding for Third Level education [also known as higher or university education outside of Ireland]. This policy is also related to children leaving care on turning 18, then not being granted legal immigration status. They are then returned to DP or deported, yet they would have spent a big chunk of their life here. This policy is not only inhuman, it contradicts all that talk about human rights and the child welfare and protection legislation in the state.'

Roti, a Black female social worker, stated:

'Yes, I have provided them information regarding their rights and entitlements and where they can seek redress should they be denied the enjoyment of these rights, but I cannot change any of the policies that I find oppressive to such clients. It's sad really that I must tell them I only follow the law as laid in policies and legislation.'

The disproportionate number of Black African children in state care also illustrated how the workings of the capitalist racial state can be interpreted as impacting on and shaping the seemingly mundane quotidian, as this relates to service provision for children and families. Rese, a Black African female respondent, argued:

'Firstly, I think this is to do with how we assess Black African families and the assessment tools we use. I mean, it's like trying to fit a square peg in a round hole: this does not work ... We use the same assessment tools for Irish families as for Black African families, but these families come from different cultural backgrounds. Now how does that make sense? I don't believe we are being fair to these families.'

Trio, a Black African female respondent, related present ways of engaging with Black African families to ways in which oppressive state institutions engaged with marginalised and stigmatised groups in the past in Ireland (see also Chapter 5). She also argued that social work interventions needed to take on a much more supportive and less punitive character. Expanding at length, she maintained:

'I think the high numbers of children taken into care are indicative of injustice in the distribution of social, cultural, political and economic power. To me, the high numbers are also indicative of a historically abusive and punitive system. I mean, look at what happened in the Magdalene Laundries, look at what is happening in DP, it's the same old story: the poor are punished for being poor and it is as though they are the cause of their own problems but surely this is not true. A system and culture that controls and punishes families exists especially in child protection in Ireland. Now don't get me wrong, I am not saying that people should be allowed to abuse their children or anything like that. But there is a role for social workers to educate families if they feel they are doing something that gets them in trouble with the law. More importantly, I think that there is need for a change in mind-set in how we assess the "significant harm" that leads to children being taken into "care". On paper, in legislation, we are assured that taking a child into care is the last resort, but where Black African children are concerned, yet we seem to resort to taking kids into state care very quickly without putting in enough family support first or exploring options to allow children to remain at home. Most Black African families experience migratory issues, including resettlement into a new country, and so taking children [from such families] into care without adequately educating them about the laws of the land is neglectful on the part of social work.'

Anne, a White respondent, confided:

'It is difficult to know [why there are a disproportionate number of Black African families in contact with child protection services] and it wouldn't be fair to say that it is due to cultural misunderstandings etc. Tusla are working to bring in "Signs of Safety" as an assessment framework. Developed in Western Australia, it recognises family strengths and it is a framework that works to identify and acknowledge cultural needs and differences. There are some positive changes happening.' (See also Turnell, 2011)

Alice, a White Irish practitioner, also pointed to more historically entrenched ways of working with those viewed as troublesome, even parasitic, groups in the past:

'DP implicitly creates a view of those in such provision as, at best, having a contested claim to asylum in this country and possibly "spongers" and "free loaders": a contemporary equivalent of "least eligibility" central to the Poor Law (1834). It is linked also to the work of Bentham and the notion of the Panopticon later critiqued by Foucault. "We" will be overrun by economic migrants [said ironically] … That "we" was part of the colonising apparatus in Africa and, with our current western economic and developmental policies and their environmental impact, "we" have responsibilities in relation to these people who are looking for asylum or a "better way of life".'

Rese, a Black African respondent, was also keen to make the connection between the past and the present. The perception of – and dominant modalities of managing – asylum seekers, for example, had to been understood in the context of past practices in Ireland:

'I think the issue of so-called "direct provision" symbolises a perpetuation of a culture of institutional abuse that has long-standing roots in Irish society. Except this time around what is disappointing is that, despite past failures by the state to protect the vulnerable members of society, no lessons seem to have been learned. DP has been signalled as the "21st century Magdalene Laundries". [However] there are mixed views from the public about DP: some people feel that DP is justified, and it should remain that way. Others have lobbied for the system to be shut.'

Breck, a Black African social worker, argued that

'The structural conditions that come with DP lead to child protection issues and this has led to negative stereotypes being held by the public and professionals on child rearing and protection practices of *all* people of Black African stock. The system is not likely to end if someone or some entity is profiting from it. If it became a liability cost-wise it would be gone yesterday!'

Many of the comments from the respondents reflected their views on how institutionally racist structures (evidenced by historically embedded organisational cultures, policies, practices and theoretical underpinnings within the Bourdieusian 'field') inform social work responses to working with Black African service users. In this context, their frequently insightful remarks also relate to the role of social work's contemporary regulatory body, CORU, and to professional supervision. Alice, a White respondent, referred to the potential role of the social work Code of Ethics (CORU, 2019) and existing policies and so-called 'best practices' in addressing issues of 'race'.

'Yes [these may assist], but, since issues of dominant epistemologies are not explicitly addressed, these ethics and policies are imbued with such epistemological naivety, yet they currently guide professional practice and so the circle begins again. Social work sees itself as the "good un" wanting to "empower" clients and so on, but until matters such as our own history and culture, as a profession, are critically addressed, I don't have much faith in the possibility that Codes of Ethics and related policies are likely to result in the "empowerment" of anyone!'

In commenting on the same issue and how it 'played out' on the ground in professional interactions 'in the office', one of the Black African respondents, Rese, reported:

'We do not discuss these issues at team meetings. It is as if issues of "race" and racism don't exist and yet these issues are alive and well in Ireland and in social work — at least the families we work with experience these issues. We live in a very racist country, but no, we don't talk about these issues, at least not within our organisational structures.'

This view was shared by Wayne, a White Irish male respondent:

'I believe in conversations about "race" and cultural differences in organisational settings, there are policies (such as "Dignity at Work" policies) which are meant to address such issues, but their implementation depends on the Team Leader or Principal Social Worker. Such policies also have weaknesses, as the burden of proof is on the complainant and effectiveness can, thus, depend on the attitude of managers and this can, of course, vary across organisations. I have seen situations where complainants are asked to name witnesses. If you are the only Black person in that organisation you can have difficulties having any of the White colleagues seen to be taking sides against their own, especially if the alleged offender is another senior manager. So, the current structures are weak and can be manipulated as they can turn out to be a game of numbers, [with much depending on] who is willing to stick their neck out in support of the complainant.'

Despite the rhetoric often featured in the various 'mission statements', the majority of respondents seemed rather sceptical in respect of the role of various regulatory bodies in dealing effectively with issues circulating around racism. Trio, a Black African respondent, added:

> 'there is not a mention of such issues in either the CORU standards or the IASW guidelines for social workers. There is a functional tendency to refer to generic anti-oppressive and anti-discriminatory practice expressed in very "liberal" ways, yet this does not radically alter the status quo. Racial inequality for Blacks does not seem to attract the same interest and attention as equality for LGBTs. Whilst not, of course, minimising any oppressions and inequality suffered by LGBT communities, as a Black African I speak for a lot of us when I say racial discrimination is the top mechanism of oppression for us Black Africans in Ireland!'

Vito offered this view:

> 'The only positive aspect of CORU regulations for the majority of my Black clients is the "fitness to practice" thing. They feel it goes a long way in protecting them from open racial abuse/actions from White social workers who now have to think twice before openly saying/doing anything that can be proved to be racist. But again, it's like a double-edged sword, as it can also be used by White clients/supervisors to victimise Black practitioners.'

In their comments on professional supervision, most respondents felt some supervisors, especially the older generation, did *not* seem to understand its supportive role. In some cases, supervision seemed to become merely a tool to control, victimise or frustrate the supervisee; particularly if the practitioner had previously made complaints against the supervisor. Some Black African respondents also suggested that in situations where a White supervisor would have preferred a White practitioner to supervise, supervision could become a mechanism to undermine and frustrate the Black practitioner.

Professional supervision often appeared to be something of a 'ritual' aimed at merely monitoring if the front-line practitioner was meeting their 'output targets' in line with the neoliberal 'business logics' now prevalent within social work in Ireland and elsewhere (see also Chapter 5). Relatedly, in the context of multicultural practice, the respondents contended that, often, regular professional supervision furnished very little by way of useful advice, as the supervisors themselves were largely White, with no sense or understanding of Black African diasporic communities and their diverse cultures. Rese, a female Black African respondent, claimed:

'Supervision, to me is like a shopping list. You go in, you discuss how many cases you have on your caseload, then you might be given more cases or some you will be advised to close, and that's it. The new system makes managers more interested in closing more cases to show that they are meeting targets and demonstrating "efficiency" in terms of productivity.'

Anne, a White Irish respondent, felt that there was an identifiable generational dimension impacting on supervision when issues pertaining to 'race' and culture were significant issues impacting on social work assessments and intervention planning:

'I don't have any Black African clients now. However, in previous roles I was not supported in practice on how to respond to different cultures. It also depends on your supervisor's understanding of the role of supervision. Most supervisors actually practised a long time ago, before Ireland was a multicultural society, and they have no idea how to support a practitioner who is experiencing challenges of a cross-cultural nature. This predisposes them to apply the 'one size fits all' in dealing with cultural diversity because that is all they know from when they last practised. It is not surprising that they are often defensive of the status quo and feel uncomfortable that as senior staff there is something new, they do not know or can talk about authoritatively. There are some, of course, of the same age group who have worked outside the country or are just naturally well disposed to difference. These have been helpful in relation to cross-cultural advice.'

Debates within society at large and the role of the media – and its focus on the presence of foreigners, particularly Black Africans – were also interpreted as impacting on organisational responses. Nearly all the respondents agreed that the role and impact of the media was very negative. Anne felt that dominant perceptions of migrants occasionally filtered down into social work interactions with users of services who were White Irish:

'Immigrants and refugees are viewed very negatively in the media and are portrayed as a "drain on society". Particularly with the US government dominating the media: immigrants and refugees are discussed within a fear-based agenda [and there is the dominant idea] that people should "stay in their own countries". It can impact our work, particularly when working with Irish clients. Some have sometimes expressed frustration at their needs not being met and those of "foreign nationals" being met and with their being "given everything for nothing".'

All of the respondents agreed that the images of Africa, in the past and present, were negative and they largely blamed the historical and ideological construction of Black Africans as an 'inferior race' for being partly responsible for the way the Black African diaspora has been and continues to be presented and treated in most western countries. Marko, a Black respondent, argued:

'For decades Africa has been presented as a country in need of "help" and "charity". It is always presented as a "dependent", lacking capacity and agency. This has been very undermining of dialogue and respect between Europe and Africa. Indeed, even speaking of this huge continent as though it were "one thing" is itself indicative of cultural ignorance.'

Anne, a White respondent, also noted that those from Black Africa were frequently perceived as being marinated in poverty and other hardships and such depictions could negatively impact on interactions involving social workers and members of the Black African diaspora: "Africa is often discussed in the media in relation to famine and poverty and these stereotypes and perceptions are present today. It can lead people to *assume* the life story of an African person before *hearing it*." Alice sarcastically commented: "It would be unlikely if the historical and contemporary images ... 'poor child victim needing to be rescued from starvation' and 'sponger/economic migrant who is here taking our social welfare' ... did not impact on perceptions of African social work clients in Ireland."

Turning to the idea of Afrophobia, a majority of respondents were – perhaps surprisingly – hearing of it for the first time during the research interviews. More generally, they agreed that they could never 'talk about racism without condemning it'. Having encountered racism, racist service users *and* racist colleagues, some of the Black African respondents had very strong and emotional views. White Irish respondents who had worked overseas and had experience of having to face racism identified with the 'pain' and 'discomfort' associated with racism now encountered by members of the Black African diaspora in Ireland.

Trio, a female Black practitioner, acknowledged witnessing Afrophobia among her White counterparts, especially when they had to interview men who were Black or from a minority ethnic group:

'It exists. You can see and hear that fear and almost "touch" it. You witness the extra "precautions" they take. This often includes alerting colleagues to be "on standby". Sometimes, they [White colleagues] request someone to sit with them in the room and they ensure that all the panic alarms are working prior to such meetings. What is interesting is that they rarely take such "extra measures" when interviewing White

Irish men. They seem to think I am brave because I see male Black African clients without taking such "extreme precautions" as they do. So yes, Afrophobia exists among some White social workers.'

Despite not volunteering specific 'case' examples, some of the respondents detected fearfulness of Black African service users. Maguire, a White Irish respondent, reported:

'I was embarrassed when some White colleagues had to request four police officers to go and remove a young girl from a Black African family. The excuse was that there were fears of violent resistance from Black African families. Hence, the justification for an excessive show of force to "send the message" that any violent resistance was futile. One of my White colleagues remarked that "Blacks were more prone to be violent than White people"!'

Significantly, given some of the main preoccupations in this book, White Irish practitioners who had no migration diasporic experience themselves tended to be defensive and suggested there was 'no way' Irish people could be 'racist', given that they too had been colonised by England. Reflecting some of the issues that we raised in Chapter 5, one of the respondents asserted that, had it not been for the 'heroic efforts' of Irish missionaries and Irish foot soldiers in faraway places such as India and other parts of the colonial empire, British colonialism would probably not have succeeded to the extent that it did.

Especially because of the 'non-coverage' of this issue by the mainstream media in Ireland, all of the Black African respondents viewed the term Afrophobia and Michael's (2016) associated research as largely helpful in highlighting the racism specifically targeting Black Africans. According to some respondents, though, using terms such as 'Afrophobia' risked discursively camouflaging its ugly material impact. For example Vito, a male Black African practitioner, maintained:

'Characterising racism as just a "phobia" amounts to relegating it to just another "fear" of ordinary things or as "illusions", and perhaps [this implies that it does not warrant] urgent policy interventions at structural levels? The implication is that it can potentially be addressed through "clinical" or other "psychological interventions" at a merely individual level.'

Breck argued:

'Racism is about subjugation or ill-treatment. I believe it is built on feelings of lack adequacy about oneself: hence the need to be better than someone else. For there to be a "superior" anything there must be an "inferior" something. In other words, conceptually, "superiority" cannot exist in the absence of "inferiority". Perhaps that explains the need to construct "inferior races" even if they do truly not exist ... For racial "superiority" as a concept and "property" of Whiteness (associated with "privilege") not to vanish, it needs the "inferior other" that "Blackness" has been conveniently constructed for. The writings of Marimba Ani (1994) and the *Critique of Black Reason* (Mbembe, 2017) bear me out. Michael (2016), though, did a good job.' (See also Chapter 4 for a critical discussion on Ani's work)

When asked about Afrophobia, one White respondent, Jamie, remarked:

'Yes! I have heard of the term and it practically exists. I mean the "fear". It is an irrational fear or anxiety of Black bodies. It mostly originates from fears of colonial-era anxiety of savage slaves seeking retribution. However, when it comes to current racism what I know, as a White person who hears a lot of pub talk, is that there is a deep seated fear of being "swamped" or "outbred" by foreigners to the point of the White Irish becoming a minority in a country they call their own ... like what happened to the Aborigines.'

Some of the White respondents conceded that Afrophobia might amount to a genuine fear, while other, mostly Black, respondents dismissed this view as errant and racialised 'nonsense'. Vito's sarcastic and tongue-in-cheek response was as follows: "If it's true that they [White people] have such fears of becoming a minority one day, then that should be an incentive for them to treat us well now, so that when the tables turn in future, they won't have anything to worry about in terms of retribution!" A number of White Irish social workers felt that when immigrants arrived in Ireland they should try to 'fit in' to existing organisational and social structures. Wayne, a White male respondent, asserted:

'Is it not common sense that "when in Rome, you do as the Romans do"? So, when "foreigners" come to Ireland, they should try to fit into whatever structures they find in place. Our job as social workers should be to try to facilitate them to do that by attending to transitional individual maladaptive behaviours. By coming to Ireland, they have consciously or unconsciously chosen to identity with Ireland, or at least embrace things that identify with being "Irish". The same applies to my Black African social work colleagues: when they come here and work for the Health Service Executive (HSE), they assume the same social work identity as me and, as employees, they are bound by whatever organisational cultures and structures that are already in place. The current organisational structures, whilst not perfect in my view, promote a standard social identity for immigrant clients and a standard professional identity for social workers, "Black" and "White" alike.'

Two other White respondents made similar points: if, it was argued, one is a *guest* in another person's home, is it not conventional wisdom that you follow the host's 'house rules'? This logic implied, of course, that immigrants are merely Irish 'guests', expected to unquestioningly follow local laws and hegemonic cultural mores. Most of the Black African social workers, along with some of their White Irish colleagues, such as Maria, disagreed with this notion. She maintained:

'There has to be a serious questioning of professional identity, its origins and the practices that flow from a "standard identity": does "one size fit all"? Must everyone who lives in Rome become a Roman and/ or act as if he or she were Roman? Why the assumption that it is the immigrants who fail to adapt without even pausing to think that it could be our "traditional" organisational structures and systems, that were designed based on our societal ethnic culture and norms at a time when there no ethnic minorities in our societies, that are now failing to accommodate them in meeting their culturally different needs? What does that kind of thinking say about the education and training of our social workers?'

Grace, a Black African social worker, also referred to 'double standards' at work here: in expecting Black Africans to do what '(White) Romans' do when in '(White) Rome', yet, when the same '(White) Romans' arrived in what we might term '(Black) Rome' (Black Africa) they rarely appear to 'do' as the '(Black) Romans'. She further questioned why it was always Black people – everywhere – who had to adapt to accommodate White people. Addressing the organisational structures at universities providing social work education, she observed that:

'The existing status quo, represented by current organisational structures at social work universities, contradicts the often-heard and lofty rhetoric of "social justice", "equality", the "humanitarian" ethos, "anti-oppressive practice", "anti-discriminatory practice" and so on that social work supposedly stands for. In terms of educational justice, there are no mechanisms to guard against the continued biased recruitment of White students, White lecturers, White social services managers and the continued teaching of exclusively White ethnocentric theories. If enough Black students are not recruited, where are the Black practitioners, lecturers and managers going to come from?'

Vito, a Black African male practitioner, echoed Grace's sentiments:

'In social work employing agencies it's time there were more minorities in middle and top management positions, such as Team leaders and Principal Social Workers. As the largest social work employing organisation (as well as being a state entity), the HSE was supposed to "set the ball-rolling". However, there is no visible change at present.'

Perhaps alert to the setting up of the ASWI and the African Scholars' Association, Maria, a White social worker, offered a slightly different view. She suggested that Black African social workers should, instead, establish their own advocacy organisations:

'I hate the idea of White people continuing to speak and act on behalf of Black Africans and their problems. Sometimes this is fronted by "handpicked", pliant Black people representing the "master's voice" in a way reminiscent of current neocolonial practices in some parts of Africa. In such situations, the invisible "White hand" continues to pull the strings, from a distance, whilst hiding behind a convenient "Black face" ... [As] White people, we should only wait to be invited as partners if needed at all. Why the obsessive messianic complex? Is it not the same thinking that sees us spending huge sums of money on overseas aid or building houses for homeless people in South Africa when we are struggling with our own homelessness in Dublin?'

As well as relating to the inauguration of organisations like the ASWI, such ideas can be connected to the efforts of Black social workers in UK urban centres (such as Liverpool) in the 1980s who collectively established their own autonomous Black social workers' groups within social services in order to champion the rights of Black practitioners and service users.

Neoliberalism

All respondents acknowledged the deleterious impact of neoliberal socioeconomic policies on *all* users of social work services (see also Chapter 5). However, they suggested that Black African service users were more likely to experience neoliberal policies at their most 'extreme'. Hence, certain respondents reported that Black and ethnic minority service users were more likely to lose their jobs, face precarious employment or be unemployed when compared to White, Irish service users. This led them to be seen to be more 'welfare dependent' (Garrett, 2015; 2019). Policies, such as the HRC, created to prevent social welfare payments being paid to immigrants resulted in their struggling to sustain a 'normal' life. For example, this left them highly vulnerable to becoming homeless. Gnawing anxiety also tended to produce serious, chronic and debilitating mental health problems. It was pointed out that the HRC also affects, to a certain extent, returning Irish emigrants. However – unlike Black and other minority ethnic service users – most of these returnees will have family networks to support them in Ireland.

The impact of racism on the health and well-being of Black African people was also highlighted, especially by the majority of Black African social workers (and some of their White colleagues) who reported encountering Black service users who complained that racism was continually inducing psychological difficulties. Anti-racist and wider social policies, rhetorically based on equality and anti-discriminatory intent, remained largely 'unenforced' and this was partly to blame, it was argued. Overall, entrenched neoliberal rationality negatively impacted on and undermined decent social services – and related – provision. Maguire, a White male respondent, reflected this view:

'At organisational and individual service delivery levels, the paradoxes of current neoliberal policies of "austerity" are exposed. On one hand, in keeping with tenets of the policy, we are supposed to offer clients "choices" and other specific "client centred care packages": options which require substantial resources to effectively implement. On the other hand, budgets are cut: for example, in hospitals, meeting the needs of clients with different cultural, linguistic and religious needs requires a considerable investment in resources. Significant financial, human and other resources are needed to cater for special diets and medical care consistent for clients who are culturally diverse. We have, for example, Islamic women refusing to be seen by male doctors, a need to provide *halal* meals and so on. Culturally defined conceptualisations of health and health needs cannot be met within an "austerity" policy framework.'

Some of the practitioners suggested that it would be helpful to commission studies that explored, in forensic detail, the pernicious impact of neoliberal policies in Ireland (see, in this context, Bhattacharyya, 2015). Meg, a White female respondent, commented:

'I am not familiar with the research findings on "outcomes" for Black African clients of existing social and economic policies. My intuition, however, tells me that, one, policies are usually aimed at including the "excluded", but only to the point where the "excluded" (as a critical mass) do not infringe on the hegemony of the "included": particularly those who hold power among the "included". Two, these policies, for the main part, operate on implicit assumptions about "autonomy" and "the capacity of the individual" to overcome *all* and *every* adversity with the right "guidance" and "support". Conventionally, social work is constructed on a similar premise. This raises questions about the construction of "identity" and "subjectivity". For example, everyone is supposed to be capable of "human reason" as understood since the Enlightenment ... Whose fault is it if the individual "fails"? Again, these are questions which are conventionally considered to be "too academic" or "too intellectual" for social work practice.'

The areas most highlighted for radical change by practitioners were related to 'reforming' social work education and policies concerning the reception and resettlement of migrants. As for approaches to social work education and the professional formation of new social workers, Grace, a Black African respondent, argued that Whiteness, explored earlier in Chapter 3, warrants much deeper interrogation:

'We must find more radically persuasive strategies that link in with other international situations, as the problems we encounter have global dimensions that play out locally. The globalised anti-Black racism and unregulated capitalism that spawn "dual societies" also plays out locally and requires critical global engagement by public intellectuals. They should interrogate the nexus of Whiteness, White privilege and White epistemologies of ignorance and racism. I concur with arguments that premise philosophy of "race" and Whiteness on the deep ignorance of White people in matters of "race" and racism. I am also aware how racial capitalism and the consequent inheritance of habits of privilege and ignorance are further enhanced by unchallenged, skewed cognitive frameworks abetted by "White solipsism" affliction that emanates from assumptive notions of universality of the White perspective. The suggested cure ... Social work must return to *structural* social work as basis for effective policy and practice.'

Two other respondents, Maria and Trio, supported Grace's stance of reigniting what was termed 'radical placard waving activism' (see also Garrett, 2021). Both Maria and Trio referred to the success of the 2014 'No to cheap labour' campaign organised by SWAN and supported by various alliances drawn from service user groups and other civic organisations as a template for such future actions (Cuskelly et al, 2014). The majority agreed that the solidarity they had in the past was compromised by falling victim to the tensions inherent in trying to serve 'two masters': the state was their employer, yet they also tried to remain 'true' to the humanitarian and progressive values of the profession.

Regarding the reception and resettlement of migrants, there were concerns that the current policy is incoherent in that it was manifestly not anchored in a 'human rights' rights approach. The economic crash of 2008 was blamed for 'rolling back' earlier progress. A few respondents, such as Alice, a White Irish social worker, asserted: "I think we need to *stop* making policies and start thinking again about our own history as a dominant and subjugated people and begin to become aware, more than we presently are, of the historical and contemporary forces that construct the micro-physics of power."

The social work educators

Social work education and theoretical perspectives

All of the educator respondents agreed that their cultural and racial background – for Bourdieu, their 'habitus' – was a significant factor in shaping their approaches to social work education and the theoretical approach that they taught. The focal response was captured by Michael: "It is impossible to escape one's own cultural background and socialisation. It is an inevitable factor. Indeed, much of the conventional underlying social theory is rooted within a western cultural perspective." Relatedly, all the social work educators confirmed the absence of Black African teaching staff on social work courses in Ireland, generally and at their own educational institutions. While there may be some Black African students, their numbers are disproportionately low, given the demographic composition within Ireland. Thomas reported: "The staff group is culturally quite homogeneous – the clear majority are White Irish. The student group, however, is far more diverse. Over the last four years in particular, a significant number of students from Africa are attending." Commenting on the situation of teaching staff in more detail, Tina maintained that:

> 'In some Irish universities, Black African postgraduate students have been given "casual-teaching-assistant" roles on some social work courses, giving some an impression of intent and willingness to embrace cultural diversity, but even these Black African individuals have met with resistance from some, White lecturers and White students alike. It was also revealed that, most Black African social workers with PhD qualifications (and substantial social work experience) have ended up confined to teaching social care in Institutes of Technology colleges (not in Universities) ... The often-heard excuse is Ireland is relatively new to the idea of embracing diversity at various levels and that more time is needed. However, I disagree. Even when you hear that one of the Irish universities was taken to court for not promoting women to

be senior lecturers, none of these women were Black African women or Irish Travellers. That says it all.'

Echoing Tina's observation, two of the educator respondents felt that it was simply a 'matter of time' before Black Africans began to be adequately represented in these strategic roles within the Irish social work sector. It was also the view that there could be an unwillingness to embrace such 'practical diversity' on account of worries about the 'foreigners taking over'. Both also referred to how long it took for a gay man of Indian descent (who also, as we saw in Chapter 5, happens to be a mainstream neoliberal apparatchik) to become *Taoiseach* [Irish Prime Minister]. Respondents also suggested that most of the people who made key decisions about recruitment and promotion within the social work academy and practice would seem to need to evolve a new form of 'habitus' and sensibility grounded in a desire to generate racial equality within the field (see also the discussion on Bourdieu in Chapter 3). Some respondents also believed that 'affirmative action' policies might have a role to play if social work were to undergo transformation.

Three of the four educators interviewed felt that, in recent years, social work education had not adequately changed in order to respond to issues of 'race' and ethnicity. The fourth, Kim, argued that there was very little the educators could do beyond instructing their students to treat people equally and in a humane manner, based on the available teaching resources. She continued: "It could, however, mean what we are teaching is not solid enough to unsettle or make our students 'unlearn' prior negative conceptions of equality of 'races'/cultures they bring to college with them from their homes and communities."

Equality studies tended to be taught from a perspective that did not critique or radically question the dominance of Eurocentric epistemologies and practice methods. Some even dismissed the teaching of 'anti-oppressive practice' as not going far enough to interrogate the history and origins of the oppression, in that it tended to ignore the structural and racialised oppression embedded in social institutions. Michael maintained that it was crucial to recognise that 'diversity' does not merely signal a willingness to enrol culturally diverse students:

'That is the easy bit! The real challenge is to make the course itself culturally diverse. The challenge is that you must relativise the dominant hegemony and admit into equal or at least respectful consideration diverse discourses and practices. That is very problematic for academics trained within the hegemonic discourse and is very unsettling to western assumptions of superiority ... These assumptions of dominance and superiority are very much grounded in claims to be "scientific" ... Other discourses, especially those from "less advanced" cultural groups, can be categorised as instances of "culture" and "diversity", but not as equally valid claims on "truth" itself. As for culturally diverse courses, a truly open, diverse course is, therefore, very hard to achieve. It needs a diverse set of teachers, styles and accommodations.'

Some respondents suggested that there was a universal gender oppression/ inequality dynamic at play, but it was far more damaging to be a woman *and* to be Black. Some also pointed to how a more individualistic, career-orientated 'lean-in' feminism may have helped some White women to get a measure of 'equality' and dilute aspects of traditional patriarchy (see also the critique of this strand of feminism in Fraser, 2013). They viewed most Black African societies and cultures as continuing to be more patriarchal than western ones. For example, Michael commented:

'Many African cultures appear more "patriarchal" than western "liberal" ones. This can raise questions for Black African female students when addressing issues ... In my experience, so far, most if not all of the Black African female students are critical of patriarchy. However, western individualism is not an obvious "good" thing either.'

Tina maintained:

'Yes, you can think of all the oppressions that are gender based – it's worse when you add the colour Black. From what my female Black students say, even with racism and Afrophobia, women are disproportionately targeted in terms of physical violence and verbal abuse, as Black men are considered naturally violent in the minds of most White Irish people and are therefore perceived as likely to retaliate in kind if attacked.'

The educators' main responses to the notion of 'cultural competence' identified with Strier's (2004) definition, and they all acknowledged the nature of the 'competences' required for intercultural communication: attention to prosody (different accents), proxemics (distance from a person when speaking), gestures and facial expressions, such as eye contact, as well as cognitive competences. They did not believe such models, alone, would make practitioners respond better to 'cultural others'. Thomas argued:

"Cultural competence" and "intercultural competence" I think primarily suggest a capacity to recognise and then respond to cultural difference. This is wrapped up, for me, in the concept of attempting to understand each person in terms not only of their individuality but also of their gender, ethnicity, culture and so on. It is difficult to fully evaluate how successful I and my colleagues have been in creating a culturally open learning environment at this college. I suspect we cannot ultimately escape our underlying assumptions.'

All the White lecturer respondents acknowledged the value of more culturally inclusive knowledge that might expand western paradigms. Kim, one of the female lecturers, maintained:

'Enlarging the knowledge base [within social work education] and including non-western theories and knowledge systems would mean that students would expand their knowledge base and learn about theories from both the Global South and the Global North. At present, social work training in Ireland is based on teaching mainly theories and philosophies that have evolved from the Global North. A more nuanced and broader perspective on service user groups [that newly qualified social workers encounter in present-day multicultural Ireland] is required.'

Referring to specific examples of models of working generated beyond the northern hemisphere, Thomas added:

'Both family group conferencing and restorative justice concepts, now widely used in child protection social work and in probation services, respectively, originated from non-western cultures (see also Hayes and Houston, 2007). These are just two examples demonstrating that "traditional social work" can be enriched by other cultural knowledge systems. I'm not sure many know this! [laughs] More importantly, having *one* cultural knowledge system to cater for *all* cultures, especially in a multicultural environment, suggests a hierarchy of cultures. [Yet] inequality of any kind is against what social work stands for.'

All the respondents reported that it 'made sense' to teach different worldviews emanating from the Global North *and* South, as this would be entirely in keeping with democratic tenets and notions of inclusivity. Doing so would also be consistent with the social justice imperatives embedded throughout the social work literature. Tina commented: "The only recommendation I can make is to teach both Black African and European perspectives in the classroom. This should be easily done. Teaching only one worldview from one 'race' in my view amounts to some form of racism ... perhaps even 'epistemic racism' or 'cultural oppression'." All four respondents agreed that these 'differences' were largely underpinned by notions of the liberal

Enlightenment and logical positivism as manifested through the philosophy of 'individualism'. This, the social work educators suggested, often clashed with Black African philosophies that are often rooted in a more 'collectivist' and 'communal' approach to life (see also Chapter 4). For example, as previously discussed, the Black African philosophy of *Ubuntu* is rooted in the understanding that a person is entirely constituted as a 'self' through their relationship with others. One of the respondents described *Ubuntu* philosophy, as defined by Swanson (2007), as suggesting that personal 'strength' comes out of community support, with a sense of dignity and identity achieved through mutualism, empathy, generosity and community commitment. The often-cited African adage 'it takes a village to raise a child' is aligned with the 'spirit' and intent of *Ubuntu* and a humble 'togetherness' is perceived as a source of 'solidarity in crisis times' (Swanson, 2007). Old age is frequently viewed as degeneration in western culture. In contrast, within most Black African cultures, the elderly are often valued for their life-long experientially acquired wisdom (see also the critical discussion on such themes in Chapter 4).

Praxis

The lecturer respondents were unanimous that the presence of Black African and other minority ethnic students 'enriched' class discussions, and in the process, some of them confided, they themselves had also learned 'something new' or had their earlier misconceptions 'clarified'. For example, Kim maintained: "Yes, we have Black African students in each of our programme stages/years. I think this has been quite positive for everyone. I'm not aware of any difficulties that have arisen. I think it has enriched our programme and made us all more alert to cultural difference and assumptions." In contrast, and reflecting some of the emerging research and conversations occurring among Black African students, Tina asserted:

'While we do our best to paint a picture that in academia we are more enlightened and hence more tolerant, sometimes there have been difficulties in hearing what Black African students are saying, due to their heavy accents, particularly those from West Africa. Equally, sometimes you get a sense they are not challenging what is said in class, no matter how offensive ... maybe this is related to cultural taboos about challenging authority or just out of fear that the White lecturer/White students will be offended. Perhaps there is concern too about how their response may be used against them. I just don't know. This may not, though, apply to all Black social work students.' (See also Chapter 5)

Thomas added:

> 'The Black students I have taught are very cautious how they get involved in discussions. They try to be as polite as possible and usually use their own experiences/stories and what they have heard, but they wait for White students to speak first, like they're "testing the waters". Most of the mature ones have poor computer literacy/typing skills and are often slow in completing assignments. Their excuse has often been they had no access to home computers in their countries of origin. Moreover, some work to send money to family members back home despite being on a full-time course.'

Organisational structures within the capitalist racial state

Most of the academic respondents admitted that they found it 'uncomfortable' talking about or teaching racism within their organisational setting and that it was more convenient and easier to discuss the need to 'treat all people equally and fairly' in the context of teaching 'human rights', 'equality studies' and generic 'anti-oppressive' and 'anti-discriminatory' theory. When asked about specific teaching on racism and anti-racism, Tina stated:

> 'This depends on how comfortable the individual lecturer is talking about issues of "race"/racism. Some of us are obviously embarrassed and prefer to give the impression that, as Irish people, we can never be seen in the same light as perhaps the English or other Europeans with a colonial and racist history. The fact that we teach social work values professing a humanitarian ethos of equality and repudiate any form of oppression means we are duty bound to expose structural issues such as "institutional racism" and neoliberal racism manifested in punitive social policy such as DP and the HRC. In other words, it's "politically correct" for social work lecturers to be heard condemning any form of injustice, as that accords with their mandate. The question perhaps is, beyond what we teach [and should focus on], how many of us, as lecturers, have joined the street protests to, for example, press for the end or DP or to end the deportation of children, previously taken into "care", when they turn 18?'

As for DP, all the educator respondents felt that it had a wholly negative impact on professional and public perceptions of Black Africans. They were not sure why – despite its wide condemnation for violating human rights – the state had not produced a more humane alternative (see also Government of Ireland, 2021). Tina, for example, commented:

'Many who have been lobbying for the system to be shut down see it as the ugly face of big business which, under the guise of helping, is profiting from the misery of asylum seekers. This system also portrays Black Africans as people who are "dependent" and who, without paying for it, receive "free" accommodation and food. This perception is often used [to argue] against Ireland accepting more asylum seekers or refugees based on the view that they are here as "welfare tourists after resources meant for the locals". This breeds resentment towards Black Africans generally, even those who are not asylum seekers.' (See also Chapter 5)

Relatedly, all of the respondents felt that the often relentlessly 'negative' past and present images of Black Africa and its inhabitants influenced how Black African social work service users are perceived today. They largely attributed this to biased teaching of the history of early European colonialism and, not infrequently, the appropriation of the Bible and scripture to suggest that it was appropriate to maintain a hierarchy of "races". The White "race" is at the apex with a "primitive" Blackness, variously evoked as "child-like" and "dependent" and/or "evil" at the bottom. Respondents also believed that the current global media focus on poverty as exclusive to Black Africa (as represented in international aid advertisements) implies that "poverty has one colour" and that "colour is Black". In a politically convenient way, and entirely in tune with the neoliberal project, this presentation also erases the plight of the millions of impoverished White people residing is the so-called "developed" western world and in ostensibly "rich countries" such as the US.

All the social work educators cited possible cultural misunderstandings, poverty and shortcomings due to policies (failing to reflect the presence of other cultures) as the chief reasons for the disproportionate number of Black African children in 'care'. Kim said:

'Four factors I think contribute to the high number of Black African children being taken into care, namely: (1) cultural misunderstandings, (2) poverty and socioeconomic disadvantage and (3) "institutional racism" and, I think, (4) the ethnocentric design of the child welfare system impacts negatively on the equitable assessment of Black African families. I would like to also add that Black African children are at risk of becoming over-represented in the child protection system in Ireland when ethnocentric, rather than culturally appropriate, assessment criteria are used to judge whether "maltreatment" has occurred. "Culture" is more at risk of taking the blame for over-representation in the child protection system than "institutional racism" where organisational practices and policies, such as the Children First national guidelines (Department of Children and Youth Affairs, 2017) preserve only the dominant culture. It is important that "culture" is not mistaken for "maltreatment" and that "maltreatment" is not mistaken for "culture".' (See also Chapter 5)

Kim elaborated:

'Lack of clarity on these issues can lead to over-representation of [Black African] children [in "care"]. It is difficult to say for sure that social workers are using non- ethnocentric assessment measures to assess Black African families in child protection matters because currently ... there is little in practice guidelines or policies about "culturally competent" practice. In fact ... amongst the competencies that social workers are assessed on, which qualify them for practice, "cultural competency" is not one of them. Now I know there are arguments about how to assess one's level of "cultural competency", but the fact these issues are not part of the assessment of social workers leaves a lot to be desired.'

The common view expressed by these educators was that racism was 'not unique' to Ireland and that there was no way any 'sane person', let alone a social worker, could 'talk about racism without condemning it'. Three of the respondents believed that increased racism targeting Black Africans was attributable to being 'more visibly different' than, say, Eastern European migrant workers. One respondent maintained:

'Most people are unaware that the majority of older Irish people could have been irreparably indoctrinated by the "pennies for Black babies" collections [in church parishes and schools in the 1960s and 1970s], yet this possibly fostered an enduring mind-set about Black Africans' "dependency" [see also Chapter 5]. Ireland was also part of the White world despite itself being colonised. [As a consequence, it was] also subjected to prevailing socialisations of White supremacy prevalent in the western hemisphere for centuries. [All of this was] further reinforced by missionaries who sent back home stories of "Black savages" who needed to be "saved from themselves". Do not forget that in the Bible and scripture "Black" is also often equated with death, decay, sin and so on. [Such deep-rooted ideas have not been adequately] contested in our inherited constructions.' (See also Chapter 2)

Thomas, alert to the issues of labour shortages in parts of the Global North, responded slightly differently:

'Demographic studies indicate that White people will be a minority in countries such as the US in few decades. This, I believe, coupled with falling birth rates in Europe, suggests that the real reason countries such as Germany took in a lot of refugees was not out of altruism, but to mitigate labour shortages arising from the "greying" of the German labour force threatening the country's economic competitiveness and, hence, its economic status in the world. At the same time there are also fears of being "outbred" and "swamped" in some quarters.'

It was also suggested that the election of Donald Trump in 2016 demonstrated that White 'fear of decline' had emboldened those with certain views to 'come out' and openly express their fears about the so-called 'browning' of the US (Vice News Tonight, 2017). Thomas remarked:

'Afrophobia is not just an Irish problem … it is on the rise in most western countries disguised as the "ultra-nationalism" of right-wing parties. It's similar, in some ways, to new forms of cultural racism like Islamophobia and both are often expressed through policies that seek to retreat from multiculturalism. The pretext is that multiculturalism as an ideal is impractical, given the huge cultural differences. What is not highlighted, though, is that such sentiments and movements mostly thrive in situations of declining economic conditions, with the visibly different often getting the blame.'

All agreed that organisations such as CORU and the IASW played a key role in setting 'basic standards' and fulfilling a 'watchdog' role in maintaining some semblance of uniformity in education and practice. The respondents were critical of these bodies for not 'taking the lead' in energetically pressing for more diversity in the social work curriculum, student recruitment and relevant training so as to ensure that students (that is to say, future practitioners) get exposure to working in *all* our communities. Some even saw CORU as endeavouring to control and mould what a professional practitioner should 'come across' in terms of their intellectual and political allegiances (Garrett, 2021). Michael reported:

'I wonder why "theory" is so often removed from under-grad education … If you can present the discipline or profession as a series of "techniques" to be learned, then you do not have to make explicit, never mind defend, its assumptions. Just look at CORU's "proficiency standards for social care" − it entirely focuses on "technique" and does not acknowledge that there may be multiple modes of practising "social care".'

Similarly critically, Kim avowed:

> 'If one has to be brutally honest, organisations such as IASW and
> CORU suffer from what I prefer to call "insular afflictions". Despite
> both having substantial Black subscription/registration fee-paying
> members they have done very little to ... reflect this racial and cultural
> diversity. It's not uncommon for these organisations to have all White
> people on their websites or magazine/journal covers. They also show
> little interest in the experiences of Black and other minority ethnic
> social work clients. Naturally, they should have been the ones to argue
> for the implementation of the culture-gram as a family assessment
> tool in Irish social work. This does not mean they are racist, or ill-
> intentioned, it's just plain insensitivity arising from unconscious bias
> ... Hopefully this will change with time.'

Neoliberalism

All of the social work educator respondents suggested that Black African
service users were more 'at risk' of having their lives undermined by the
impact of the neoliberal regime of capital accumulation and the pernicious
social order that it generates. This included their lacking 'proper' information,
not understanding the welfare system and the impact of 'institutional
racism': this third element included exclusion from the labour market
through discrimination or being more 'at risk' of being the first to be 'let
go' following neoliberal moves to 'slim down' workforces.

These educators also maintained that the 'negative' media presentation
of Black Africans could be perceived as having deleterious consequences
in term of the wider public debates on immigration, asylum seekers and
refugees. Thomas, for example, argued:

> 'I'm not sure I'm influenced by this. However, there is no doubt that
> the current focus on migration and the political responses are a very
> important backdrop to our life at present. This clearly is an issue we
> must pay attention to and firmly address using the core humanist values
> of social work as a frame of reference.'

Michael differed slightly:

> 'While it's true that some media has influenced the public perception
> of Blacks and asylum seekers negatively, it also true that not all media
> have done that. Some sections of the media have run some "positive
> stories" highlighting how asylum seekers have defied the difficult
> situations and worked hard to be successful citizens. It could be just

that the "negative stories" have been highlighted by those with an agenda *against* immigrants.'

In keeping with the idea that large-scale immigration is a recent experience in Ireland, and the country may still have a lot to learn from other jurisdictions with longer histories of immigration, Kim argued that there is a

'need for an integration policy encompassing policies on education, health, social welfare, housing, public and civic participation and so on. The current understanding of integration policy is often confused with immigration policy that seeks to control who has access to enter, and live in, Ireland. There should be a clearly defined policy with programmes that link in with all other services and perhaps a new social work role of " 'resettlement social worker", specialising in supporting new arrivals beyond refugees and asylum seekers, might be considered.'

The other policy reform, suggested by Tina, was to commence a through and ongoing 'decolonisation' of much of what is taught within the Irish educational system:

'Policy reform interventions should also take cognisance of and address emerging research evidence suggesting there is value in other cultural ways and methods. However ... there is need to go beyond changing what we teach and unlearning old ways of thinking and teaching new perspectives. A policy framework that targets changing the entrenched "habitus" of practitioners and institutions through "conscientisation" is a more sustainable and effective long-term solution More importantly, the contradictions of neoliberal hegemony need to be exposed.'

Conclusion

Having garnered here the views of social work practitioners and educators, in the final chapter we review our findings and discuss some of the implications for social work and the wider society in Ireland. It will also be argued that the 'messages' conveyed by our respondents have more universal and generic resonances for global social work. We will also briefly summarise the book's main theme and point to some of the key issues highlighted.

Recognising the inescapable omissions in our own exploration, we will also signal areas for research initiatives. For example, future projects might focus on service user perspectives. There may also be multiple 'stories' and differing experiences attributable to the specific place of origin of Black Africans (Gatwiri, 2020) and their religious affiliation. Intersectional questions, pivoting on class, gender and 'race', similarly warrant further study.

Reflection and talk box 6

How do the views and perceptions of the practitioners, featured in this chapter, relate to the situation in the country in which you are situated?

Are there any factors that you view as significant that the research participants do not address?

How do the comments of the social work educators relate to your experiences as either a social work student or academic?

How might social work education evolve in order to better meet the needs of racially diverse communities?

7

Conclusion

Introduction

In this book, our chief aspiration has been to thoroughly examine factors that constrain social work, in Ireland, in responding to issues of 'race' and ethnicity in providing services to members of the Black African diaspora. In this final chapter, beginning with a reflection on the empirical work, we will briefly reflect on some of the main issues we have addressed. The concluding section of the chapter then turns to consider the future possibilities for anti-racist social work in Ireland. However, we hope that some of the 'messages' that we try to convey have more global implications.

Looking backwards

In the previous chapter we provided the space for 21 respondents to air their views and to speak expansively about their own experiences. Importantly, we opted to present their words with little by way of editorial commentary; the chapter focused on four themes derived from the relevant literature and our own experience within the field of social work. More specifically, we dwelt on: social work education and theoretical perspectives; praxis; organisational structures within the capitalist racial state; neoliberalism.

While the small size of the sample of practitioners and educators could be considered as unreflective of the profession as a whole, it still provides insights and addresses issues that have not, to date, been investigated within the academic literature of social work. Other limitations associated with this empirical material are fairly clear: for example, while we have often tended to identify White Irish, White American and White English among the respondents, we have not replicated this with our Black African sample. We could, for example, have chosen to delineate their background and heritage in greater detail and make clear which part of Africa they originated in. Indeed, a future study might explore if there are particular themes and preoccupations more associated with those from, say, Zimbabwe, or South Africa or the Ivory Coast and so on (see, for instance, how Kathomi Gatwiri, 2020 has opted to differentiate her respondents in this way). We were sensitive to this issue, but also alert to the need to safeguard the respondents' anonymity. There are so few Black African social workers in Ireland that it would have been easy to – accidentally – surrender too much biographical information and, thus, heighten the risk of inadvertently revealing their actual identities. Differentiating the White respondents certainly helps to illuminate the fact that being a White social worker did not automatically translate to inexperience and ideological incompetence in responding to Black African users of services. Indeed, as we have seen, some of the White respondents were critically self-reflexive, perhaps especially if they had spent time overseas as immigrants themselves.

The experiences of Black African social workers from other western countries might also have introduced another enriching dimension. The absence of full-time social work lecturers working in Irish universities who are Black Africans also constitutes something of a 'gap' because this meant that we were able to garner the views only of White Irish social work educators. The reason for this lacuna is that, apart from availing themselves of 'casual', 'sessional' and precarious teaching 'gigs', Black Africans are not – at the time of writing – teaching on accredited social work programmes in the Republic of Ireland. Indeed, this is a structural factor of great concern, given that social work rhetorically lauds inclusivity, recognition of difference and equality.

The 'voices' that we have heard in the previous chapter indicate that, in Ireland, the social work response to the Black African diaspora remains highly problematic. Social work education (often imbued with a largely Eurocentric worldview), practice and organisational structures (largely forged and maintained and tethered to 'business logics' and a stifling neoliberal outlook) form a constellation of factors undermining responses in both macro and micro contexts.

Values and ethical claims-making

As we observed in Chapter 5, the IFSW (2014) maintains that social work

> promotes social change and development, social cohesion, and the empowerment and liberation of people. Principles of social justice, human rights, collective responsibility and respect for diversities are central to social work. Underpinned by theories of social work, social sciences, humanities and indigenous knowledges, social work engages people and structures to address life challenges and enhance wellbeing.

Arguably, the way that Irish social work is organised and carried out (in teaching, practice and research) indicates that it fails to sufficiently take into account non-western indigenous knowledge systems. Consequently, there seems to be little space for 'cultural diversity' in any meaningful onto-epistemological sense. In short, current approaches to the Black African diaspora do not appear, at the either the praxis or educative levels, to reflect the global definition of social work, its values and ethical claims-making.

Indeed, this exclusion of knowledge systems derived from other places in the world – in teaching, research and practice – appears to run entirely counter to the global definition and its rhetorical and more pluralistic call for inclusion of other knowledge systems in social work. Most of the practitioners interviewed suggested that they had graduated with little interest in or knowledge of any other paradigm outside of primarily mainstream Eurocentric ones. This entails a further layer of complexity, because here 'Eurocentric' might be better and more accurately perceived as *specific* European views that reflect or fail to interrogate the imperatives of capitalism. For example, there is a lack of engagement with figures from the Global South such as de Sousa Santos, but there is also a failure to incorporate some of the iconic figures associated with the *critical* European corpus of theory and with figures, such as Marx and Gramsci. Arguably, the lacuna within social work education in Ireland tells as much about a pervasive lack of criticality as it does about a purported unthinking Eurocentrism. For us, this is a vital point to grasp and respond to as we head further into the second decade of the twenty-first century.

The comments featured in the previous chapter also suggest that social work's inadequacy, in its interventions with members of the Black African diaspora, possibly emanates from this insular reliance on theories and knowledge often situated outside the lived experiences of people from Black Africa. The findings further suggest that social work in Ireland risks being perceived as politically compliant and impotent to promote 'social change' and the 'liberation' of people (see also Brockmann and Garrett, 2022). Clearly, at the vibrant and dissenting margins there are the activist groups, such as SWAN, but the profession as a whole, overseen by a conservative regulatory body and a liberal but largely compliant cadre of professors, seems overly keen to not 'rock any boats'. From their articulations, it is clear that respondents are aware of this problem and feel rather stultified, constrained and unsupported. There are also powerful indications that policy frameworks and institutional cultures are far too grounded in neoliberal business logics that valorise compliant 'top-down' decision making and largely uncontested, rigid hierarchical lines of authority. So, on account of this, there is little 'space' for conceptual innovation and, hence, considerable limitations exist in terms of what more progressive educators and practitioners can achieve (Garrett, 2021).

We also need to remind ourselves of the profession's dual and contradictory role as both 'state agents' and potentially radical 'change agents' (Cooper, 1977). Within Ireland, the 2014 successful 'NO to cheap labour!' campaign, which galvanised opposition and ultimately prevented the introduction of a new 'lower scale' rate of pay for newly qualified social workers, indicates that progressive sections within the profession can – if organised on a collective basis – create chains of solidarity and actually 'win' skirmishes inside the neoliberal social order (Cuskelly et al, 2014). Similar forms of action could contribute to the struggles to, for example, immediately end DP – and not in a few years as is the plan of the current Irish government – and the associated mental health problems that often lead to some families losing their children to state care. As for the 'official' social work response to the DP, it is striking just how many years it has taken for this issue to appear on what we might term the 'social work radar'.

Generally, there have been no sustained attempts by social work – as a Bourdieusian 'field' – to enhance the well-being of Black African and other minority ethnic families. Moreover, the teaching of 'diversity' from 'liberal' and 'conservative' perspectives may well serve to actually impede students' and practitioners' willingness and ability to mount challenges directed at the imperatives of the capitalist racial state.

Social work education, social work praxis

Social Work with the Black African Diaspora places centre-stage the cultural oppression prevalent in monocultural social work education and practice. This can be associated with enduring – if often latent and subtle – racist assumptions that many of the respondents address. Turning to onto-epistemological pluralism, Ireland is situated within a western European socio-cultural context that is saturated in historical and contemporary notions of western racial and cultural superiority. When applied to social work, such a neocolonial ideological orientation is, as we have argued, at odds entirely with the profession's rhetorical egalitarian claims. Some of our respondents, for example, blamed lack of interest in other onto-epistemologies on the very lecturers who were supposed to 'enlighten' them. More conceptually, this may reveal a good deal about the resilience and solidity of – what Bourdieu might term – 'doxic' knowledge or – after Foucault – dominating 'truth regimes' within the social work sector (see also Chapter 3).

The ineffectiveness of current teaching is evidenced by several respondents who felt that mainstream approaches seek to mostly champion arid and anachronistic 'liberal' practice models that palpably fail to change the situation 'on the ground' as it relates to transcultural interactions and encounters. Is it because White liberals find such approaches convenient in that they fail to grapple with the historic power dynamics that could lead on to 'uncomfortable' topics such as slavery and its legacy of racism? Relatedly, Terrance MacMullan (2015) argues that 'colour blind, White, liberals' may want to pretend that racism is now 'non-existent' or is 'no longer an issue'. Meanwhile, political conservatives, both in social work and the wider society, are keen to claim that the 'pendulum has swung too far' and that we are increasingly in thrall to 'political correctness', those who are 'woke' and a pervasive, debilitating 'cancel culture' (see also Fairclough, 2003). Across a wider canvas, a more subtle and opportunistic neoliberal strategy involves the 'corporate extraction of value from the struggles for recognition led by historically oppressed populations' (Kanai and Gill, 2021, p 11). Hence the corporate advertising has, in recent years, tried to annex and exploit the struggles of the oppressed in order to more successfully sell commodities to particular ethnicised market niches.

In our earlier discussion on Boaventura de Sousa Santos, it was suggested that the sociology of 'emergences' can potentially help us to see that the prevailing oppressive social order is not 'natural' – or, indeed, imbued with 'permanence' – and can be changed through human agency that seeks to counter silencing and exploitation with activism (see also Chapter 3). Indeed, the conceptualisations of this Portuguese intellectual remind us that which currently exists canonically is not the only way of understanding the social world. Alternative and more socially and economically progressive forms of knowledge, formerly subjected to historical enforced absences, can always begin to emerge. In this sense, social work teaching might also begin to try to furnish examples of knowledge systems whose absence has been historically enforced.

'Traditional' teaching in social work instructs students to have empathy by 'putting themselves in the shoes of the client'. This book, however, exposes the fact that, in working with Black Africans, most White practitioners have no knowledge of or lack familiarity with relevant ethnic cultures. This may be related, in fact, to the gradual, but uncritical, adoption of 'cultural competence' models derived from, for example, the US. There is, of course, nothing wrong in adopting foreign models, but these should deepen and expand our thinking, not stupefy us. Relatedly, in theory-to-practice areas, such as counselling, social work in Ireland might have much to gain from exposing the limitations of Carl Rogers' 'unconditional regard' when applied to 'clients' from a more collectivist-oriented culture shunning individualism. Alerting students and practitioners to similar problems with other traditional theoretical pillars for practice is also vital. More pervasively, as one respondent pointed out, policies impacting on social work tend to operate on implicit assumptions about 'autonomy' and the 'capacity of the individual' to overcome all and every adversity with the right guidance and support. Social work conventionally is constructed on a similar premise and is overly keen to blandly promote keywords, such as 'resilience', that merely amplify such deeply ideological perceptions (Garrett, 2016).

The respondents in Chapter 6 also express concerns that the way that social work is taught lays insufficient emphasis on the political nature of the profession. This was blamed for 'turning out' graduates who had little, if any, interest in critical politics, and this rendered them neoliberal compliant and averse to dissent (Fenton, 2018). Underpinning this book, therefore, is something of a 'call' for social work to view critical praxis as a way of disrupting the current orthodoxies (Garrett, 2021). This might be done by, for example, beginning to politically exploit the tensions inherent within the rhetoric of 'fundamental rights', 'human rights' and so on (see also Brockmann and Garrett, 2022). Recent evidence reveals that the 'human rights' have further been devalued in that, as mentioned in Chapter 5, CORU (2019) has deleted them from Irish social work's ethical code.

Organisational structures housing social work

Organisational culture may be defined as the shared norms, values and beliefs that develop in an organisation as members interact with each other. As indicated in Chapter 6, organisational structures mirror values reflecting both a western culture of individualised service provision and neoliberal 'business logic'. These fuse to sustain workplace culture and dominant leadership styles. Relatedly, the practices of Human Resources (HR) translate this 'culture' and 'style' into practices of recruitment and promotion and, in some instances, they aid the continuance of abusive, even racist practices. Top-down decision making, premised on rigid hierarchical lines of authority, was also identified by our respondents as a wholly negative characteristic of organisational structures prevalent within the 'field' of social work in Ireland.

In workplaces, 'dignity at work' policies (rhetorically benign, even socially progressive) are entirely ill equipped to deal with issues such as racism, as they rely heavily on the attitude of managers (themselves the individuated 'products' of neoliberal, racialised structures) to meaningfully address complaints. Oftentimes, the ways mapped to resolve problems are also manifesting as impractical, given that the modalities in place to deal with complaints and grievances place the onus on the complainant to accumulate a sufficient number of witnesses. This can, of course, be difficult for Black African workers, who might be outnumbered and socially marginalised in many organisations. In marked contrast to the stated 'mission' statements, most social services organisations have policies and practices that risk remaining, in reality, discriminatory and oppressive, given how they are experienced by many service users *and* practitioners. Relatedly, some the practitioners interviewed were, as we have seen, trying to provide more benign and supportive services that evoke Lipsky's 'street level bureaucrats' (see also Ash, 2010; Conneely and Garrett, 2015).

The social devastation wrought by neoliberalism provides the social work profession with sufficient evidence to re-evaluate its ambivalence regarding activist scholarship and radical activism. It is exceedingly difficult – perhaps especially if one is from a Black minority ethnic background – to be identified with 'radical' or 'critical' causes. Oftentimes, this can result in marginalisation within social work offices and university social work departments. Leftist activism can produce the low-level hum of bullying and harassment from ideological opponents. In an Australian context, Christine Morley (2018) has written with brave lucidity on this theme. Within this toxic context, some social work educators have, perhaps, become (voluntarily or unconsciously) the ideological 'gatekeepers' of the very oppressive organisational and institutional arrangements that are founded on the desire to contradict and eradicate aspirations for social justice. A decline in numbers of progressive social work educators – Gramsci's 'organic intellectuals' – has, of course, far reaching implications. If there are an insufficient number of critical intellectuals, unable to imbed and nurture the much-needed emancipatory consciousness, the future of the social work profession as a socially progressive activity is in jeopardy (Garrett, 2021).

Bourdieu expressed this concern in theoretical terms in that one of his main preoccupations was that previously autonomous or quasi-autonomous 'fields' were becoming contaminated and corroded by the imperatives of neoliberal capitalism. This has great resonance for contemporary social work, in that the transformation from 'field' to 'apparatus' occurs when 'under certain historical conditions ... the dominant manage to crush and annul the resistance and reactions of the dominated, when all movements go exclusively from the top down' (Bourdieu in Bourdieu and Wacquant, 2004, p 102). That is to say, apparatuses – in which critique has been extinguished and compliance guaranteed – are 'the *pathological* state of fields' (Bourdieu in Bourdieu and Wacquant, 2004, p 102, emphasis added). Nevertheless, as we have reported, many of our respondents featured in Chapter 6 are – against the odds – lucid and remarkably articulate critics of the capitalist racial state and its organisational imperatives. This may suggest that some individuals within the profession have not yet transmogrified into social technicians within the omnipresent 'apparatus'.

Previous studies

Previous related studies, along with our personal and professional experience, raise important questions. Generally, social work with Black and minority ethnic groups in the western world – and here specifically in Ireland – struggles to provide adequate services for those who are culturally and visibly different. The often-cited excuse, in the case of Ireland, is, as we saw in Chapter 6, 'more time is needed' to evolve better interventions, given the country's very recent history of sizeable inward migration. It might also be countered that the Travelling community has been here for a 'long time' and their treatment does not suggest 'culturally sensitive' responses from social work and state institutions are imminently likely (Pavee Point, 2013; Logan, 2014).

Social Work with the Black African Diaspora identifies with other studies that challenge the dominance and inadequacy of unquestioning Eurocentric monocultural practice methods in social work practice. The thrust of our interpretation of the findings in Chapter 6 suggests that we need to begin to valorise hitherto subjugated knowledge derived from other cultural locations and to develop forms of transcultural social work. Perhaps unlike previous Irish contributions, this book also points to the deleterious impact of the colonisation of Africa on contemporary social work's way of *thinking* and *acting*. Hence, the continuity between the past colonial hegemony and the present hegemony and its associated oppressive structures. History is, of course, tremendously significant because of the potent residues discernible in our contemporary times, as Gramsci recognises. Indeed, an interrogation of the institutional abuses in Ireland's past has begun to surface in the 21st century (Garrett, 2017). Exposing the links between the past and the present also helps us to grasp how colonial history provides the seed for contemporary 'normalised' unequal racialised power relations and social structures. Inescapable here are two intertwined imperatives: to recognise cultural difference and to combat neoliberal politics within, and beyond, the profession of social work.

While noting its potential strategic utility for those seeking change, we differ from many previous books in that we, like many of our respondents, are deeply sceptical about the emphasis on 'cultural competence'. Largely originating in the Global North, we view the centrality of the 'cultural competence' concepts and their associated tools and ephemera as mostly helping to deflect attention from economic exploitation and a differential distribution of power within capitalist racial states (see also Chapter 2).

Looking forwards

Perhaps, more generally, changes are beginning to take place and there are identifiable departures from uncritical Eurocentric perspectives within social work. On World Social Work Day 2021, the IFSW highlighted *Ubuntu*, along with the tagline 'I am because we are: strengthening social solidarity and global connectedness'. On the organisation's web page, the president avowed that *Ubuntu* 'resonates with the social work perspective' that recognises the 'interconnectedness of all peoples and their environments'. In this way *Ubuntu* 'speaks to the need for global solidarity and also highlights indigenous knowledge and wisdom'.

Similarly on a more positive note, in Ireland, a range of other smaller and less officially trumpeted initiatives, such as the 'sanctuary' movement, very clearly identify with a more emancipatory politics (Places of Sanctuary Ireland, 2020). Specifically in terms of social work, the IASW (2021) produced *A new way forward: Dismantling racism in 21st-century Irish social work – ISAW anti-racism strategic plan 2021–2023*. This three-year plan is 'inspired' by the Black caucus within the IASW and it reflects a desire to move beyond merely 'tokenistic statements' (IASW, 2021, p 4). In an Irish context this is an immensely significant development because it can potentially combat the 'inertia' that has characterised the profession's response to racism (see also Chapter 5). As the drafters of the strategy explain, there has been a palpable 'lack of political will to support anti-racist initiatives and tackle racism at the level of the state and its institutions' (IASW, 2021, p 6). In contrast, the values and vision of the profession 'based on egalitarian and social justice ethos find expression in this strategic plan's thrust towards achieving racial justice through dismantling racism and its various manifestations' (IASW, 2021, p 3).

This strategy has been prompted by the painstaking hard work and tenacity of Black African and other minority ethnic activists within the field. These pivotal figures have also been supported by socially progressive White activists – a number of whom have been active in SWAN over many years. As the plan explicitly states, it was formulated by 'individuals with lived experience of racism and their White allies' (IASW, 2021, p 8). The BLM movement, and wider moves to combat racism, provide the galvanising impetus energising and emboldening those seeking change at this conjuncture (see also Chapter 1). Indeed the BLM movement, with which this book is unequivocally aligned, does not merely aim to 'stop premature deaths that result from police violence but to foster economic, social and political power and resources that will sustain Black life more broadly' (Benjamin, 2019, p 119). In this context, partly embedded in fascinating empirical work with practitioners and educators, *Social Work with the Black African Diaspora* has been a modest intervention aiming to ensure that Black lives matter both in terms of the knowledge base of social work and in its daily practices (Taylor, 2016). Indeed, the motif 'Black lives matter' must become a more focal and defining feature of social work in future (Baines, 2021; Joseph, 2021; Michael and Joseph, 2021).

Given the perspective developed in this book, we entirely support the IASW initiative and, indeed, one of us (Washington) has been tirelessly involved in constructing and amplifying its 'messages'. If the strategy is to be supportively criticised, this would be on account of a failure to locate racism in the context of capitalism and its current manifestation, neoliberalism (see also Chapter 5). Relatedly, as numerous contributions of Nancy Fraser persuasively highlights, the cultural and the material are invariably intertwined and inseparable (Fraser, 2003). Indeed, as this book went to press a motion being circulated by social work students and progressively-orientated social work practitioners recognises this intersectional dimension. Hence, an inspiring #FeesMustFall campaign is calling for reduction in fees across all social work programmes in Ireland. The motion, in detail, is as follows:

While recognising that there is great variability in fees throughout the state, we call on Directors of Social Work programmes and associated staff to advocate that universities in Ireland reduce fees. This is important because such a move would:

a) be a very practical measure rooted in a commitment to developing anti-racist practices and it is congruent with social work values associated with social inclusivity and combatting social exclusion;
b) potentially open up access to such programmes for members of Black and ethnic minority communities, such as Irish Travellers, who are frequently unable to afford the cost of current fees on account of structural racism and discrimination that undermines their, and the families', ability to afford to embark on social work studies;
c) potentially help to transform the composition of the social work workforce by introducing more students, and subsequently practitioners, who are not White and middle-class;
d) aid the efforts of working-class class students who are also presently largely excluded from applying to social work programmes because of expensive fees and the additional costs associated with fieldwork placements.

As Esme Choonara (2021, p 2) forcefully points out in a UK context, and as we have argued in *Social Work with the Black African Diaspora*, racism has to be understood as 'firmly bound to the functioning and perpetuation of capitalism'. Hence, a 'wider vision of change is needed to effectively challenge racism. This involves an understanding of how racism is structured into capitalism and how power resides not in interpersonal relationships or in Whiteness, but in the economic and social relations of a system that derives profit from exploitation' (Choonara, 2021, p 11). Entirely in tune with this analysis, Angela Davis (2020) summarises: 'racism is integrally linked to capitalism' and it is a 'mistake to assume that we can combat racism by leaving capitalism in place'. This is an understanding that large corporations seek to deny in their cynical efforts to harness themselves to the vitality and vision of the BLM movement and other progressive movements seeking change (Sobande, 2019; 2020).

Clearly, the COVID-19 pandemic illuminates the fact that we cannot decouple racism and capitalism. This is illustrated by the figures published in Britain in June 2020 revealing that '94 per cent of doctors and 71 per cent of nurses' who had died from COVID-19 were from Black and other minority ethnic backgrounds (Choonara, 2021, p 9). Although we lack comparable Irish data, Black and minority ethnic workers are less 'likely to be promoted, they are more likely to be in direct patient-facing roles, with greater risk of exposure to COVID-19. Black health workers, including nurses and doctors, have also reported having less access to personal protective equipment (PPE) and feeling less able to speak out over safety issues at work' (Choonara, 2021, p 9).

Recognising the core centrality of the capitalism/racism nexus need not prompt strident and rhetorically monotonous denunciations of capitalism that lead us nowhere. Rather, the twofold aim should be this: first, to intellectually make the connection between racism and capitalism, as this relates to particular manifestations in policy and micro-encounters; second, the intention should be to incessantly seek to build what we might term a political 'rainbow coalition' of groups committed to challenging *all* facets of oppression within the fabric of capitalism (see also Garrett, 2021). Such an understanding and strategy is founded, therefore, on a rejection of the narrow insularity that is solely focused on questions of identity. We also remain alert of the dangers of ethno-particularism and, indeed, this is the major problem with a good deal of the literature on 'the African American trend', dubbed Afrocentrism, that we turned our critical attention to in Chapter 4 (Hountondji, 2002, p 217). Here also we explored the work of Paul J. Hountondji, and we would argue that his contributions might aid how we theorise, teach and practise social work within the 'diaspora space' that is contemporary Ireland (Brah, 1996; see also Chapter 1). The comments of Achille Mbembe on Afropolitanism are also important:

> Afropolitanism emerges out of that recognition of the multiple origins of those who designate themselves as 'African' or as 'of African descent'. Descent here, or descendants, or genealogy, is a bit more than just biological or racial, for that matter. For instance, we have in Africa a lot of people of Asian or Indian origin. We have people who are Africans but they are Africans of European origin in South Africa, and other former settler colonies like Angola, Mozambique. We have Africans who are of Middle Eastern origin, for example in West Africa, Senegal, and Côte d'Ivoire. And more and more, we have Africans of Chinese origin. (Mbembe in Balakrishnan, 2016, p 30)

That is to say, the Afropolitanism, if it is anchored in intersectional considerations may, help us to think beyond the 'racial'. However, we also have affinities with Gregor McLennan (2001, p 405) in calling for 'critical universalism'. This notion is even more apt in the context of the global COVID-19 pandemic. In focusing on Black Africans in Ireland and their encounters with and within social work services, our approach has likewise been influenced by the remarks of Césaire:

> I'm not going to confine myself to some narrow particularism. But I don't intend either to become lost in a disembodied universalism ... I have a different idea of a universal. It is a universal rich with all that is particular, rich with all the particulars there are, the deepening of each particular, the coexistence of them all. (Césaire in Kelley, 2000, pp 25–26)

We reject the notion that there is a seamless unanimity among Black Africans, across a range of beliefs, because their lifeworlds are complex and multifarious. Perceiving such lifeworlds as being all the same also gives rise to – frequently implicit – reductive ideas that *all* Black African parents share the same opinions on how best to care for and rear children. Such views risk generating and sustaining the false assumption that Black African parents have a 'natural' proclivity to physically chastise their offspring. More fundamentally, we are suspicious of any ideas rooted in 'attempts to link explicitly or implicitly such and such a system of values to such and such a geographical zone or region of the globe' (Hountondji, 2002, p 137). Perhaps now embedded – in a Gramscian sense – in the 'common sense' of the social work profession and the wider public, such ideas may well have resulted in children from Black African families being disproportionately targeted by child protection services (Child Care Law Reporting Project, 2015). Progressives within the field of social work in Ireland must, therefore, incessantly question and collectively confront such reasoning. In Africa, and among the diaspora, it is 'impossible for everyone to be in agreement with everyone else' (Hountondji, 2002, p 107). However, some of our respondents indicated that parts of the field of social work have difficulty in acknowledging the reality of pluralism.

There is a need to acknowledge that what we might term 'Afro-Hibernian lifeworlds' are pluralistic and complex, and social work services must begin to engage with those inhabiting and creating such worlds in a much more nuanced and informed way. In short, there has to be a much more intellectually curious, rigorous, pluralistic form of social work inquiry and practice. At the heart of such a project should be an acknowledgement that it is a pressing professional and civic duty to uncover simplified, arid notions of culture. As Hountondji (2002, p 134) counsels, it is vital to recognise the 'complexity, diversity, tensions, contradictions, internal dynamics of each culture, [and that we see] in that a source of richness and creativity'.

The assertion, by White social work educators in the previous chapter, that the presence of Black African students enriched class discussions and that Black African practitioners played a significant role as 'cultural resources', mediating situations of misunderstanding, further highlights the urgent need for a truly diverse social work workforce. It is also important to take into account Ebun Joseph's (2021, p 23) comment that Black activists are 'routinely invited to share their stories, reveal their vulnerability, the pain and shame of being victims of racism. Yet there are real dangers that attend the public telling of stories of racism. The danger is that it can make them victims of gaslighting, denial, accusation of exaggerating, trolling or worse, with colleagues seeing them as objects of pity'.

Clearly, social work practice and education in Ireland and elsewhere needs to be comprised of a workforce that is racially and culturally diverse. While essential, this does not necessarily mean that Social Work – as institution, field and discipline – will become more benign and beneficially responsive to the needs of the Black African diaspora. The situation is much more complex and it is sociologically and politically naive to conclude that recruitment of more Black African social workers is a magic-bullet 'solution'. The assumption that Black and ethnic minority social workers could 'solve' the problem of anti-Black racism betrays an entrenched lack of productive awareness and presents us with a rather odd – and racialised – inflection of human capital theory. Relatedly, based in Scotland, Alison Bowes and Naira Dar (2000) suggest that White social workers lack knowledge of minority ethnic communities or have difficulties working with them. These practitioners also view such work as risky, given that they may unintentionally offend service users and this might prompt accusations of their being labelled 'racist' (Bowes and Dar, 2000). This is confirmed by Burman et al (2004), who reveal that White social workers intervening with South Asian families in child protection cases express similar anxieties and tend to withdraw from this work and unduly rely on their Black colleagues. Given these findings, it is not unlikely that newly trained and recruited Black social work practitioners might find themselves exclusively working with more 'difficult cases' within Black and minority ethnic ghettoised enclaves.

In the US city of Baltimore, in 2015, Freddie Gray, a 25-year-old African-American, was arrested and suffered severe injuries leading to his death. This led to widespread protests across the city. However, almost all positions of power in the city were filled by African-Americans, including the mayor, the police commissioner, the attorney general and a majority of the city council. Three of the six police officers involved in the brutal and ultimately lethal arrest were African-American (Choonara, 2021). Here, the point we are making is that the dominance of Black people in positions of power failed to eradicate the lethal brutality of the police and structurally embedded racism. In short, the function of the police was not transformed (Dobuzinskis, 2019). If we translate this understanding to social work, we might also conclude that fundamental changes within the field of social work will not result, merely by the introduction of more Black African social workers. Rather, there needs to be a more encompassing strategy that reorientates the field to truly address the needs of the Black African people and others who are (dis)similarly exploited and rendered voiceless. This would entail substantial economic transformations, the dispossession of the super-rich and – at present a pressing requirement in Ireland – a major public housing programme. That is to say, the transformation of social work must take place as part of a more encompassing transformative programme strategy intent on remaking the state and its economic and social imperatives (Garrett, 2021).

Even within the narrow field of social work, it is important to recognise the constraints hampering new ways of working. As our respondents make apparent, certain reductive and stereotypical perceptions of Black Africans – and, indeed, of Africa – continue to haunt the social work imaginary. This factor aside, we can also observe that a more in-depth engagement with Black African families, by both White and Black African practitioners, demands that social workers produce more immersive and time-consuming assessments. This involves reactivating something of a traditional social work emphasis on heightened attentiveness, intensive listening, clear communication and relationship building. Aspiring to work in this way runs directly counter to neoliberal imperatives that prompt 'fast' working on the social work 'production line'. This development was highlighted across a number of countries at the century's commencement, and it has become subsequently more pronounced (Jones, 2001; Baines, 2004a; 2004b). Indeed, this requirement to work speedily and to process 'cases' quickly remains one of the insufficiently examined facets connected to the UK death of the Black African child Victoria Climbié in 2000 (Garrett, 2006).

One of the 'messages' conveyed by this book, therefore, is that anti-racist social work, if it is to respond more adequately to the complex issues relating to cultural identity – and always entangled material factors – requires new temporal regimes in which slower and more reflexive work is valorised. Bernler et al (1993) argue that the nexus of social work is a relationship between two parties through communication. Hence, conversation is *the* medium through which users of services express their needs and grievances and describe their life situations. It follows, therefore, that differences in the social worker's and service user's culture might play a significant role in influencing their mutual relationship and interaction (Laird, 2008). More fundamentally, we need a form of social work that is grounded in a willingness to question, and oftentimes dissent from, established paradigms and canonical streams of thought within the profession (Garrett, 2021).

Conclusion

In this book we have covered a lot a theoretical and empirical ground! We sincerely hope that the messages conveyed have universal and generic resonances for global social work. Recognising the inescapable omissions in our exploration, future research projects might focus on service user perspectives. There may also be differing experiences attributable to the specific place of origin of Africans and their religious affiliation. Intersectional questions, pivoting on entanglement of class, gender and 'race', similarly warrant further study within social work. *Social Work with the Black African Diaspora* might, therefore, furnish a helpful foundation for these future explorations.

Reflection and talk box 7

How might having regard to history help the profession of social work to evolve into a more socially progressive force?

How might social workers begin to address issues connected to racist policing?

What is presently being done in your field and national setting to create anti-racist forms of social work?

How might 'rainbow coalitions' be constructed to combat racism, patriarchy and diverse forms of capitalist exploitation?

'Outsiders within': a short reflection on the interviews in the book

Washington Marovatsanga

As someone who has worked in the health and social care/social work field for many years in different parts of Ireland, I had no difficulties accessing respondents. My membership of various social work organisations was also helpful. I mostly relied on e-mailing potential recruits, and these included team leaders and principal social workers. In this context, 'snowballing' helped to generate sufficient respondents. Within the research sites, my status was shaped by not only my previous social work practice experience; it was also associated with my cultural location as an 'ethnic minority' with lived experience in North America and other parts of Europe as well as in Ireland.

Of course, no social research activity is 'value free', and there exist possibilities of bias when researching one's own profession. I recognise, following Bourdieu (2003 [1977]), that I am enmeshed in the 'doxa' current within the 'field' of social work. Additionally, being a social worker, I was aware of, and sympathetic toward, some of the limitations imposed on those promoting progressive change by economic and other structural factors. I am also aware of the difficulty and risk, for the respondents, in providing research interviews that were clearly 'political'.

While familiar with social work–related culture and language, I am equally alert to facets of the lifeworld associated with Black African racialised minorities in Ireland (Garrett, 2009). In this sense, my own background, and that of Black African social workers whose 'voices' we 'hear' in Chapter 6, give us a glimpse of the wider perceptions of the Black African minority ethnic group in Ireland. I, and the Black African social workers, are positioned as 'outsiders within' (see also Fanning and Michael, 2019). This implies that we may be able to function both from 'within' and 'outside' dominant structures, and so potentially possess a 'double vision' better enabling us to focus on the 'marginal' in social work research and practice. Subordinated groups may have a capacity to see the dominant societal structures through the 'eyes of the stranger' (Robe, 1998). Ruth Frankenberg (1993; 1997) argues that the oppressed can see with the greatest clarity not only their position but also the 'shape' or contours of the wider social system. For marginalised groups to survive in such society where they are oppressed by societal structures, they must be attentive to both the perspectives of the dominant group and their own. In other words, they need to develop a 'double vision'. Due to their privileged stance, those from the dominant group, positioned at the centre of social structures, do not develop a similar 'double vision', and solely focus on the 'dominant' view of society. So, when their version of reality is compared to that of marginalised groups, despite its hegemonic character, it remains partial, even strategically deployed to maintain its dominant position.

This 'double vision' may apply to Black African social workers, given their 'fleeting' access to dominant structures. Patricia Hill Collins (1986) argues that bringing an 'outsider within' status into the centre of analysis is helpful in revealing obscured, even suppressed, perspectives (Collins and Bilge, 2016). Additionally, despite sharing the same cultural identity with the Black African respondents and possibly carrying the same 'baggage', in terms of perceptions of what was happening in policy and practice, I still tried to leave room for the possibility that there could be other as yet unknown factors influencing what was occurring.

I am also aware that I may not always have obtained 'truthful' accounts when investigating issues of 'race' and racism in a context where respondents could have been very guarded due to, for example, the manifest incompatibility of racist views with the 'official' values of their profession. We need to be reminded of Atkinson and Silverman's (1997, p 305) cautionary comments regarding the 'neo-Romantic celebrations of the speaking subject', which are frequently implicit in some of the literature on research interviews.

Norman Denzin (2001, p 24) observes that the 'reflexive interview is not an information gathering tool *per se*. It is not a commodity that you hire someone to collect for you, or that you pay someone to give you. It belongs to a moral community'. Relatedly, I worked hard to nurture *Ubuntu*-imbued research. As Jacob Mugumbate (2020, p 420) states, such an approach in entirely at odds with top-down imposed research processes and it aspires to give the 'research process a humane face'. Those of us who advocate for this form of engagement advocate 'collaboration with the participants and community' and attentiveness and respect for 'their spirituality, values, needs, norms and mores' (Mugumbate, 2020, p 420). A researcher such as myself becomes very much 'a *Munhu ane hunhu* (humane person)' who seeks to dilute or remove power imbalances in the research interaction. *Ubuntu*-imbued research strives to arrive at an ontology that is relational and collaborative.

I also remained entirely guided by the research ethics protocols within the university where I initially began to conduct the research project that later gave rise to *Social Work and with the Black African Diaspora*; for example, in safeguarding research participants' anonymity and the handling of sensitive information. As a registered social worker, I also subscribed to and was obligated to uphold similar ethical standards pertaining to confidentiality and non-maleficence, as are demanded by CORU, the Irish professional regulatory body (see also Marovatsanga, 2020 for a more detailed articulation of questions pertaining to ethics, methodology and data analysis techniques).

References

Adcock, M. and White, R. (1985) *Good enough parenting*, London: BAAF.

Adeleke, T. (2009) *The case against Afrocentrism*, Jackson, MS: University of Mississippi.

Adeleye T., Adeniran D., Fidel, M. and Watson, C. (2020) 'Discrimination and apathy: Students describe culture of racism on campuses', *University Times*, 18 July, www.universitytimes.ie/2020/07/discrimination-and-apathy-students-describe-culture-of-racism-on-campuses/

Adjei, P.B. and Minka, E. (2018) 'Black parents ask for a second look: Parenting under "white" child protection rules in Canada', *Children and Youth Services Review*, vol 94, pp 511–524.

AFRUCA (2018) 'New AFRUCA report calls for ban on smacking children', press release, 28 September, https://afruca.org/press-release/6072-2/

Ahluwalia, P. (2002) 'The struggle for African identity: Thabo Mbeki's African renaissance', *African and Asian Studies*, vol 1, no 4, pp 265–278.

Ahluwalia, P. (2010) *Out of Africa*, New York: Routledge.

Ahmad, B. (1990) *Black perspectives in social work*, Birmingham: Venture press.

Akinyela, M.M. (1995) 'Rethinking Afrocentricity: The foundation of a theory of critical Africentricity', in A. Darder (ed) *Culture and difference*, New York: Bethon & Garvey Press, pp 21–39.

Akinyele, M.M. and Aldridge, D.P. (2003) 'Beyond Eurocentrism, Afrocentricity and multiculturalism', *Race, Gender & Class*, vol 10, no 2, pp 58–70.

Alexander, J.C., Eyerman, R., Giesen, B., Smelser, N.J. and Sztompka, P. (eds) (2004) *Cultural trauma and collective identity*, California: California University.

Allen, K. (2007) *The corporate takeover of Ireland*, Dublin: Irish Academic Press.

Allen, K. (2012) 'The model pupil who faked the test', *Critical Social Policy*, vol 32 no 3, pp 422–440.

Allen, K. (2020) 'The politics of COVID-19', *Irish Marxist Review*, vol 9, no 27 file:///C:/Users/0103674s/Downloads/372-1471-1-PB%20(2).pdf

Allen, T.W. (1994) *The invention of the white race: Volume one*, London: Verso.

Allen, T.W. (1997) *The invention of the white race: Volume two*, London: Verso.

Althusser, L.A. (1971) *Lenin and philosophy and other essays*, London: New Left Books.

Amnesty International (2018) *Trapped in the Matrix* www.amnesty.org.uk/files/reports/Trapped%20in%20the%20Matrix%20Amnesty%20report.pdf

Anderson, R. (2012) 'Molefi Kete Asante: The Afrocentric idea and the cultural turn in intercultural communication studies', *International Journal of Intercultural Communication Studies*, vol 35, pp 760–769.

Ani, M. (1994) *Yurugu: An African centred critique of European cultural thought and behaviour*, Trenton, New Jersey, USA: Africa World Press.

Aniagolu, C. (1997) 'Being black in Ireland' in E. Crowley and J. Mac Laughlin (eds) *Under the belly of the tiger*, Dublin, Irish Reporter Publications, pp 43–53.

Annamma, S.A. (2015) 'Whiteness as property', *The Urban Review*, vol 47, pp 293–316.

Anthias F. and Yuval-Davis, N. (1993) *Racialised boundaries*, London: Routledge.

Aradau, C. and Tazzioli, M. (2021) 'Covid-19 and rebordering the world', *Radical Philosophy*, Summer, vol 2, no 10, pp 3–11.

Arendt, H. (1998) *The human condition*, Chicago, USA: University of Chicago. (Originally published in 1958).

Arnold, S. (2012) *State sanctioned child poverty and exclusion*, www.irishrefugeecouncil.ie/Handlers/Download.ashx?IDMF=10c78084-d67c-4b86-b6d6-3b1b48fb85ed

Asante, M.K. (1980) *Afrocentricity*, Buffalo, New York, USA: Amuliefi.

Asante, M.K. (1998) *The Afrocentric idea*, Philadelphia, USA: Temple University. (Second edition).

Asante, M.K. (2006) 'A discourse on black studies', *Journal of Black Studies*, vol 36, no 5, pp 646–662.

Ash, A. (2010) 'Ethics and the street-level bureaucrat', *Ethics and Social Welfare*, vol 4, no 2, pp 201–209.

Askeland, G.A. and Payne, M. (2006) 'Social work education's cultural hegemony', *International Social Work*, vol 49, no 6, pp 731–743.

Atkinson, D.R. and Lowe, S.M. (1995) 'The role of ethnicity, cultural knowledge, and conventional techniques in counselling and psychotherapy', in J.G. Ponterotto, J.M. Casas, L.A. Suzuki, & C.M. Alexander (eds) *Handbook of multicultural counselling*, Thousand Oaks, CA: Sage, pp 387–414.

Atkinson, P. and Silverman, D. (1997) 'Kundera's Immortality: The Interview Society and the Invention of the Self', *Qualitative Inquiry*, vol 3, no 3, pp 304–325.

Badiou, A. (2008) *The meaning of Sarkozy*, London: Verso.

Baines, D. (2004a) 'Pro-market, non-market: vol 24, no 1, pp 5–29.

Baines, D. (2004b) 'Caring for nothing', *Work, Employment and Society*, vol 12, no 2, pp 267–295.

Baines. D. (2021) 'Soft cops or social justice activists: Social work's relationship to the state in the context of BLM and neoliberalism', *British Journal of Social Work*, published online 11 October, DOI: 10.1093/bjsw/bcab200

Baines, D., Bennett, B., Goodwin, S. and Rawsthorne, M. (2019) *Working across difference*, London, Red Globe

Baker, M. (2012) 'Modernity/coloniality and Eurocentric education', *Policy Futures in Education*, vol 10, no 1,

Baker, N. (2021) 'Residents at Cork direct provision centre refuse meals in protest at standards', *The Irish Times*, 17 January www.irishtimes.com/news/social-affairs/cork-direct-provision-residents-refuse-meals-over-low-standard-1.4488868

Balakrishnan, S. (2016) 'Pan-African legacies, Afropolitan futures: a conversation with Achille Mbembe', *Transition*, 120, pp 28–37.

Balakrishnan, S. (2020) 'Afrocentrism revisited', *Souls*, vol 22, no 1, pp 71–88.

Ball, S.J. (2013) *Foucault, power, and education*, New York, USA: Routledge.

Bar-On, A. (1999) 'Social work and the "missionary zeal to whip up the heathen along the path of righteousness"', *British Journal of Social Work*, vol 29, no 5, pp 5–26.

Barry, K. (2014) *What's food got to do with it: Food experiences of asylum seekers in Direct Provision* www.nascireland.org/wp-content/uploads/2014/05/WhatsFoodFINAL.pdf

Barry, U. and Conroy, P. (2012) Ireland 2008–2012: Untold story of the crisis – gender, equality and inequalities www.tascnet.ie/upload/file/MurphyGenderGovernance.pdf

Bartoli, A., Kennedy, S. and Tedam, P. (2008) 'Black African student experience of practice learning in a social work setting', *Journal of Practice Teaching and Learning*, vol 8, no 2, pp 75–90.

Bauman, Z. (1989) *Modernity and the Holocaust*, Cambridge: Polity.

BBC News (2020) 'George Floyd death: Clashes as protests spread across US', 30 May, www.bbc.com/news/world-us-canada-52857334

Becker, H.S. (1982) 'Culture: a sociological view', *Yale Review*, pp 513–27.

Beirne, L. and Jaichand, V. (2010) *Breaking down barriers*, Irish Centre for Human Rights, National University of Ireland: Galway.

Bell, J.M. (2014) *The black power movement and American social work*, New York: Columbia University Press.

Benjamin, R. (2019) *Race after technology*, Cambridge: Polity.

Bernler, G., Johnsson, L., Skårner, A. (1993) *Behandlingens villkor. Om relatione och förväntningarna i det sociala arbetet*, Stockholm: Natur och Kultur.

Bernstein, B. and Solomon, J. (1999) 'Pedagogy, identity and the construction of a theory of symbolic control – Basil Bernstein questioned by Joseph Solomon', *British Journal of Sociology of Education*, vol 20, no 2, pp 265–279.

Bhambra, G.K. (2007) *Rethinking modernity*, Houndsmill: Palgrave Macmillan.

Bhambra, G.K., Gebrial, D. and Nisancioglu, K. (2018) 'Introduction', in G.K. Bhambra, D. Gebrial and K. Nisancioglu (eds) *Decolonising the university*, London: Pluto, pp 1–19.

Bhattacharyya, G. (2015) *Crisis, austerity, and everyday life*, London: Palgrave Macmillan.

Bidgood, B., Holosko, M.J. and Taylor, L.E. (2003) 'A new working model of social work practice: A turtle's view', *Research on Social Work Practice*, vol 13, no 3, pp 400–408.

Biestek, F.P. (1975 [1957]) 'Client self-determination', in F.E. McDermott (ed) *Self-determination in social work*, London: Routledge & Kegan Paul.

Bissoondath, B. (1994) *Selling illusions: The cult of multiculturalism in Canada*, London: Penguin.

Boccagni, P. (2015) '(Super)diversity and the migration – social work nexus', *Ethnic and Racial Studies*, vol 38, no 4, pp 608–20.

Bohrer, A.J. (2019) *Marxism and intersectionality*, Bielefeld, Germany: Transcript-Verlag.

Bojarczuk, S., Marchelewska, E. and Prontera, M. (2015) *Ethnic minorities and mental health in Ireland*, Dublin: Cairde https://cairde.ie/wp-content/uploads/2009/08/CAIR_001_Document_P7.pdf

Bonnett, A. (2000) *White identities*, Harlow: Prentice Hall.

Boucher, G. (2008) 'Ireland's lack of a coherent integration policy', *Translocations*, vol 3, no 1, pp 5–28.

Bourdieu, P. (1986) 'The forms of capital', in J.G. Richardson (ed) *Handbook of theory and research for the sociology of education*, New York: Greenwood Press, pp 241–58.

Bourdieu, P. (1991) *Language and symbolic power*, Cambridge: Polity.

Bourdieu, P. (2003 [1977]) *Outline of a theory of practice*, Cambridge: Cambridge University.

Bourdieu, P. and Wacquant, L. (1999) 'On the cunning of imperialist reason', *Theory, Culture & Society*, vol 16, no 1, pp 41–59

Bourdieu, P. and Wacquant, L. (2001) 'NewLiberalSpeak: Notes on the new planetary vulgate', *Radical Philosophy*, Jan/Feb, 105, pp 2–6.

Bourdieu, P. and Wacquant, L. (2004) *An invitation to reflexive sociology*, Cambridge: Polity.

Bourdieu, P., Accardo, A., Balazas, G., Beaud, S., Bonvin, F., Bourdieu, E., Bourgois, P., Broccolichi, S., Champagne, P., Christin, R., Faguer, J.P., Garcia, S., Lenoir, R., Oeuvrard, F., Pialoux, M., Pinto, L., Podalydes, D., Sayad, A., Soulie, C. and Wacquant, J.D. (2002) *The weight of the world: Social suffering in contemporary society*, Polity: Cambridge (first reprint).

Bowes, A. and Dar, N. (2000) 'Researching social care for minority ethnic older people: Implications of some Scottish research', *British Journal of Social Work*, vol 30, no 3, pp 305–321.

Bowlby, J. (1990) *Child care and the growth of love*, Harmondsworth: Penguin (third edition).

Brah, A. (1996) *Cartographies of diaspora*, London: Routledge.

Branigan, R. and Madden, C. (2020) *Spending review 2020: Tusla residential care costs*, Dublin: Department of Children and Youth Affairs file:///C:/Users/0103674s/Downloads/90898_7509a985-73a8-4963-a2eb-522285714ab2.pdf

Brenner, R. (2020) 'Escalating plunder', *New Left Review*, issue 23, pp 5–25.

Briggs, S. and Whittaker, A. (2018) 'Protecting children from faith-based abuse through accusations of witchcraft and spirit possession: Understanding contexts and Informing practice', *British Journal of Social Work*, 48, pp 2157–217.

British Association of Social Workers (BASW) (2016) *Code of ethics for social work*, www.basw.co.uk/system/files/resources/Code%20of%20Ethics%20Aug18.pdf

Brockmann, O. and Garrett, P.M. (2022) '"People are responsible for their own individual actions": dominant ideologies within the Neoliberal Institutionalised Social Work Order', *European Journal of Social Work*, DOI: 10.1080/13691457.2022.2040443

Brown, W. (2015) *Undoing the demos*, New York: Zone Books.

Browne, S. (2015) *Dark matters: On the surveillance of blackness*, Durham, NC and London: Duke University.

Bruce-Jones, E. (2017) 'A body does not just combust', *World Policy Journal*, vol 34, no 2, pp 31–35.

Bryman, A. (2012) *Social research methods*, Oxford: Oxford University (second edition).

Burman, E., Smailes, S.L. and Chantler, K. (2004) '"Culture" as a barrier to service provision and delivery: Domestic violence services for minoritised women', *Critical Social Policy*, vol 24, no 3, pp 332–357.

Burr, V. (2015) *Social construction*, London: Routledge.

Byrne, D. (2017) 'Beyond mere equality – a politics of class analysis not "evidence"', *Soundings*, 64, pp 105–117.

Cahill, D. (2011) 'Beyond neoliberalism? Crisis and the prospects for progressive alternatives', *New Political Science*, vol 33, no 4, pp 479–492.

Cameron, D. (2011) PM's speech at Munich Security Conference, 5 February, www.number10.gov.uk/news/pms-speech-at-munich-security-conference/

Canadian Association of Social Workers (CASW) (2019) *Statement of apology and commitment to reconciliation*, www.casw-acts.ca/sites/default/files/Statement_of_Apology_and_Reconciliation.pdf

Central Statistics Office (2020) Census of Population 2016 – Profile 8 Irish Travellers, Ethnicity and Religion, www.cso.ie/en/releasesandpublications/ep/p-cp8iter/p8iter/p8e/

Césaire, A. (2000 [1955]) *Discourse on colonialism*, New York: Monthly Review Press (trans J. Pinkham).

Chakrabarty, D. (2000) *Provincializing Europe*, Princeton, NJ: Princeton University Press.

Charbeneau, J.M. (2009) 'Enactments of whiteness in pedagogical practice', Ann Arbor: University of Michigan (unpublished doctoral dissertation).

Chaturvedi, V. (ed) (2012) *Mapping subaltern studies and the postcolonial*, London: Verso.

Chibber, V. (2013) *Postcolonial theory and the specter of capital*, London, Verso.

Chigudu, S. (2021) 'The long shadow of Cecil Rhodes', *The Guardian*, The long read, 14 January, pp 5–9.

Child Care Law Reporting Project (2015) *Final report*, www.childlawproject. ie/wp-content/uploads/2015/11/CCLRP-Full-final-report_FINAL2.pdf

Choonara, E. (2021) 'Theorising anti-racism in health and social care', *Critical Radical Social Work*, published online 18 January, doi.org/10.1332/ 204986021X16109919364036

Christie, A. (2003) 'Unsettling the "social" in social work: Responses to asylum seeking children in Ireland, *Child and Family Social Work*, vol 8, no 3, pp 223–231.

Christie, A. (2005) 'Social work education in Ireland: Histories and challenges', *Portularia*, vol 1, pp 111–130.

Christie, A. (2006) 'From racial state to racist state: Questions for social professionals', *Irish Journal of Social Studies*, vol 7, no 2, https://arrow. tudublin.ie/cgi/viewcontent.cgi?article=1021&context=ijass

Christie, A. (2010) 'Whiteness and the politics of "race" in child protection guidelines in Ireland', *European Journal of Social Work*, vol 13, no 2, pp 199–215.

Colic-Peisker, V. and Tilbury, F. (2007) 'Integration into the Australian labour market: The experience of three "visibly different" groups of recently arrived refugees', *International Migration*, vol 45, no 1, pp 59–86.

Cole, M. (2009) 'Critical race theory comes to the UK: A Marxist response', *Ethnicities*, vol 9, no 2, pp 246–284.

Collins, P.H. (1986) 'Learning from the outsider within: The sociological significance of Black feminist thought', *Social Problems*, vol 33, no 6, pp 14–32.

Collins, P.H. and Bilge, S. (2016) *Intersectionality*, Cambridge: Polity.

Commission to Inquire into Child Abuse (2009) *Commission to Inquire into Child Abuse Report*, Dublin: Stationery Office.

Committee on the Elimination of Racial Discrimination (CERD) (2019) *Concluding observations on the combined fifth to ninth reports of Ireland*, 12 December, CERD/C/IRL/CO/5-9, https://tbinternet.ohchr.org/ Treaties/CERD/Shared%20Documents/IRL/INT_CERD_COC_IRL_ 40806_E.pdf

Conneely, E. and Garrett, P.M. (2015) 'Social workers and social justice during a period of intensive neoliberalization: a preliminary investigation from the Republic of Ireland', *Journal of Progressive Human Services*, vol 26, no 2, pp 126–147.

Connell, R. (2007) *Southern theory*, Cambridge: Polity.

Cooper, S. (1977) 'Social work: A dissenting profession', *Social Work*, vol 22, no 5, pp 360–367.

Coquelin, O. (2005) 'Politics in the Irish Free State: The legacy of a conservative revolution', *The European Legacy*, vol 10, no 1, pp 29–39.

CORU (2019) *Social workers registration board code of professional ethics*, www.coru.ie/files-codes-of-conduct/swrb-code-of-professional-conduct-and-ethics-for-social-workers.pdf

Coulter, C. and Reynolds, J. (2020) 'Good times for a change? Ireland since the general election', *Soundings*, issue 75, pp 66–81.

Council of Europe (2013) *Advisory Committee on the Framework Convention for the Protection of National Minorities: Third opinion on Ireland adopted on 10 October 2012*, www.coe.int/t/dghl/monitoring/minorities/3_FCNMdocs/PDF_3rd_OP_Ireland_en.pdf

Crabtree, S.A., Husain, F. and Spalek, B. (2008) *Islam and social work: Debating values, transforming practice*, Bristol: Policy Press.

Crehan, K. (2002) *Gramsci, culture and anthropology*, London: Pluto.

Crehan, K. (2011) 'Gramsci's concept of common sense: A useful concept for anthropologists?', *Journal of Modern Italian Studies*, vol 16, no 2, pp 273–287.

Crehan, K. (2016) *Gramsci's common sense*, Durham, NC: Duke University.

Crosbie, B. (2009) 'Ireland, colonial science, and the geographical construction of British rule in India, c. 1820–1870', *The Historical Journal*, vol 52, no 4, pp 963–987.

Cross, T., Bazron, B.J., Dennis, K.K. and Isaacs, M.R. (1989) *Towards a culturally competent system of care*, Washington, DC: Howard University.

Cullen, P. (2020) 'Ireland has one of the highest rates of Covid-19 deaths in care homes in world', *The Irish Times*, 22 May, www.irishtimes.com/news/health/irelandhas-one-of-the-highest-rates-of-covid-19-deaths-in-care-homes-in-world-1.4260140

Cullen, P. (2021) 'HSE vaccination portal to correct ethnicity error', *The Irish Times*, 7 June, p 1.

Cuskelly, K., Lavin, E. and Conneely, E. (2014) 'Respect social workers, NO to cheap labour!', *Critical and Radical Social Work*, vol 2, no 2, pp 251–255.

Dalikeni, C. (2013) 'Making sense of each other: Lived experiences and told stories of child protection social workers and asylum-seeking families', Belfast: Queens University (unpublished PhD thesis).

Dalikeni, C. (2021) 'Child-rearing practices: Cross cultural perspectives of African asylum-seeking families and child protection social workers in Ireland', *European Journal of Social Work*, vol 24, no 1, pp 8–20.

Danaher, G., Schirato, T. and Webb, J. (2000) *Understanding Foucault*, London: Sage.

Danso, R. (2016) 'Migration studies: Resuscitating the casualty of the professionalisation of social work', *British Journal of Social Work*, vol 46, no 6, pp 1741–1758.

Data for Black Lives (D4BL) (2020) *COVID-19 pulse check report – April 2020*, file:///C:/Users/0103674s/Downloads/D4BL%20COVID19%20 Movement%20Pulsecheck%20Report%20(Print)%20(1).pdf

Davis, A. (2020) 'Angela Davis on abolition, calls to defund police, toppled racist statues and voting in 2020 election', *Democracy Now!*, 12 June, www. democracynow.org/2020/6/12/angela_davis_on_abolition_calls_to

Davis, S.K., Williams, A.D. and Akinyela, M. (2010) 'An Afrocentric approach to building cultural relevance in social work research', *Journal of Black Studies*, vol 41, no 2, pp 338–350.

de Sousa Santos, B. (2012) 'Public sphere and the epistemologies of the south', *African Development*, vol 37, no 1, pp 43–67.

de Sousa Santos, B. (2014) *Epistemologies of the South*, London: Routledge.

De Tona, C. and Lentin, A. (2011) 'Networking sisterhood, from the informal to the global: AkiDwA, the African and Migrant Women's Network, Ireland', *Global Networks*, vol 11, no 2, pp 242–261.

Dean, R.G., and Fleck-Henderson, A. (1992) 'Teaching clinical theory and practice through a constructivist lens', *Journal of Teaching in Social Work*, vol 6, no 1, pp 3–20.

Delgado, R. (2003) 'Crossroads and blind alleys: A critical examination on recent writing about race', *Texas Law Review*, vol 82, no 1, pp 121–152.

Delgado, R. and Stefancic, J. (2012) *Critical race theory*, New York: New York University (second edition).

Denzin, N.K. (2001) 'The reflexive interview and a performative social science', *Qualitative Research*, vol 1, no 1, pp 23–46.

Denzin, N.K. and Lincoln, Y.S. (1998) *Collecting and interpreting qualitative materials*, London: Sage.

Department of Children and Youth Affairs (2017) *Children First Guidance*, www.tusla.ie/uploads/content/Children_First_National_Guidance_2017. pdf

Department of Children, Equality, Disability, Integration and Youth (2020) *Anti-racism Committee: Interim report to the minister for children, equality, disability, integration and youth*, www.gov.ie/pdf/?file=https://assets.gov.ie/ 132151/ed3f39e2-4aa1-4991-aa06-52beae8310db.pdf#page=null

Department of Health (2020) 'Minister Zappone publishes statistical spotlight #4 young Travellers in Ireland', 14 April, www.gov.ie/en/ press-release/7d4267-minister-zappone-publishes-statistical-spotlight-4- young-travellers-/

Dettlaff, A.J., Weber, K., Pendleton, M., Boyd, R., Bettencourt, B. and Burton, L. (2020) 'It is not a broken system, it is a system that needs to be broken: The upEND movement to abolish the child welfare system', *Journal of Public Child Welfare*, published online 6 September, DOI: 10.1080/15548732.2020.1814542

Devore, W. and Schlesinger, E.G. (1991) *Ethnic-sensitive social work practice*, New York: Macmillan.

Dobuzinskis, A. (2019) 'More racial diversity in US police departments unlikely to reduce shootings: study', Reuters, 23 July, www.reuters.com/article/us-usa-police-race-idUSKCN1UI017

Du Toit, L. and Coetzee, A. (2016) 'Gendering African philosophy, or: African feminism as decolonizing force', in A. Afolayan and T. Falola (eds) *The Palgrave handbook of African philosophy*, New York: Palgrave Macmillan, 333–371.

Dübgen, F. and Skupien, S. (2019) *Paulin Hountondji: African philosophy as critical universalism*, Cham, Switzerland: Springer.

Dyer, R. (1997) *White*, London: Routledge.

Earhart, B. (1993) *The religious traditions of the world*, San Francisco, CA: Harper.

Earner, I. (2007) 'Immigrant families and public child welfare', *Child Welfare*, vol 86, no 4, pp 63–91.

Economic and Social Research Institute (ESRI) (2018) *Annual Report, 2018*, www.esri.ie/publications/esri-annual-report-2018

Elkins, C. (2005) *Imperial reckoning*, New York: Henry Holt.

European Union Agency for Fundamental Rights (2020) *Roma and Travellers in six countries*, file:///C:/Users/0103674s/Documents/EU%20Fundamental%20Rights%20Agency,%20Roma%20&%20Travellers%206%20Countries,%20Sept%202020.pdf

Eze, E.C. (ed) (1997) *Race and the enlightenment: A reader*, Oxford: Blackwell.

Fairclough, N. (2003) '"Political correctness": The politics of culture and language', *Discourse and Society*, vol 14, no 1, pp: 127–28.

Fanning, B. (2002) *Immigration and social change in the Republic of Ireland*, Manchester: Manchester University Press.

Fanning, B. (2011) *Immigration and social cohesion in the Republic of Ireland*, Manchester: Manchester University Press.

Fanning, B. (2012) *Racism and social change in the Republic of Ireland*, Manchester: Manchester University Press (second edition).

Fanning, B. and Michael, L. (eds) (2019) *Immigrants as outsiders in the two Irelands*, Manchester: Manchester University Press.

Fanon, F. (1986 [1952]) *Black skin, white masks*, London: Pluto (trans C.L. Markham).

Fanon, F. (1989 [1959]) *Studies in a dying colonialism*, London, Earthscape (trans H. Chevalier).

Fanon, F. (2004 [1961]) *The wretched of the earth*, New York: Grove Press (trans R. Philcox).

Fanon, F. (2018 [1953–1956]) 'Our journal', in J. Khalfa and R.C.J. Young (eds) *Alienation and freedom: Frantz Fanon*, London: Bloomsbury, pp 311–349 (trans S. Corcoran).

Farah, W. (2020) 'New right, old racism – the battleground of COVID-19', The Institute of Race Relations, 30 May, www.irr.org.uk/news/new-right-old-racism-the-battlefield-of-covid-19/

Farmer, N. (2020) '"I never felt like an illegal immigrant until social work turned up at the hospital": No recourse to public funds as necropolitical exception', *British Journal of Social Work*, published online 27 September, DOI: 10.1093/bjsw/bcaa151

Fenton, J. (2018) 'Putting old heads on young shoulders', *Social Work Education*, vol 37, no 8, pp 941–954.

Ferguson, S.C. (2016) *African-American philosophy and the African diaspora*, Basingstoke: Palgrave Macmillan (first edition).

Foreman, M. (2008) 'HIV and "direct provision" – learning from the experiences of asylum seekers in Ireland', *Translocations*, vol 4, no 1, pp 67–85.

Forgacs, D. (1988) *A Gramsci reader*, London: Lawrence and Wishart.

Foucault, M. (1972) *The archaeology of knowledge*, New York: Pantheon.

Foucault, M. (1997) 'The ethics of the concern for the self as a practice of freedom', in P. Rainbow (ed) *Ethics, subjectivity and truth*, London: Penguin, pp 281–301.

Frankenberg, R. (1993) *White women, race matters*, Minneapolis, MN: University of Minnesota.

Frankenberg, R. (ed) (1997) *Displacing whiteness*, Durham, NC: Duke University.

Fraser, N. (2003) 'Social justice in an age of identity politics', in N. Fraser and A. Honneth (eds) *Redistribution or recognition?* London: Verso.

Fraser, N. (2013) *Fortunes of feminism*, London: Verso.

Fraser, N. (2016) 'Capital and care', *New Left Review*, no 100, pp 99–119.

Freire, P. (1970) *Pedagogy of the oppressed*, New York: Continuum.

Frost, N. and Dolan, P. (2021) 'Theory, research and practice in child welfare', *Child and Family Social Work*, published online 21 January, https://doi.org/10.1111/cfs.12824

Furedi, F. (2004) *Therapy culture*, London: Routledge.

Gair, S., Thomson, J., Miles, D., and Harris, N. (2003) 'It's very "white" isn't it! Challenging mono-culturalism in social work and welfare education', *Advances in Social Work and Welfare Education*, vol 5, no 1, pp 37–52.

Gallagher, A. (2020) 'Pads for pooches with serious (bow) wow factor', *The Irish Times*, 22 November, www.irishtimes.com/life-and-style/homes-and-property/interiors/dog-s-life-pads-for-pooches-with-bow-wow-factor-1.4413782

Gallagher, C. and Pollack, S. (2021) 'Gardai fear declining relations with Black community', *The Irish Times*, 9 April, p 4.

Garrett, P.M. (1998) 'Notes from the diaspora: Anti-discriminatory social work practice, Irish people and the practice curriculum', *Social Work Education*, vol 17, no 4, pp 435–448.

Garrett, P.M. (2004) *Social work and Irish people in Britain*, Bristol: Policy Press.

Garrett, P.M. (2005) 'Social work's "electronic turn": Notes on the deployment of information and communication technologies in social work with children and families', *Critical Social Policy*, vol 25, no 4, pp 529–554.

Garrett, P.M. (2006) 'Protecting children in a globalised world: "Race" and place in the Laming Report on the death of Victoria Climbié', *Journal of Social Work*, vol 6, no 3, pp 315–336.

Garrett, P.M. (2007) 'Neoliberalism and "welfare" in the shadow of the prison' in R. Sheehan and J. Ogloff (eds) *Working with the forensic paradigm: Cross-discipline approaches for policy and practice*, London: Routledge, pp 85–98.

Garrett, P.M. (2009) 'Questioning Habermasian social work: A note on some alternative theoretical resources', *British Journal of Social Work*, vol 39, no 5, pp 867–883.

Garrett, P.M. (2012) 'Adjusting "our notions of the nature of the state": A political reading of Ireland's child protection crisis', *Capital & Class*, vol 36, no 2, pp 263–281.

Garrett, P.M. (2013) 'A "catastrophic, inept, self-serving" Church? Re-examining three reports on child abuse in the Republic of Ireland', *Journal of Progressive Human Services*, vol 24, no 1, pp 43–65.

Garrett, P.M. (2015) 'Words matter: Deconstructing "welfare dependency" in the UK', *Critical and Radical Social Work*, vol 3, no 3, pp 389–406.

Garrett, P.M. (2016) 'Questioning tales of "ordinary magic": "Resilience" and neoliberal reasoning', *British Journal of Social Work*, vol 46, no 7, pp 1909–1925.

Garrett, P.M. (2017) 'Excavating the past: Mother and Baby Homes in the Republic of Ireland', *British Journal of Social Work*, vol 47, no 2, pp 358–374.

Garrett, P.M. (2018) *Social work and social theory*, Bristol: Policy Press (second edition).

Garrett, P.M. (2019) 'Welfare words, neoliberalism and critical social work', in S.A. Webb (ed) *The Routledge handbook of critical social work*, London: Routledge, pp 3–15.

Garrett, P.M. (2020) 'Faulty "tools"? Why social work scholarship needs to take a more critical approach to Michel Foucault', *Journal of Social Work*, vol 20, no 4, pp 483–500.

Garrett, P.M. (2021) *Dissenting social work: Critical theory, resistance and pandemic*, London: Routledge.

Gartland, F. (2016) 'Fewer male social workers leads to gender bias, says TCD academic', *The Irish Times*, 22 February, www.irishtimes.com/news/social-affairs/fewer-male-social-workers-leads-to-gender-bias-says-tcd-academic-1.2543216

Gatwiri, K. (2020) 'Racial microaggressions at work: Reflections from Black African professionals in Australia', *British Journal of Social Work*, published online 25 December, https://academic.oup.com/bjsw/article/51/2/655/6048178?rss=1

Gelling, L. (2015) 'Qualitative research', *Nursing Standard*, vol 29, no 30, pp 43–47.

Gilbert, J. (2015) 'Disaffected consent', *Soundings*, 60, pp 29–42.

Gilmore, R.W. (2007) *Golden gulag prisons: surplus, crisis and opposition in globalizing California*, Berkeley and Los Angeles, CA: University of California Press.

Gilroy, P. (1993) *The Black Atlantic*, London: Verso.

Gilroy P. (1994) 'Forward', in I. Gaber and J. Aldridge (eds) *In the best interests of the child: Culture, identity and transracial adoption*, London: Free Association.

Gilroy, P. (1998) 'Race ends here', *Ethnic and Racial Studies*, vol 21, no 5, pp 838–847.

Gilroy, P. (2000) *Between camps*, London: Penguin.

Gilroy, P. (2013) '"We got to get over before we go under … ": fragments for a history of black vernacular neoliberalism', *New Formations*, vol 80/81, pp 23–39.

Gilroy, P. (2019) 'Never again: Refusing race and salvaging the human', The 2019 Holberg Lecture, https://holbergprisen.no/en/news/holberg-prize/2019-holberg-lecture-laureate-paul-gilroy

Giroux, H.A. (1997a) 'Insurgent multiculturalism and the promise of pedagogy', in D.T. Goldberg (ed) *Multiculturalism: A critical reader*, Oxford: Blackwell (third reprint).

Giroux, H.A. (1997b) 'Rewriting the discourse of racial identity: Towards a pedagogy of whiteness', *Harvard Educational Review*, vol 67, no 2, pp 285–321.

Go, J. (2013) 'Decolonizing Bourdieu', *Sociological Theory*, vol 31, no 1, pp 49–74.

Goldberg, D.T. (2002) *The racial state*, London: Wiley-Blackwell.

Goldstein, D.M. (2012) 'Decolonising "actually existing neoliberalism"', *Social Anthropology*, vol 20, no 3, pp 304–309.

Gopal, P. (2019) *Insurgent empire*, London: Verso.

Gore, E. (2020) 'COVID-19 and racial capitalism in the UK', Sheffield Political Economy Research Institute, 1 May, http://speri.dept.shef.ac.uk/2020/05/01/covid-19-and-racial-capitalism-in-the-uk-why-race-and-class-matter-for-understanding-the-coronavirus-pandemic/

Gotanda, N. (2000) 'A critique of "our constitution is colour-blind"', in R. Delgado and J. Stefancic (eds) *Critical race theory*, Philadelphia, PA: Temple University, pp 35–38 (second edition).

Government of Ireland (2021) *White paper to end direct provision and to establish a new international protection support service*, www.gov.ie/en/publication/7aad0-minister-ogorman-publishes-the-white-paper-on-ending-direct-provision/

Graham, M. (1999) 'The African-centred worldview: Developing a paradigm for social work', *British Journal of Social Work*, vol 29, no 2, pp 252–267.

Graham, M. (2001) 'Expanding the philosophical base', in V.E. Cree (ed) *Social work: A reader*, Birmingham: Venture, pp 63–74.

Gray, B. (2000) 'Gendering the Irish diaspora', *Women's International Review*, vol 23, no 2, pp 167–185.

Gray, M., Coates, J., Yellow Bird, M. and Hetherington, T. (eds) (2013) *Decolonizing social work*, Farnham: Ashgate.

Gregory, J.R. (2020) 'The imperative and promise of neo-abolitionism in social work', *Journal of Social Work*, published online 26 August, doi.org/10.1177/1468017320952049

Gusciute, E. (2021) 'Míle fáilte? Discrimination in the Irish rental housing market towards Black applicants', in L. Michael and E. Joseph (eds) *The sociological observer: Black lives matter*, Maynooth, Ireland: Sociological Association of Ireland, pp 30–37.

Gusciute, E., Mühlau, P. and Layte, R. (2020) 'Discrimination in the rental housing market: A field experiment in Ireland, *Journal of Ethnic and Migration Studies*, DOI: 10.1080/1369183X.2020.1813017

Gyekye, K. (1995) *African philosophical thought: The Akan conceptual scheme*, Philadelphia, PA: Temple University.

Hall, S. (1990) 'Cultural identity and diaspora', in J. Rutherford (ed) *Identity: Community, culture, difference*, London: Lawrence and Wishart, pp .

Harmon, A. and Garrett, P.M. (2015) 'It's like Weber's "iron cage": Irish social workers' experience of the habitual residence condition (HRC)', *Critical and Radical Social Work*, vol 3, no 1, pp 35–52.

Harrington, H. (2017) 'No one-size-fits-all approach: Complexities in working with African children and families', Galway: National University of Ireland Galway (unpublished MA dissertation).

Harris, C.I. (1993) 'Whiteness as property', *Harvard Law Review*, vol 106, no 8, pp. 1707–1791.

Harris, C. and Boddy, J. (2017) 'The natural environment in social work education: A content analysis of Australian social work courses', *Australian Social Work*, vol 70, no 3, pp 337–349.

Hart, W.A. (2002) 'Africans in eighteenth-century Ireland', *Irish Historical Studies*, vol 33, no 129, pp 19–33.

Harvey, A.R., and Rauch, J.B. (1997) 'A comprehensive Afrocentric rites of passage program for black male adolescents', *Health & Social Work*, vol 22, no 1, pp 30–37.

Harvey, D. (2020) 'Anti-capitalist politics in the time of COVID-19', 19 March, http://davidharvey.org/2020/03/anti-capitalist-politics-in-the-time-of-covid-19/

Haug, E. (2005) 'Critical reflections on the emerging discourse of international social work', *International Social Work*, vol 48, no 2, pp 126–135.

Hayes, D. and Houston, S. (2007) ' "Lifeworld", "system" and family group conferences', *British Journal of Social Work*, vol 37, no 6, pp 987–1006.

Health Information and Quality Authority (HIQA) (2015) *Findings of inspection of the child protection and welfare services provided to children living in direct provision*, https://static.rasset.ie/.../news/hiqa-report-on-child-protection-and-welfare-services.pdf

Hearne, R. (2020) *Housing shock: The Irish housing crisis and how to solve it*, Bristol: Policy Press.

Hickman, M.J., Morgan, S., Walter, B. and Bradley, J. (2005) 'The limitations of whiteness and the boundaries of Englishness', *Ethnicities*, vol 5, no 2, pp 160–182.

Higgins, M.D. (2015) Speech at an event celebrating 30 years of the Pavee Point Traveller and Roma Centre, 18 November, www.president.ie/en/media-library/speeches/speech-at-an-event-celebrating-30-years-of-the-pavee-point-traveller-roma-c

Higgins, M.D. (2021) 'Empire: instincts, interests, power and resistance "versions of the 'other' – As tool in the culture of imperialism, and rationalisation for sources of violence"', Machnamh 100 Seminar II, 25 February, https://president.ie/en/media-library/speeches/machnamh-100-seminar-ii-empire-instincts-interests-power-resistance

Hoare, Q. and Nowell Smith, G. (eds) (2005) *Antonio Gramsci: Selections from Prison Notebooks*, London: Lawrence and Wishart (tenth reprint).

Holborow, M. (2015) *Language and neoliberalism*, London: Routledge.

Holohan, C. (2011) *In plain sight: Responding to the Ferns, Ryan, Murphy and Cloyne Reports*, Dublin: Amnesty International Ireland.

hooks, b. (1984) *Feminist theory*, Boston, MA: South End Press.

Hountondji, P.J. (1973) 'Pluralism, true and false', *Diogenes*, vol 94, pp 101–118.

Hountondji, P.J. (1983) 'Knowledge appropriation in a post-colonial context', in C.A. Odora Hoppers (ed) *Indigenous knowledge and the integration of knowledge systems*, Claremont, SA: New Africa Books, pp 23–39.

Hountondji, P.J. (1995) 'Producing knowledge in Africa today', *African Studies Review*, vol 38, no 3, pp 1–10.

Hountondji, P.J. (1996 [1976]) *African philosophy*, Bloomington and Indianapolis: Indiana University Press (second edition).

Hountondji, P.J. (2000) 'Tradition, hindrance or inspiration?', *Quest*, vol 24, no 1–2, pp 5–12.

Hountondji, P.J. (2002) *The struggle for meaning*, Athens, OH: Ohio University Press.

Houston, S. (2003) 'Moral consciousness and decision-making in child and family social work', *Adoption & Fostering*, vol 27, no 3, pp 61–71.

Howe, S. (1998) *Afrocentricism: Mythical pasts and imagined homes*, London, Verso.

Howe, S. (2003) *Ireland and empire*, Oxford: Oxford University.

Hudis, P. and Anderson, K.B. (eds) (2004) *The Rosa Luxemburg reader*, New York: Monthly Review Press.

Humphries, B. (2004) 'An unacceptable role for social work: Implementing immigration policy', *British Journal of Social Work*, vol 34, pp 93–107.

Hutchings, A. and Taylor, I. (2007) 'Defining the profession? Exploring an international definition of social work in China', *International Journal of Social Welfare*, vol 16, pp 382–390.

Hutchinson, D.L. (2000) 'Out yet unseen: A racial critique of gay and lesbian legal theory and political discourse', in R. Delgado and J. Stefancic (eds) *Critical race theory: The cutting edge*, pp 325–333 (second edition).

Hylton, K. (2012) 'Talk the talk, walk the walk: Defining critical race theory in research', *Race, Ethnicity and Education*, vol 15, no 1, pp 23–41.

Ignatiev, N. (1995) *How the Irish became white*, London: Routledge.

Inglis, T. (1998) *Moral monopoly*, Dublin: University College Dublin.

Institute for Policy Studies (2020) *Billionaire bonanza 2020*, https://inequality.org/wp-content/uploads/2020/04/Billionaire-Bonanza-2020-April-21.pdf

International Federation of Social Workers (2014) *Global definition of social work*, http://ifsw.org/get-involved/global-definition-of-social-work/

Ioakimidis, V. and Trimikliniotis, N. (2020) 'Making sense of social work's troubled past', *British Journal of Social Work*, published online 2 August, DOI: 10.1093/bjsw/bcaa040

Irish Association of Social Workers (IASW) (2021) *A new way forward: Dismantling racism in 21st-century Irish social work – ISAW anti-racism strategic plan 2021–2023*, file:///C:/Users/0103674s/Downloads/IASW%20Anti%20Racist%20Strategy%202021-2023.pdf

Irish Refugee Council (2020) *Powerless: Experiences of direct provision during the Covid-19 pandemic*, https://irishrefugeecouncil.eu.rit.org.uk/Handlers/Download.ashx?IDMF=419a9b2f-c405-4cc8-93c7-c27a618beb07

Jafri, B. (2018) 'Intellectuals outside the academy', *Social Justice*, vol 44, no 4, pp 119–131.

James, A., Jencks, C. and Prout, A. (1998) *Theorising childhood*, Cambridge: Polity.

Janz, B.B. (2016) 'The geography of African philosophy', in A. Afolayan and T. Falola (eds) *The Palgrave handbook of African philosophy*, New York: Palgrave Macmillan, pp 155–167.

Jessop, B. (2007) 'From micro-powers to governmentality', *Political Geography*, vol 26, pp 34–40.

Jones, C. (1996) 'Anti-intellectualism and the peculiarities of British social work education', in N. Parton (ed) *Social theory, social change and social work*, London: Routledge, pp 190–211.

Jones, C. (2001) 'Voices from the front line: State social workers and New Labour', *British Journal of Social Work*, vol 31, pp 547–562.

Jones, C.P. (2000) 'Levels of racism: A theoretic framework and a gardener's tale', *American Journal of Public Health*, vol 90, no 8, pp 1212–1215.

Joseph, E. (2017) 'Whiteness and racism: Examining the racial order in Ireland', *Irish Journal of Sociology*, vol 26, no 1, pp 46–70.

Joseph, E. (2021) 'Disposable workers: Responses to #BLM and Covid 19 as temporary disruption to the status quo', in L. Michael and E. Joseph (eds) *The sociological observer: Black lives matter*, Maynooth, Ireland: Sociological Association of Ireland, pp 20–30.

Jubilee Debt Campaign (2020) 'Sixty-four countries spend more on debt payments than health', 12 April, https://jubileedebt.org.uk/press-release/sixty-four-countries-spend-more-on-debt-payments-than-health

Kaime, T. (2009) 'The foundations of rights in the African charter on the rights and welfare of the child', *African Journal of Legal Studies*, vol 3, no 1, pp 120–136.

Kanai, A. and Gill, R. (2021) 'Woke? Affect, neoliberalism, marginalised identities and consumer culture', *New Formations*, vol 102, pp 10–27.

Kaseke, E. (2011) 'The poor laws colonialism and social welfare: social assistance in Zimbabwe', in J. Midgley and D. Piachaud (eds) *Colonial and welfare*, Cheltenham: Edward Elgar, pp 119–131.

Keena, C. (2015) 'Development of nursing homes needs a helping hand as banks fail to fund sector', *The Irish Times*, Business Section, 26 June, p 5.

Kelley, R.D.G. (2000) 'Introduction', in A. Césaire, *Discourse on colonialism*, New York: Monthly Review Press (trans J. Pinkham).

Kilkelly, U. (2000) 'Child protection and the European Convention on Human Rights', *International Journal of Human Rights*, vol 3, no 2, pp 1–12.

Kitano, H.H. (1980) *Race relations*, Englewood Cliffs, NJ: Prentice Hall.

Kitchin, R., O'Callaghan, C., Boyle, M. and Gleeson, J. (2012) 'Placing neoliberalism: The rise and fall of Ireland's Celtic Tiger', *Environment and Planning A*, vol 44, no 6, https://doi.org/10.1068/a44349

Kleibl, T., Lutz, R., Noyoo, N., Bunk, B., Dittmann, A. and Seepamore, B. (eds) (2019) *The Routledge handbook of postcolonial social work*, London and New York: Routledge.

Kovel, J. (1988) *White racism*, London: Free Association Books

Kriz, K. and Skivenes, M. (2010) 'Lost in translation: How child welfare workers in Norway and England experience language difficulties when working with minority ethnic families', *British Journal of Social Work*, vol 40, no 5, pp 1353–1367.

Kumagai, A. and Lypson, M. (2009) 'Beyond cultural competence: Critical consciousness, social justice, and multicultural education', *Academic Medicine*, vol 84, no 6, pp 782–787.

Kvale, S. (1996) *InterViews*, London: Sage.

Kymlica, W. (1995) *Multicultural citizenship*, Oxford: Clarendon Press.

Laird, S.E. (2008) *Anti-oppressive social work*, London: Sage.

Lash, D. (2017) *When the welfare people come: Race and class in the US child protection system*, Chicago, IL: Haymarket Books.

Lavalette, M. and Penketh, L. (eds) (2013) 'Introduction', in M. Lavalette and L. Penketh (eds) *Race, racism and social work: Contemporary issues and debates*, Bristol: Policy Press, pp 1–17.

Lea, J. (2000) 'The Macpherson Report and the question of institutional racism', *The Howard Journal*, vol 39, no 3, pp 219–233.

Lee, C. (1992) 'Profile of an independent Black institution', *The Journal of Negro Education*, vol 61, pp 60–177.

Lee, J-A. and Lutz, J.S. (2005) *Situating 'race' and racisms in scholars*, Montreal, Canada: McGill Queen's University.

Legault, G. (1997) 'Social work practice in situations of intercultural misunderstandings', *Journal of Multicultural Social Work*, vol 4, no 4, pp 49–66.

Lemelle, S.J. (1993) 'The politics of cultural existence: Pan-Africanism, historical materialism and Afrocentricity', *Race & Class*, vol 35, no 1, pp 93–113.

Lentin, R. (2007) 'Ireland: Racial state and crisis racism, *Ethnic and Racial Studies*, vol 30, no 4, pp 610–627.

Lentin, A. and Titley, G. (2011) *The crises of multiculturalism*, London: Zed.

Lentin, R. and Moreo, E. (eds) (2012) *Migrant activism and integration from below in Ireland*, Basingstoke: Palgrave Macmillan.

Letseka, M. (2013) 'Anchoring *Ubuntu* morality', *Mediterranean Journal of Social Sciences*, vol 4, no 3, pp 351–360.

Lewis, D. (2011) 'Representing African sexualities', in S. Tamale (ed) *African sexualities: A reader*, Oxford: Pambazuka Press, pp 199–117.

Liberty (2019) *Policing by machine*, www.libertyhumanrights.org.uk/policy/report-policing-machine

Lindner, K. (2010) 'Marx's Eurocentrism', *Radical Philosophy*, 161, pp 27–42.

Littlewood, R. and Lipsedge, M. (1997) *Aliens and alienists*, London: Routledge (third edition).

Lloyd, D. (1999) *Ireland after history*, Cork: Cork University.

Logan, E. (2014) *Garda Síochána 2005 (Section 42) Special Inquiries relating to Garda Síochána Order 2013*, http://specialinquiry.ie/wp-content/uploads/2014/06/Special-Inquiry-July-2014.pdf

Lorenz, M. (1994) *Social work in changing Europe*, London: Routledge.

Low, S. (2009) 'Maintaining whiteness', *Transforming Anthropology*, vol 17, no 2, pp 79–92.

Loyal, S. and Quilley, S. (2018) *State power and asylum seekers in Ireland*, London: Palgrave Macmillan.

Lum, D. (1999) *Culturally competent practice*, Pacific Grove, CA: Brooks/Cole.

Mac an Ghaill, M. (2002) 'Beyond a black–white dualism: Racialisation and racism in the Republic of Ireland and the Irish diaspora experience', *Irish Journal of Sociology*, vol 11, no 2, pp 99–123.

Mac Laughlin, J. (1996) 'The evolution of anti-Traveller racism in Ireland', *Race & Class*, vol, 37, no 3, pp 47–64.

MacMullan, T. (2015) 'Facing up to ignorance and privilege', *Philosophy Compass*, vol 10, no 9, pp 646–660.

Malešević, V. (2019) 'Religious regulation in Ireland', *The Oxford research encyclopedia of politics*, https://doi.org/10.1093/acrefore/9780190228637.013.805

Mandela, N. (1994) *A long walk to freedom*, Boston, MA: Little Brown.

Marable, M. (1993) 'Beyond racial identity politics', *Race & Class*, vol 35, no 1, 113–131.

Marovatsanga, W. (2020) 'When in Rome, you do as the Romans do? Black Africans and social work in the Republic of Ireland', National University of Ireland Galway (unpublished PhD thesis).

Maruyama, G. and Ryan, C.S. (2014) *Research methods in social relations*, Chichester: Wiley (eighth edition).

Marx, K. (1981 [1857–58]) *Grundrisse*, London: Penguin.

Masolo, D.A. (2016) 'Africanizing philosophy: Wiredu, Hountondji, and Mudimbe', in A. Afolayan and T. Falola (eds) *The Palgrave handbook of African philosophy*, New York: Palgrave Macmillan, pp 61–75.

Massey, D. (2015) 'Vocabularies of the economy', in S. Hall, D. Massey and M. Rustin (eds) *After neoliberalism*, London: Lawrence and Wishart, pp 24–37.

Matarese, M.T. and Caswell, D. (2018) ' "I'm gonna ask you about yourself, so I can put it on paper": Analysing street-level bureaucracy through form-related talk', *British Journal of Social Work*, vol 48, no 3, pp 714–733.

Mathema, Z. (2007) 'The African worldview: A serious challenge to Christian discipleship', *Ministry Magazine*, www.ministrymagazine.org/archive/2007/10/the-african- worldview.html

Matsuda, M.J., Lawrence III, C.R., Delgado, R. and Crenshaw, K. (1993) *Words that wound*, Boulder, CO: Westview Press.

Maylea, C. (2020) 'The end of social work', *British Journal of Social Work*, published online 3 December, DOI: 10.1093/bjsw/bcaa203

Mbembe, A. (2003) 'Necropolitics', *Public Culture*, vol 15, no 1, pp 11–40.

Mbembe, A. (2017) *Critique of Black reason*, Durham, NC and London: Duke University.

Mbigi L. (1997) *Ubuntu: The African dream in management*, Randburg, South Africa: Knowledge Resources.

McClintock, A. (1995) *Imperial leather: Race, gender and sexuality in the colonial conquest*, London: Routledge.

McDermott, S. (2020a) 'Over 32,000 people sign petition calling for government to end Direct Provision', *thejournal.ie*, 5 June, www.thejournal.ie/direct-provision-petition-5115670-Jun2020/

McDermott, S. (2020b) 'Dublin Lord Mayor calls on public to become "anti-racist" following attacks on Chinese people in Ireland', *thejournal.ie*, 18 August, www.thejournal.ie/hazel-chu-interview-anti-racism-asian-attacks-5178303-Aug2020/

McGregor, C., Dalikeni, C., Devaney, C., Moran, L. and Garrity, S. (2020) 'Practice guidance for culturally sensitive practice in working with children and families who are asylum seekers: Learning from an early years study in Ireland', *Child Care in Practice*, vol 26, no 3, pp 243–256.

McKeown, M. and Wainwright, J. (2019) 'Echoes of Frantz Fanon in the place and space of an alternative black mental health centre', *Critical and Radical Social Work*, published online 16 December, DOI: 10.1332/204986019X15724516823395

McLaren, P. (1994) 'White terror and opposition agency', in D.T. Goldberg (ed) *Multiculturalism: A critical reader*, Oxford: Blackwell, pp 45–74.

McLellan, G. (2001) 'Can there be a critical multiculturalism?', *Ethnicities*, vol 1, no 3, pp 389–422.

McNally, D. (2012) *Monsters of the market: Zombies, vampires and global capitalism*, Chicago, IL, Haymarket (first published by Brill, 2011).

McNamee, S. and Gergen, K.J. (1992) *Therapy as social construction*, London: Sage.

Mead, M. (1962) 'A cultural anthropologist's approach to maternal deprivation', in World Health Organization, *Deprivation of maternal care: A reassessment of its effects*, Geneva: WHO, pp 45–63.

Mercille, J. (2014) 'The role of the media in fiscal consolidation programmes: The case of Ireland', *Cambridge Journal of Economics*, vol 38, pp 281–300.

Mercille, J. and O'Neill, N. (2020) 'The growth of private home care providers in Europe: The case of Ireland', *Social Policy & Administration*, published online 1 September, DOI: 10.1111/spol.12646

Metz, T. (2011) '*Ubuntu* as a moral theory and human rights in South Africa', *African Human Rights Law Journal*, vol 11, no 2, pp 532–559.

Metzl, J.M. (2010) *The protest psychosis: How schizophrenia became a Black disease*, New York: Beacon Press.

Michael, L. (2016) *Afrophobia*, ENAR Ireland, https://static.rasset.ie/ documents/news/afrophobia-in-ireland.pdf

Michael, L. (2021a) 'Policing black lives in Ireland', in L. Michael and E. Joseph (eds) *The sociological observer: Black lives matter*, Maynooth, Ireland: Sociological Association of Ireland, pp 56–64.

Michael, L. (2021b) *Reports of racism in Ireland 2020: Data from iReport. ie*, Dublin: Irish Network Against Racism, https://inar.ie/wp-content/ uploads/2021/03/2020_iReport-Reports-of-Racism-in-Ireland.pdf

Michael, L. and Joseph, E. (eds) (2021) *The sociological observer: Black lives matter*, Maynooth, Ireland: Sociological Association of Ireland, www. sociology.ie/uploads/4/2/5/2/42525367/sociological_observer_2.pdf

Michael, L. and Schulz, S. (ed) (2019) *Unsettling whiteness*, Leiden, Brill.

Midgley, J. (1981) *Professional imperialism: Social work and the third world*, London: Heinemann.

Mignolo, W. (2007) 'Delinking', *Cultural Studies*, vol 21, no 2/3, pp 449–514.

Miles, R. (1987) *Capitalism and unfree labour*, London: Tavistock.

Mills, C.W. (1998) *Blackness visible*, Ithaca, NY: Cornell University Press.

Mills, C.W. (2009) 'Critical race theory: A reply to Mike Cole', *Ethnicities*, vol 9, no 2, pp 270–281.

Milner, R.H. (2008) 'Critical race theory and interest convergence as analytic tools in teacher education policies and practices', *Journal of Teacher Education*, vol 59, no 4, pp 332–346.

Mirsepassi, A. (2000) *Intellectual discourse and the politics of modernization*, Cambridge: Cambridge University Press.

Morley, C. (2018) 'Beyond silence and conformity: A reflection on academic activism as resistance to managerialism in the contemporary university', in A.L. Black and S. Garvis (eds) *Women activating agency in academia: metaphors, manifestos and memoir*, London: Routledge, pp 79–89.

Morley, C., Ablett, P., Noble, C. and Cowden, S. (eds) (2020) *The Routledge handbook of critical pedagogies for social work*, London: Routledge.

Morrison, T. (1992) *Playing in the dark: Whiteness and the literary imagination*, London: Picador.

Mugumbate, J. (2020) 'Samkange's theory of *Ubuntu* and its contribution to social work pedagogy', in C. Morley, P. Ablett, C. Noble, C. and S. Cowden, S. (eds) *The Routledge handbook of critical pedagogies for social work*, London: Routledge, pp 412–424.

Mugumbate, J. and Nyanguru, A. (2013) 'African philosophy: The value of Ubuntu in social work', *African Journal of Social Work*, vol 3, no 1, pp 82–101.

Mukanjari, M. (2020) 'Racism and parenting: The experiences and resilience of Afro-origin parents raising children in Gothenburg', Sweden: University of Gothenburg (unpublished thesis, International MA in Social Work and Human Rights).

Mullings, D.V., Clarke, J., Bernard, W.T., Este, D. and Giwa, S. (eds) (2021) *Africentric social work*, Winnipeg, Canada: Fernwood.

Munck, R. (2011) 'Ireland in the world, the world in Ireland', in B. Fanning and R. Munck (eds) *Globalization, migration and social transformation*, Farnham: Ashgate.

Mungai, N.W. (2013) 'Afrocentric approaches to working with immigrant communities', *International Journal of Social Work and Human Services Practice*, vol 1, no 1, pp 45–53.

Munn, W. (2020) 'African Americans are contracting and dying from COVID-19 at higher rates. We know why', North Carolina Justice Center, 28 April, www.ncjustice.org/publications/african-americans-are-contracting-and-dying-from-covid-19-at-higher-rates-we-know-why/

NASC (2013) *In from the margins: Roma in Ireland*, www.nascireland.org/wp-content/uploads/2013/05/NASC-ROMA-REPORT.pdf

Nash, J.C. (2019) *Black feminism reimagined*, Durham, NC and London: Duke University.

Navarro, Z. (2006) 'In search of a cultural interpretation of power: The contribution of Pierre Bourdieu', *IDS Bulletin*, vol 37, no 6, pp 11–22.

Ndukaire, R. (2019) 'Challenges encountered by social workers supporting African children with intellectual disabilities and their families', Galway: National University of Ireland Galway (unpublished MA dissertation).

Ngũgĩ wa Thiong'o (2014) *Globalelectics: theory and the politics of knowing*, New York: Columbia University Press.

Ní Chonaill, B. (2021) 'Black lives matter and higher education in Ireland', in L. Michael and E. Joseph (eds) *The sociological observer: Black lives matter*, Maynooth, Ireland: Sociological Association of Ireland, pp 49–56.

Nordberg, A. and Meshesha, B.T. (2018) 'African diasporan experiences of US police violence', *British Journal of Social Work*, online 28 August, DOI: 10.1093/bjsw/bcy074

Nylund, D. (2006) 'Critical multiculturalism, "whiteness" and social work', *Journal of Progressive Human Services*, vol 17, no 2, pp 27–41.

O'Hagan, K. (2001) *Cultural competence in the caring professions*, London: Jessica Kingsley.

O'Leary, N. (2020) 'Protesters highlight killings in police custody throughout Europe', *The Irish Times*, 8 June, www.irishtimes.com/news/world/europe/protesters-highlight-deaths-in-police-custody-throughout-europe-1.4272985

O'Reilly, Z. (2018) '"Living liminality": everyday experiences of asylum seekers in the "Direct Provision" system in Ireland', *Gender, Place & Culture*, vol 25, no 6, pp 821–842.

O'Sullivan, A. (2021) 'Black lives matter and the global history of Irish anti-imperialism', in L. Michael and E. Joseph (eds) *The sociological observer: Black lives matter*, Maynooth, Ireland: Sociological Association of Ireland, pp 10–15.

Obasi, C. (2021) 'Black social workers: Identity, racism, invisibility/ hypervisibility at work', *Journal of Social Work*, published online 4 June, DOI: 10.1177/14680173211008110

Odirih, A. (2019) 'The social work practice placement experience of Black African minority students in Ireland', Galway: National University of Ireland Galway (unpublished MA thesis).

Office for the Minister for Integration (2008) *Migration nation*, www.integration. ie/website/omi/omiwebv6.nsf/page/AXBN-7SQDF91044205-en/$File/ Migration%20Nation.pdf

Ohlmeyer, J. (2020) 'Ireland has yet to come to terms with its imperial past', *The Irish Times*, 29 December, www.irishtimes.com/opinion/ ireland-has-yet-to-come-to-terms-with-its-imperial-past-1.4444146

Okafor, V.O. (1991) 'Diop and the African origin of civilization: An Afrocentric analysis', *Journal of Black Studies*, vol 22, no 2, pp 252–268.

Okpokiri, C. (2020) 'Parenting in fear: Child welfare micro strategies of Nigerian parents in Britain' *The British Journal of Social Work*, published online 15 December, https://doi.org/10.1093/bjsw/bcaa205

Okpokiri, C. (2021) 'Nigerian parents have fears of "parenting-while-Black", in Britain', The Conversation, 6 January, https://theconversation.com/ nigerian-parents-have-fears-of-parenting-while-black-in-britain-152197

Ombudsman for Children's Office (2021) *Safety and welfare of children in direct provision: An investigation by the Ombudsman for Children's Office*, www. oco.ie/app/uploads/2021/04/Safety-and-Welfare-of-children-in-Direct-Provision.pdf

Omi, M. and Winant, H. (1986) *Racial formation in the United States*, New York: Routledge.

Onyejelem, C. (2017) 'Tusla "biased against" ethnic families', *Metro Éireann*, 1 March, www.metroeireann.com/news/810/tusla-biased-against-ethnic-families-social-workers-claim-care-rates-for-african-children-disproportionately-high.html

Orbe, M.P. (1998) *Constructing co–cultural theory*, London: Sage.

Otto, H. and Keller, H. (eds) (2014) *Different faces of attachment*, New York: Cambridge University Press.

Otukoya, B. (2021) 'Shooting of George Nkencho raises questions', *The Irish Times*, 28 January, p 28.

Owomoyela, O. (1987) 'Africa and the imperative of philosophy', *African Studies Review*, vol 30, no 1, pp 79–99.

Oxfam (2018) *Reward work, not wealth*, www.oxfam.org/sites/www.oxfam.org/files/file_attachments/bp-reward-work-not-wealth-220118-en.pdf

Oxfam Ireland (2021) 'Mega-rich recoup Covid-losses in record-time yet billions will live in poverty for at least a decade', press notice, 25 January, www.oxfamireland.org/blog/davos-2021

Park, Y. (2005) 'Culture as deficit: A critical discourse analysis of the concept of culture in contemporary social work discourse', *Journal of Sociology and Social Welfare*, vol 32, pp 11–33.

Parker, D. (2000) 'The Chinese takeaway and the diasporic habitus', in B. Hesse (ed) *Un/settled Multiculturalism*, London: Zed Books, pp 73–95.

Parveen, N. and Akinwotu, E. (2021) 'Idris Elba and Naomi Campbell sign letter backing gay rights in Ghana', *The Guardian*, 1 March, www.theguardian.com/world/2021/mar/01/idris-elba-and-naomi-campbell-sign-letter-backing-gay-rights-in-ghana

Patel, L. (2014) 'Anti-colonial educational research: From ownership to answerability', *Educational Studies*, vol 50, no 4, pp 357–377.

Pavee Point (2013) *Travelling with austerity*, Dublin: Pavee Point, http://paveepoint.ie/sitenua/wp-content/uploads/2013/04/Pavee-Point-Austerity-PDF-1.pdf

Phelan, S. (2007) 'The discourses of neoliberal hegemony: The case of the Irish Republic', *Critical Discourse Studies*, vol 4, no 1, pp 29–48.

Pile, S. (1990) *The private farmer: Transformation and legitimation in advanced capitalist agriculture*, Aldershot: Dartmouth.

Pinderhughes, E.E. (1989) *Race, ethnicity and power*, New York: The Free Press.

Pirtle, W.N.L. (2020) 'Racial capitalism: A fundamental cause of novel coronavirus (COVID-19) pandemic inequities in the United States', *Health, Education and Behavior*, vol 47, no 4, pp 504–508.

Pitika Ntuli, P. (2002) 'Indigenous knowledge systems and the African renaissance', in C.A. Odora Hoppers (ed) *Indigenous knowledge and the integration of knowledge systems*, Claremont, SA: New Africa Books, pp 53–66.

Places of Sanctuary Ireland (2020) 'Sanctuary in higher education seminar attracts over 250 registrations', 17 November, https://ireland.cityofsanctuary.org/2020/11/17/sanctuary-in-higher-education-seminar-attracts-over-250-registrations

Pon, G. (2009) 'Cultural competency as new racism', *Journal of Progressive Human Services*, vol 20, no 1, pp 59–71.

Presbey, G.M. (2016) 'Oruka and sage philosophy', in A. Afolayan and T. Falola (eds) *The Palgrave Handbook of African Philosophy*, New York: Palgrave Macmillan, pp 75–97.

Public Health England (2020) *Beyond the data: Understanding the impact of COVID-19 on BAME groups*, https://assets.publishing.service.gov.uk/government/uploads/system/uploads/attachment_data/file/892376/COVID_stakeholder_engagement_synthesis_beyond_the_data.pdf

Quinn, N. and Mageo, J.M. (eds) (2013a) *Attachment reconsidered*, New York: Palgrave Macmillan.

Quinn, N. and Mageo, J.M. (2013b) 'Attachment and culture: an introduction', in N. Quinn and J.M. Mageo (eds) *Attachment reconsidered*, New York: Palgrave Macmillan, pp 3–33.

Rancière, J. (1999 [1995]) *Dis-agreement.* Minneapolis, MN: University of Minnesota Press.

Ransby, B. and Matthews, T. (1993) 'Black popular culture and the transcendence of patriarchal illusions', *Race & Class*, vol 35, no 1, pp 93–113.

Razack, N. (2001) 'Diversity and difference in the field education encounter', *Social Work Education*, vol 19, no 2, pp 219–32.

Reder, P. and Duncan, S. (2003) 'Understanding communication in child protection networks', *Child Abuse Review*, vol 12, no 2, pp 82–100.

Reid, W. and Maclean, S. (2021) (eds) *Outlanders: Hidden narratives from workers of colour*, Lichfield: Kirwan Maclean Associates.

Roberts, D.E. (2014) 'Child protection as surveillance of African American families', *Journal of Social Welfare and Family Law*, vol 36, no 4, pp 426–437.

Robertson, H. and Travaglia, J. (2020) 'The necropolitics of COVID-19', LSE Blogs, 18 May, https://blogs.lse.ac.uk/impactofsocialsciences/2020/05/18/the-necropolitics-of-covid-19-will-the-covid-19-pandemic-reshape-national-healthcare-systems/

Roediger, D. (1994) *Towards the abolition of whiteness*, London: Verso.

Roediger, D. (2017) *Class, race and Marxism*, London: Verso.

Rogers, C. (1980) *A way of being*, Boston, MA: Houghton Mifflin Company.

Ross, L. (2010) 'Notes from the field: Learning cultural humility through critical incidents and central challenges in community-based participatory research', *Journal of Community Practice*, vol 18, pp 315–335.

Ruch, E.A. and Anyanwu, K.C. (1981) *African philosophy: An introduction to the main philosophical trends in contemporary Africa*, Rome: Catholic Book Agency.

St Louis, B. (2002) 'Post-race/post-politics? Activist-intellectualism and the reification of race', *Ethnic and Racial Studies*, vol 25, no 4, pp 652–675.

Samkange, S. and Samkange, T.M. (1980) *Hunhuism or Ubuntuism: A Zimbabwe indigenous political philosophy*, Salisbury, Zimbabwe: Graham Publishing.

Samuel, M. (2020) 'Black and ethnic minority social workers disproportionately subject to fitness to practise investigations', *Community Care*, 31 July, www.communitycare.co.uk/2020/07/31/black-ethnic-minority-social-workers-disproportionately-subject-fitness-practise-investigations/

Sayad, A. (2004) *The suffering of the immigrant*, Cambridge: Polity.

Schiele, J.H. (1996) 'Afrocentricity', *Social Work*, vol 41, no 3, pp 284–294.

Schiele, J.H. (1997) 'The contour and meaning of Afrocentric social work', *Journal of Black Studies*, vol 27, no 6, pp 800–819.

Schiele, J.H. (2017) 'The Afrocentric paradigm in social work', *Journal of Human Behavior in the Social Environment*, vol 27, no 1–2, pp 15–26.

Schram, F.S. and Paylovskaya, M. (2017) *Rethinking Neoliberalism*, New York: Routledge.

Schuster, L. (2003) 'Common sense or racism? The treatment of asylum-seekers in Europe', *Patterns of Prejudice*, vol 37, no 3, pp 233–256.

Scott, J.C. (1985) *Weapons of the weak*, New Haven, CT: Yale University Press.

Shahid, M. and Jha, M.K. (2014) 'Revisiting the client–worker relationship: Biestek through a Gramscian gaze', *Journal of Progressive Services*, vol 25, pp 18–36.

Silavwe, G. (1995) 'The need for a new social work perspective in an African setting', *British Journal of Social Work*, vol 25, no 1, pp 71–84.

Singh, G. (2020) '"Race", racism and resistance: Theory and politics', in G. Singh and S. Masocha (eds) *Anti-racist social work*, London: Red Globe Press, pp 13–35.

Singh, G. and Cowden, S. (2009) 'The social worker as intellectual', *European Journal of Social Work*, vol 12, no 4, pp 1369–1457.

Singh, G. and Masocha, S. (2020) 'Introduction', in G. Singh and S. Masocha (eds) (2020) *Anti-racist social work*, London: Red Globe Press, pp 1–13.

Skills for Care (2021) *Assessed and Supported Year in Employment (ASYE) child and family annual report to the Department for Education, April 2020–May 2021*, www.skillsforcare.org.uk/Documents/Learning-and-development/ASYE-child-and-family/ASYE-child-and-family-annual-report-2020-21.pdf

Smith, G. (2011) 'Selective hegemony and beyond – populations with "no productive function"', *Identities*, vol 18, no 1, pp 2–38.

Sobande, F. (2019) 'Woke-washing: "intersectional" femvertising and branding "woke" bravery', *European Journal of Marketing*, vol 54 no 11, pp 2723–2746.

Sobande, F. (2020) '"We're all in this together": Commodified notions of connection, care and community in brand responses to COVID-19', *European Journal of Cultural Studies*, vol 23, no 6, pp 1033–1037.

Sodi, T. (1998) 'A phenomenological study of healing in a North Sotho community', Cape Town, SA: University of Cape Town (PhD thesis).

Solorzano, D.G. (1997) 'Images and words that wound: Critical race theory, racial stereotyping, and teacher education', *Teacher Education Quarterly*, vol 24, pp 5–20.

Soper, S., Blomfield, G., Mullings, M. and Ndimande, S. (2016) 'Do you have to be white to pass this course?', in A. Bellinger and D. Ford (eds) *Practice placement in social work: Innovative approaches for effective teaching and learning*, Bristol: Policy Press.

Spence, L.K. (2012) 'The neoliberal turn in black politics', *Souls*, vol 14, no 3–4, pp 139–159.

Spivak, G.C. (2002) 'Resident alien', in D.T. Goldberg and A. Quayson (ed) *Relocating postcolonialism*, Oxford: Blackwell.

Srikanthan, S. (2019) 'Keeping the boss happy: Black and minority ethnic students accounts of the field education crisis', *British Journal of Social Work*, vol 49, no 8, pp 2168–2186.

Stobart, E. (2006) *Child abuse linked to accusations of spirit possession and witchcraft*, Department for Education and Skills: London (Research report RR750), http://dera.ioe.ac.uk/6416/1/RR750.pdf

Strier, J. (2004) 'Intercultural competencies as a means to manage intercultural interactions in social work', *Intercultural Communication*, 7, www.immi.se/intercultural/nr7/stier.htm

Sue, D.W., Capodilupo, C.M., Torino, G.C., Bucceri, J.M., Holder, A.M.B., Nadal, K.L. and Esquilin, M. (2007) 'Racial microaggressions in everyday life: implications for clinical practice', *American Psychologist*, vol 62, no 4, pp 271–286.

Sundberg, J. (2009) 'Eurocentrism', in R. Kitchin and N. Thrift (eds) *International encyclopaedia of human geography, Volume 3*, Oxford: Elsevier, pp 638–643.

Swanson, D.M. (2007) '*Ubuntu*: An African contribution to (re)search for/with a "humble togetherness"', *Journal of Contemporary Issues in Education*, vol 2, no 2, pp 53–67.

Tamale, S. (ed) (2011) *African sexualities: A reader*, Oxford: Pambazuka Press, pp 182.

Taylor, K-T. (2016) *From #blacklivesmater to Black liberation*, Chicago, IL: Haymarket Press.

Teasley, M.L., Schiele, J.H., Adams, C. and Okilwa, N.S. (2018) 'Trayvon Martin: racial profiling, Black male stigma, and social work practice, *Social Work*, vol 63, no 1, pp 37–46.

Tedam, P. (2014) 'When failing doesn't matter: A narrative inquiry into the social work practice learning experiences of Black African students in England', *International Journal of Higher Education*, vol 3, no 1, pp 136–45.

Tempels, P. (1969 [1959]) *Bantu philosophy*, Paris: Présence Africaine.

Thabede, D.G. (2005) 'Social casework: An Afrocentric perspective' (PhD thesis, University of Stellenbosch, South Africa).

Thabede, D.G. (2008) 'The African worldview as the basis of practice in the helping professions', *Social work/Maatskaplike Werk*, vol 44, pp 233–245.

Therborn, G. (2011) *The world: A beginner's guide*, Cambridge: Polity.

Thompson, A. (2008) 'Summary of whiteness theory', www.kooriweb.org/foley/resources/whiteness/summary_of_whiteness_theory.pdf

Tsri, K. (2016) 'Africans are not black: Why the use of the term "black" for Africans should be abandoned', *African Identities*, vol 14, no 2, pp 147–160.

Turnell, A. (2011) *The signs of safety child protection practice framework*, Government of Western Australia, www.dcp.wa.gov.au/resources/ documents/policies%20and%20frameworks/signsofsafetyframework2011. pdf

Turpel-Lafond, M.E. (2020) *In plain sight: Addressing indigenous-specific racism and discrimination in BC health care*. Victoria, BC: Government of British Columbia.

Tutu, D. (2000) *No future without forgiveness*, London: Random House.

Twine, F.W. and Gallagher, C. (2008) 'Introduction: The future of whiteness – a map of the "third wave"', *Ethnic and Racial Studies*, vol 31, no 1, pp 4–24.

Tyrrell, P. (2006) *Founded on fear*, Dublin: Irish Academic Press.

UNISON (2019) 'Crisis in social work revealed by new UNISON survey', press notice, 19 June, www.unison.org.uk/news/2019/06/ crisis-social-work-revealed-new-unison-survey/

Van der Walt, B.J. (1992) *A Christian worldview and Christian higher education for Africa*, Potchefstroom: Institute for Reformational Studies.

Vertovec, S. (2000) *The Hindu diaspora*, London: Routledge.

Vice News Tonight (2017) 'Charlottesville, "race" and terror', 14 August, https://news.vice.com/story/vice-news-tonight-full-episode-charlottesville-race-and-terror

Vicedo, M. (2013) *The nature and nurture of love: from imprinting to attachment in cold war America*, Chicago, IL: University of Chicago Press.

Viens Commission (2019) *Public inquiry commission on relations between indigenous peoples and certain public services in Quebec: Listening, reconciliation and progress – Final report*, Quebec: Government of Quebec.

Viljoen, F. (1998) 'Supra-national human rights instruments for the protection of children in Africa', *The Comparative and International Law Journal of Southern Africa*, vol 31, no 2, pp 199–212.

Wacquant, L. (1998) 'Pierre Bourdieu', in R. Stones (ed) *Key sociological thinkers*, Houndsmill: Palgrave Macmillan.

Wacquant, L. (2001) 'The penalisation of poverty and the rise of neo-liberalism', *European Journal on Criminal Policy and Research*, vol 9, pp 401–412.

Wacquant, L. (2004) 'Critical thought as solvent of *doxa*', *Constellations*, vol 11, no 1, pp 97–102.

Wacquant, L. (2009) 'The body, the ghetto and the penal state', *Qualitative Sociology*, vol 32, pp 101–129.

Walker, C.E. (2001) *We can't go home again: An argument about Afrocentrism*, New York: Oxford University Press.

Walsh, M. (2016) *Bitter freedom: Ireland in a revolutionary world, 1918–1923*, London: Faber and Faber.

Walsh, T., Wilson, G. and O'Connor (2010) 'Local, European and global: An exploration of migration patterns of social workers into Ireland', *British Journal of Social Work*, vol 40, no 6, pp 1978–1995.

Walter, B. (2001) *Outsiders inside: Whiteness, place and Irish women*, London: Routledge.

Waters, M.C. and Jiménez, T.R. (2005) 'Assessing immigrant assimilation', *New Empirical and Theoretical Challenges*, vol 31, no 1, pp 105–125.

Watkins, M. (2002) 'Seeding liberation', in D. Slattery and L. Corbett (eds) *Depth psychology*, Einsiedeln, Switzerland: Daimon.

Watts, J. (2020) 'A billion people will face intolerable heat by 2070, study show', *The Guardian*, 6 May, p 21.

Weaver, H. (1999) 'Indigenous people in a multicultural society', *Social Work*, vol 43, no 3, pp 203–211.

Webb, S. (2003) 'Local orders and global chaos in social work', *European Journal of Social Work*, vol 6, no 2, pp 191–204.

Weheliye, A.G. (2014) *Habeas viscus*, Durham, NC and London, Duke University.

Werbner, P. (2000) 'Who sets the terms of the debate?', *Theory, Culture & Society*, vol 17, no 1, pp 147–156.

White, R. (1990) *White mythologies*, London: Routledge.

White, S., Hall, C. and Peckover, S. (2008) 'The descriptive tyranny of the common assessment framework', *British Journal of Social Work*, vol 39, no 7, pp 1197–1217.

Wiebe, M. (2010) 'Pushing the boundaries of the social work practicum', *Journal of Progressive Human Services*, vol 21, no 1, pp 66–82.

Williams, C. (2020) 'Politics, preoccupations, pragmatics: A race/ethnicity *redux* for social work research', *European Journal of Social Work*, vol 23, no 6, pp 1057–1068.

Williams, C. and Graham, M.J. (2016) *Social work in a diverse society*, Bristol: Policy Press.

Williams, R. (1973) 'Base and superstructure in Marxist cultural theory', *New Left Review*, Nov–Dec, pp 3–17.

Williams, R. (1983) *Keywords*, New York: Norton (second edition).

Winant, H. (1997) 'Behind blue eyes: Whiteness and contemporary US racial politics', *New Left Review*, 225, pp 73–89.

Yosso, T.J. and Burciaga, R. (2016) *Reclaiming our histories, recovering community cultural wealth*, Los Angeles, CA: Centre for Critical studies, UCLA, https://issuu.com/almaiflores/docs/ty___rb_research_brief_final_versio

Young, I.M. (1990) *Justice and the politics of difference*, Princeton, NJ: Princeton University Press.

Young, R.J.C. (2001) *Postcolonialism: An historical introduction*, Oxford: Blackwell.

Zembe, C.R. (2019) 'Quest for a cohesive diaspora African community', in H. Adi (ed) *Black British history*, London: Zed, pp 199–218.

Žižek, S. (2002) *Revolution at the gates*, London: Verso.

Zuberi, T. (2011) 'Critical race theory of society', *Connecticut Law Review*, vol 43, no 5, pp 1573–1591.

Index

www.ingramcontent.com/pod-product-compliance
Lightning Source LLC
Chambersburg PA
CBHW070618030426
42337CB00020B/3842